A BOOK OF SCOTTISH VERSE

A BOOK OF
SCOTTISH VERSE

Selected by
MAURICE LINDSAY
and
R. L. MACKIE

Third Edition

ROBERT HALE · LONDON
1983

A Book of Scottish Verse *was first published* in The World's
Classics *in* 1934 *and reprinted in* 1942, 1947, 1949, 1956 *and*
1960. *Second edition* 1967 *and* 1968.

This edition first published in 1983

This Selection and Introduction
© *Robert Hale Ltd.*, 1983

The Publisher acknowledges subsidy from the Scottish Arts
Council towards the publication of this volume.

ISBN 0 7090 0841 4

Robert Hale Limited
Clerkenwell House
Clerkenwell Green
London EC1R 0HT

Printed in Great Britain by
St Edmundsbury Press,
Bury St Edmunds and bound
by Hunter & Foulis Ltd., Edinburgh

CONTENTS

ACKNOWLEDGEMENTS

Acknowledgements for permission to include copyright poems are due to Mr N. Lingen-Hutton for the two poems from *The Scottish Poems of Violet Jacob*; to Faber and Faber Ltd. for the two poems (from *The Turn of the Day*) by Marion Angus; to Constable & Co. Ltd. for the poem (from *The Auld Doctor*) by David Rorie; to A. & C. Black (Publishers) Ltd. for the poem (from *The End of Fiammetta*) by Rachel Annand Taylor; to Mr John Gray for 'Scotland', 'The Deil o' Bogie' (from *Sir Halewyn*) and 'On a Cat, Ageing' by Sir Alexander Gray; to Martin Secker & Warburg Ltd. for the two poems (from *Collected Poems*) by Andrew Young; to Gordon Wright Publishing for 'Shy Geordie' (from *Up the Noran Water*) and 'The Wishin' Well'; to Faber and Faber Ltd. for the seven poems (from *Collected Poems*) by Edwin Muir; to the Macmillan Publishing Co. Inc., New York, for the fourteen poems (from *Collected Poems*) by Hugh MacDiarmid; to The Trustees of the National Library of Scotland for the two poems (from *Poems in Scots*) by William Soutar; to Mr Ian Sutherland for 'Sisyphus', 'And they were richt' and 'Nemo canem impune lacessit' by Robert Garioch; to Dr George Bruce for his four poems; to Mr Norman NacCaig for his six poems; to Mr Sydney Tremayne for 'North of Berwick' and for 'The Galloway Shore' (from *The Swans of Berwick*); to Mrs Hella Young for 'The Ballant o' the Laird's Bath' and 'Last Lauch' by Douglas Young; to David Higham Associates Ltd. for 'To a very beautiful lady' (from *The Winter Solstice*) by Ruthven Todd; to Mrs Paddy Fraser for 'Flemish Primitive', 'To a Scottish Poet', 'The Traveller has Regrets' and 'On the Persistence of Humanity' by G. S. Fraser; to Mr George Campbell Hay for his two poems; to Mrs Hazel Smith for 'Loch Leven', 'Elegy XIII', 'Ye Spier me' and 'Hamewith' by Sydney Goodsir Smith; to Mr W. S. Graham for the extract from his poem *The Nightfishing*; to Dr Tom Scott for his poem; to Dr Maurice Lindsay for his four poems; to Mr Alexander Scott for his four poems; to Dr Edwin Morgan for his four poems; to Mr George Mackay Brown for his three poems; to Mr Ian Hamilton Finlay for his two poems; to Mr Alastair Mackie for his two poems; to Dr Iain Crichton Smith for his four poems; to Mr Alastair Reid for his two poems; to Mr Tom Buchan for his two poems; to Mr Stewart Conn for his two poems; to Dr James Aitchison for his poem; to Mr Douglas Dunn for his four poems; to Mr Alan Bold for his two poems; to Mr Stanley Roger Green for his two poems; to Ms Liz Lochhead for her poem; to Mr Andrew Greig for his two poems 'Sapper' and 'The Glove'; to Canongate Publishing Ltd. for 'In Galloway' by Andrew Greig; and to the Scottish Text Society for permission to use their texts as a basis for some of the medieval poems included.

The Publishers gratefully acknowledge the permission granted by Oxford University Press to use the 1934 and 1967 editions of *The Oxford Book of Scottish Verse* in the compilation of the present work.

PREFACE
TO THE
THIRD EDITION

As a result of a decision of the Oxford University Press to cease publishing the delightful pocket-sized World's Classics series, the third edition of *A Book of Scottish Verse* appears under a different imprint. I am grateful to the Oxford University Press for agreeing to the transfer and to Professor Sir Rex Richards for facilitating the process. I am particularly grateful to Mr John Hale and Robert Hale Limited for having so readily undertaken to publish this third edition with, I am happy to say, the blessing of the late R. L. Mackie's son and daughter.

R. L. Mackie's original anthology included virtually no poetry written after the First World War. I was invited to update the anthology in 1967. The resulting second edition, now out of print, has been used as a prescribed text in a number of Scottish universities and schools. The anthology is, of course, primarily intended for the general reader, although possible academic usage has been kept in my mind in making some further minor changes in the original section, as well as in the section I added for the second edition.

The poem by James (B. V.) Thomson chosen by Mr Mackie, presumably because it could be quoted in its entirety, 'To Our Ladies of Death', falls far below the level of Thomson's masterpiece

'The City of Dreadful Night'. I have therefore replaced Mackie's original choice with three substantial sections from 'The City of Dreadful Night'. I have made one substitution in the Burns section and two in the Hogg. I have also strengthened the representation of William Soutar, and added three poems by Robert Garioch who, for reasons outwith my control, could not previously be represented.

Now that the penultimate decade of the twentieth century is running towards the middle of its course, it would be absurd not to reflect the work of younger Scottish poets, even at the risk of perhaps eventually seeming partially wrong in my choice. It is always difficult to be certain which poems possess lasting qualities and which merely mirror passing fashions. To take but one example reflecting permanent social change; compare the attitudes towards the expectations of love as implied by Marion Angus and Helen Cruickshank with those of Liz Lochhead, now represented among the newcomers.

Even since the appearance of the second edition, the successful use of Scots in poetry by younger writers has conspicuously declined. Indeed, I know of no poet under forty using the language today with any real poetic resonance.

Considerations of cost have prevented me from updating the selection by most of the writers of my own generation, although in many cases there was no compelling necessity to do so. For the same reason I have had to restrict the number of younger poets additionally represented, although no one has been left out who has produced even a single poem about whose effectiveness within its own terms of reference I felt no reservations. In my view every poem in this anthology possesses in some measure what I regard as the essential quality of memorability.

Milton Hill,
Dumbarton   MAURICE LINDSAY

1983

INTRODUCTION

I

The first anthology of Scottish poetry to come
into my hands while I was still a schoolboy was
A Book of Scottish Verse edited by R. L. Mackie.[1]
It provided me with a grounding in the heritage
of Scottish poetry, and gave me much pleasure
besides. Now, more than a generation later, I
am therefore especially delighted to have been
given the opportunity of re-editing it, in order
to bring it up to date.

The basic values of the Scottish literary
tradition do not, of course, change from one
generation to another. But some of the editorial
assumptions made by R. L. Mackie no longer
hold good today. He chose to range his antho-
logy from 'the end of the thirteenth century to
the beginning of the twentieth', but it was not
to include 'the work of any author now living'.
This meant, in effect, that only verse carried

[1] Robert Laird Mackie (1885–1960), the distinguished historian,
was a Dundee man, a pupil of Dundee High School, and a
graduate of St. Andrews University. He taught at Dunstable,
and at Kirkcaldy High School for some years, then in 1913
became a Lecturer at Dundee Training College (now the
College of Education), where he remained until his retirement
in 1949. His books include *A Short Social and Political History of
Britain* (1921, revised edition, London, Harrap and Co., 1961);
A Short History of Britain (O.U.P., 1930, revised by Professor
Gordon Donaldson, Oliver and Boyd, 1963); *Letters of James
IV* (Scottish History Society, 1953); and *King James IV of
Scotland* (Oliver and Boyd, 1962), the outcome of a lifelong
study, which gained him a doctorate of letters from St. Andrews
University in 1959.

over from the nineteenth century could be included to represent our own age, although by 1934, the year in which the anthology first appeared, 'Hugh MacDiarmid' had already published *Sangschaw, Pennywheep, A Drunk Man Looks at the Thistle*, and *To Circumjack Cencrastus*; Edwin Muir had produced his *First Poems* and *Variations on a Time Theme*, and William Soutar's poems had begun to appear in magazines. In fact, the movement somewhat grandiosely dubbed the 'Scottish Renaissance' by Professor Denis Saurat was already well under way. Yet because of the stipulation that all its contributors must be dead, *A Book of Scottish Verse* could only represent the twentieth century with the work of James Logie Robertson, R. F. Murray, Sir Ronald Ross, and Harold Monro.

However unfortunate the implications of the modern re-use of the word 'Renaissance' in a Scottish context may seem to purists, the body of Scottish poetry produced in Scots, Gaelic, and English since 1920 seems to me to make this period one of the most fruitful in the seven hundred or so years during which Scotland could be said to have been producing a literature of her own. MacDiarmid stands comparison with both Dunbar and Burns, for although he lacks the technical virtuosity of the former and the compelling humanity of the latter, in the comparatively small corpus of his finest work he outstrips both poets in intellectual range and originality of imagery.

I do not much like the critic's trick of placing poets like racehorses: but those who reckon the achievements of poetry by such standards have only qualitatively to place Edwin Muir against Robert Fergusson in the eighteenth century and Robert Henryson in the fifteenth; or Norman MacCaig against James Thomson and Gavin Douglas (as the author of the original prologues to his books of Virgil's *Aeneid* rather than as a translator) to satisfy themselves that Scottish poetry in the twentieth century has no need of apologists.

Tastes, too, have widened during the past thirty years. It will not now do to dismiss the work of Sir David Lyndsay as being 'almost negligible as poety'. In an age of courtly verse he was the first Scottish poet to align himself with the point of view of the common man, a fact which no doubt had something to do with his long continuing popularity, making 'the warks o' Davie Lyndsay' almost as accepted a possession as the Bible in humble Scottish homes, until the works of Robert Burns supplanted it two hundred years later: a fact, too, which reasserted itself when Lyndsay's verse morality play *Ane Satyre of the Thrie Estaitis in Commendation of Virtue and Vituperation of Vice* was brilliantly and successfully revived at the Edinburgh International Festival on several occasions.

Today, we do not much value what Mackie called 'George MacDonald's diffuse, pietistic verse', ten examples of which he nevertheless included. Nor, in the light of what came after, is there a case for retaining the self-conscious dialect pastoralizing of 'Hugh Haliburton' (James Logie Robertson), the Tennysonian overtones of Sir Ronald Ross, or the light verse of R. F. Murray.

Otherwise, the changes I have made in the contents of the earlier version of *A Book of Scottish Verse* are comparatively minor ones. I have added 'The Ballad of Kynd Kittok', which is generally agreed to be almost certainly by Dunbar, there being no other Scottish poet known to have been alive at the time capable of exercising so darkly witty a sense of fantasy. I have strengthened the earlier section of the book with one or two lively or beautiful anonymous pieces from the Banatyne manuscript, and slightly cut down the generous representation of Drummond of Hawthornden and Sir Walter Scott to make way for such excellent minor poets as James Melville, John Stewart of Baldynnis, and Lady John Scott. I have also strengthened the representation of John Davidson.

So far as the twentieth century is concerned, I have represented fully writers belonging to, or influenced by, the Scottish Renaissance Movement, and, of course, their predecessors. Several post-Scottish Renaissance poets are also represented, though in some cases only by one or two poems where it might be argued that their fullness of time has yet to come. After much heart-searching, I decided to leave out recent work in the Glasgow *patois*, believing its interest to be sociological rather than literary.

No Scottish anthology so far produced has embraced fully the three traditions of Scots, English, and Gaelic which make up Scotland's poetic heritage. I should have liked to include here the work of the Gaelic poets in translation but, apart from any question of space, few translations exist that live in their own right. Scotland has produced no Sir Samuel Fergusson, Douglas Hyde, Robin Flower, or Kuno Meyer; and to be content with prose accounts would seem to me tantamount to an admission that the poetry lies in the literal meaning of a poem, which obviously it does not. The same is true so far as the Scottish Latinists are concerned.

This, then, is an anthology for the general reader of the Scots and English streams of poetry which make up by far the greater sweep of the river of the Scottish poetic tradition. Because it is meant to be read for pleasure and readily enjoyed, some editing of the spelling of the older poems is necessary. In his introduction, Mackie wrote:

The spelling of the earlier poems has been modernized where there seemed no risk that the altered form might disguise the original sound of the word; but all obsolete words, and obsolete inflections like final -*and* indicating the present participle, and final -*is* or -*ys* indicating the plural of the noun, have been retained. The modern equivalents of the obsolete words, however, have been given in footnotes. It should be noted that final -*e* was not sounded in Middle Scots; that final -*is*, -*ys*, and -*es* were treated as separate syllables when added to monosyllables and to dissyllables with a final accent; and that the vowel in final -*it* or -*yt*, indicating the past indicative or past participle, was sounded.[1] Neglect of these rules will work havoc with the rhythms of Dunbar and Henryson.

[1] For a full description of the characteristics of Middle Scots see the Introduction to *Specimens of Middle Scots* by G. Gregory Smith (Edinburgh, W. Blackwood & Sons, 1902).

Unfortunately, Mackie's modernizing zeal occasionally led him to violate his rules. While I would agree that 'luvers', 'lufferis', and 'lovers' all sound more or less the same creatures, the Scots 'hert' or 'hairt' cannot properly be unified into 'heart' without destroying the sound of the line. Nor can the English 'soul' be said fully to equate with the darker Scots 'saul'. I have therefore made some restorations of old spellings where sound—and, in some cases, even sense—seemed to demand it, but have conformed in general to Mackie's principle where the spelling of the additional Scots poems is concerned.

II

Apart from fragments, like the moving elegy with which this anthology begins, and the long and frequently tedious chronicle poems by Andrew of Wyntoun, John Barbour, and others, the earliest Scots poem of artistic consequence is *The Kingis Quair*, written[1] by James the First of Scotland while a prisoner of the English king. King James was a cultured man, familiar with the works of Chaucer, which considerably influenced the style of his own poem. Nevertheless, a freshly personal note sounds through the Chaucerian conventions; a ready response to nature which characterized Scottish poetry throughout the ensuing centuries, and which, in the eighteenth century, saved Scotland from the aridities of an Augustan phase.

[1] Almost certainly, although no manuscript in his own hand has survived.

The literary influence of King James when he returned to Scotland out of captivity was no doubt far-reaching. The group of poets who followed him are sometimes known as the 'Scottish Chaucerians'. It is the Scottish custom, however, to refer to them as the 'Scottish Makars' (makers), a fairer description, since, although the influence of Chaucer on all of them is obvious, it is their personal individuality that gives their work distinction.

Robert Henryson (1425?–1506?) openly acknowledged the debt by writing a sequel to Chaucer's *Troilus and Criseyde*: a sequel which has, in R. L. Mackie's words, 'a chilling and terrible beauty, like the stars by the light of which the stricken Cressida moves to her doom'. Henryson's fables translate a Chaucerian convention into an unmistakably Scots setting, while in *Robene and Makyne* the pastoral note is quite new. Not only does Henryson depict the harshness of the Scottish climate— like so many poets since, down even to our own day—but he infuses all his poetry with his own warm and kindly personality. This schoolmaster of Dunfermline must have been a good person to know.

The same cannot be said of William Dunbar (1460?–1520?), one of the three great figures in Scots poetry. His energetic fancy and his considerable technical skill could be turned to subjects as different as his amusingly scandalous discussion-piece between 'The Twa Mariit Wemen and the Wedo' over their respective husbands' sexual prowess, and the magnificent, pealing Christmas and Easter hymns, '*Rorate coeli desuper*' and 'Done is a battle on the dragon black'. Behind all his dazzling virtuosity, however, lurked a moody, disappointed man.

Sir David Lyndsay of the Mount (1490–1555) had a less accomplished technique than either Henryson or Dunbar, combining the writing of verse with an active career as a courtier and diplomat. But he was at heart a people's poet concerned with the good exercise of government in the interests of the common man. His verse morality play *Ane Satyre of the Thrie Estaitis* probably did more to create conditions favourable to the Reformation in Scotland than any other single cause.

Of the minor Makars, Alexander Scott (fl. 1547–1584) and Alexander Montgomerie (1540?–1610?), who to some extent had their English counterparts in Wyatt and Surrey, wrote musical love songs with passion and telling touches of Scottish sound and imagery.

During the fourteenth and fifteenth centuries, while the Makars were cultivating their art, the ballads were being handed down from father to son, though how they first came to be written, and by whom, is likely to remain a mystery. As M. J. C. Hodgart says: 'It is now fairly certain that communal improvisation can take place; something like it has been seen in primitive and peasant communities. But it is equally certain that it can hardly have produced the ballad versions we possess.'[1] But possess them we do, with their tough economy of gesture, their swift movement, their disregard

[1] *The Ballad* (London, Hutchinson, 1960).

for the feelings of the participants, and their sudden flashes of magical poetry.

The Eighteenth Century Scots Revival, formalized by Allan Ramsay (1686–1758), carried forward by the youthful Robert Fergusson (1750–1774), and consummated by Robert Burns (1759–1796), to some extent gained its impetus from the shock of the Treaty of Union with England in 1707 and the consequent suspension of the Scottish Parliament. The Jacobite risings of 1715 and 1745 added fuel to the politcal fire, and enabled the movement to burn well into the nineteenth century.

Burns, of course, is chronologically the second of the three great figures in the Scottish poetic tradition. He came on the scene just before the old agrarian Scotland, that had lasted without much change from medieval times, began to disintegrate under the impact of the Industrial Revolution. His mastery of the Scots tongue gives the best of the poems in his Kilmarnock collection a lithe colloquial effectiveness, while his understanding of nearly every aspect of the relationship between man and woman imbued his songs with unique qualities of tenderness and warmth. 'Tam o' Shanter' shows him to be a master of the long narrative poem. 'Holy Willie's Prayer' is surely one of the supreme masterpieces of satire in the literature of any language.

So wide was Burns's genius that the shade it cast prevented much that was original from growing beneath it. A few hardy talents, however, did manage to develop their own poetic voices, among them Lady Nairne (1766–1845) and James Hogg (1770–1835).

The Scots tradition faltered into parochial insignificance during the later part of the nineteenth century, though in the work of Violet Jacob (1863–1946) and Marion Angus (1866–1946) it revived regionally in the twentieth. The deliberate attempt by C. M. Grieve ('Hugh MacDiarmid') to re-create a literary language by using an amalgam of words from the dialects of any and every region, no doubt arose out of the same impetus as the work of these two ladies. MacDiarmid, however, is the third major figure in the Scots poetic tradition, though few would now claim that he matched the greatness of Burns's humanity. A remarkable ear has enabled him to produce a varied music out of the vocables of the Scots tongue. The cosmic imagery of his early lyrics, and his later concern with a poetry which should be all-embracing, have resulted in his intellectually re-energizing the whole process of Scottish literature. Unlike the influence of Burns, the direct nature of which produced mainly imitators, MacDiarmid's influence has been largely indirect and vastly more stimulating. Indeed, the Scottish Renaissance, of which he is the central adornment, has turned out to be, not simply a revival of the Gaelic and Scots languages growing and gathering popular strength—the forces of history have made such an outcome impossible —but a new mood of questioning sensibility applied throughout the breadth and substance of modern life, and set down in three languages: in Scots and Gaelic, but, above all, in English tuned and tempered to reflect the overtones and traditions of the older tongues whose daily use and impact unfortunately dwindles from year to year.

Scottish poets deliberately set about writing in English after the Union of the Crowns in 1603. James the Sixth and First took a number of them south to London in his train, and they soon found it advantageous to try to de-Scotticize their styles. William Drummond of Hawthornden (1585–1649) spent most of his life in his romantic Scottish home outside Edinburgh, and was the earliest Scot to achieve distinction as a poet writing in English. His manner of thought and expression, however, is really European. James Thomson (1700–1748) settled near London, and was a close friend of the leading English writers of his day. Yet *The Seasons*, in spite of its languid Augustan mannerisms, is unmistakably a Scottish poem, with its vivid depiction of Nature. Sir Walter Scott (1771–1832) aroused Scotland's sense of nationhood at a time when the country was in danger of underestimating its own history. Though his impact as a novelist was greater than his importance as a poet, he attracted the interest of Europe to Scotland.

Both James Thomson the second and John Davidson (1857–1909) reflect deviationary aspects of the grim traditions of Scottish Calvinism. The realism of Davidson's 'Thirty Bob a Week' influenced not only MacDiarmid in Scotland, but also the young T. S. Eliot. Throughout the present century, many Scots poets have found a Scots-influenced English to be their natural language.

Yet in our own day, both Muir and Mac-

Diarmid had turned sixty before they achieved anything like adequate recognition in England, while some Scots poets never seem to achieve English recognition at all. No doubt this is because their mode and manner of expression does not accord with this or that London fashion. Yet it is undoubtedly their individuality, their concern with the traditions and sights and sounds of the Scotland around them, that gives their work its strength and savour. The reader of this anthology should find no difficulty in sensing parallels of thought and feeling between some of the long-dead poets here represented, and some of those living now. But sounding clearly through this constant factor of shared nationality, he should also hear, in the words of the youngest poet of them all,* 'the unpredicted voices of our kind'. These voices should be the concern, and the delight, of us all, regardless of nationality.

III

No anthologist can ever hope totally to please. For my omissions, whether due to the inherently personal nature of taste or because of practical considerations outwith my control, I ask indulgence. What follows does present, through the only kind of life that survives time's passing, the settings, the fashions, the stories, and passions of some of the men and women who have collectively shaped the sense of entity that for us today is Scotland.

October 1965/May 1983   MAURICE LINDSAY

*In 1967, but not of course, in 1983.

ANON.

Cantus

When Alexander our kynge was dede,
    That Scotland lede in lauche and le,[1]
Away was sons[2] of alle and brede,
    Off wyne and wax, of gamyn and gle.
Our golde was changit into lede.
    Crist, borne into virgynyte,
Succoure Scotlande and ramede,
    That is stade[3] in perplexite.

      (The earliest extant piece of Scottish verse.
      Quoted in *The Orygynale Cronykil* of Andrew
      of Wyntoun, completed about 1420.)

JOHN BARBOUR
1320?–1395

Freedom

Ah! Freedom is a noble thing!
Freedom makes man to have liking;
Freedom all solace to man gives;
He lives at ease that freely lives!
A noble heart may have nane ease,
Na elles nocht[4] that may him please,
Gif[5] freedom fail; for free liking
Is yearnit[6] owre all other thing.
Na[7] he, that aye has livyt free,
May nocht knaw weill the property,

---

[1] law and peace.   [2] abundance.   [3] beset.   [4] nor anything else.
    [5] if.   [6] yearned for.   [7] nor.

The anger, na the wretchit doom
That is couplit to foul thraldom.
But gif he had assayit it,
Than all perquer[1] he suld it wit,
And suld think freedom mair to prize
Than all the gold in world that is.

(*The Bruce*, Book I, ll. 225–40.)

The Battle of Bannockburn

There was the battle stricken weill;
So great dinning[2] there was of dyntis
As wapnys[3] upon armour stintis,[4]
And of spearis so great bristing,[5]
With sic thrawing[6] and sic thristing,[7]
Sic girning,[8] granyng,[9] and so great
A noise, as they can other beat,
And cryit ensenyeis[10] on everilk side,
Gifand[11] and takand woundis wide,
That it was hideous for till[12] hear
All four the battles,[13] wicht[14] that were,
Fechtand in-till ae front wholly.[15]

Almichty God! Full douchtely[16]
Sir Edward the Bruce and his men
Amang their fais contenyt them[17] then,
Fechtand into sa good covyne[18]
So hardy, worthy, and so fine,
That their avaward[19] rushit was

---

[1] then all by heart.   [2] striking.   [3] weapons.   [4] stop.
[5] breaking.   [6] throwing.   [7] thrusting.   [8] grimacing.
[9] groaning.   [10] battle-cries.   [11] giving.   [12] to.   [13] companies.
[14] strong.   [15] Fighting together on one front.   [16] valiantly.
[17] demeaned themselves.   [18] to such good purpose.   [19] vanguard.

And, maugre theiris,[1] left the place,
And to their great rout[2] to warrand[3]
They went, that then had upon hand
So great not,[4] that they were effrayit,[5]
For Scottis men them hard assayit,[6]
That then war in ane schiltrom[7] all.
Wha happnit in that ficht to fall,
I trow again he suld not rise.
There men micht see on mony wise
Hardiment eschevit[8] douchtely,
And mony that wicht were and hardy
Doun under feet lyand all dede,
Whar all the field of blood was red.
Armouris and quyntis[9] that they bare
With blood was swa[10] defoulit there,
That they micht nocht discrivit[11] be.

Ah! Michty God! wha than micht see
The Steward Walter and his rout[12]
And the good Douglas that was stout
Fechtand into the stalwart stour[13]
He suld say that till all honour
They war worthy, that in that ficht
Sa fast pressit their fais micht[14]
That they them rushit whar they yeid[15]
There micht men see full many a steed
Fleand on stray,[16] that lord had nane.
Ah! lord! qha than good tent had tane[17]
To the good Earl of Murreff,[18]
And his, that swa great routis[19] gaf,

---

[1] in spite of them.   [2] main army.   [3] for safety.   [4] employment.
[5] afraid.   [6] attacked.   [7] one serried mass.
[8] valiant deeds achieved.   [9] armorial devices.   [10] so.
[11] described. [12] company. [13] conflict. [14] the might of their foes.
[15] went.   [16] fleeing astray.   [17] who then had taken good heed.
[18] Moray.   [19] blows.

And faucht so fast in that battale,
Tholand[1] sic pain and sic travail,
That they and theiris made sic debate,
That where they come, they made them gait![2]
Then men micht hear ensenyeis cry,
And Scottis men cry hardely,
'On them! On them! On them! they fail!'
With that so hard they can assail,
And slew all that they micht owre-ta,[3]
And the Scottis archers alsua[4]
Shot amang them so sturdely,
Ingrevand them so gretumly,[5]
That what for them that with them faucht,
And swa great routis to them raught,[6]
And pressit them full eagerly,
And what for arrows that felly[7]
Mony great woundis can them ma,[8]
And slew fast of their horse alsua,
That they vandist[9] a little way;
They dread so greatly then till dee,[10]
That their covyne was war than ere
For they that with them fechtand were
Set hardyment, and strength, and will,
With heart and courage als there-till,[11]
And all their main and all their micht,
To put them foully to the flicht.

(*The Bruce*, Book XIII, ll. 152–224.)

---

[1] enduring.   [2] made a passage for themselves.   [3] overtake.
[4] also.   [5] annoying them so greatly.   [6] dealt.   [7] cruelly.
[8] make.   [9] retreated.   [10] die.   [11] also thereto.

ANDREW OF WYNTOUN
1360?–1425?

Macbeth's Dream

A nycht he thocht in his dreming
That sittand he wes beside the king
At a seat in huntyng, swa
In till a leish had grewhundis twa:
He thowcht while he wes swa syttand
He saw three wemen by gangand;
And thai wemen than thocht he
Three werd systrys mast lik to be.
The first he hard say, gangand by,
'Lo, yhondir the Thayne of Crumbawchty!'
The tothir woman said again,
'Of Murray yhondyre I see the Thayne!'
The thrid than said, 'I see the King!'
All this he herd in his dreming.
Sone efftire that, in his youthade,[1]
Of thir thayndomis he thayne wes made;
Syne neist he thocht for to be King,
Fra Duncan's dayis had tane ending.
The fantasy thus of his dreme
Moved him maist to sla[2] his eme.[3]

> (From *The Orygynale Cronykil*: the first known
> mention of Macbeth's meeting with the
> 'weird sisters'.)

[1] youth.　　[2] slay.　　[3] uncle.

KING JAMES THE FIRST OF SCOTLAND

1394–1437

From *The Kingis Quair*

(i)

Bewailing in my chamber thus alone,
    Despaired of all joy and remedy,
For-tirit[1] of my thought, and woebegone,
    Unto the window gan I walk in hye,[2]
    To see the warld and folk that went forby;
As for the time, though I of mirthis food
Might have no more, to look it did me good.

Now was there made fast by the touris wall
    A garden fair, and in the corners set
Ane herbere[3] green, with wandis long and small
    Railit about, and so with treis set
    Was all the place, and hawthorn hedgis knet[4]
That life was nonë walking there forby
That might within scarce ony wight aspy.

So thick the boughis[5] and the leavis green
    Beshadit all the alleyes that there were.
And middis every herbere might be seen
    The sharpë, greenë, sweetë Junipere
    Growing so fair with branchis here and there,
That, as it seemit to a life[6] without,
The boughis spread the herbere all about;

And on the smallë greenë twistis[7] sat
    The little sweetë nightingale, and sang
So loud and clear, the hymnis consecrat

---

[1] wearied.   [2] haste.   [3] garden plot.   [4] twined.   [5] boughs.
[6] creature.   [7] twigs.

Of lovis use, now soft, now loud among,
That all the garden and the wallis rong[1]
Right of[2] their song, and of the copill[3] next
Of their sweete harmony, and lo! the text:

Cantus

'Worshippë, ye that loveris been, this May,
　For of your blisse the Kalendis are begun,
And sing with us, away, Winter, away!
　Come, Summer, come, the sweet seasoun and sun!
　Awake for shame! that have your heavenis won,
And amorously lift up your headis all;
Thank Love that list you to his mercy call.'

When they this song had song a little thraw,[4]
　They stent[5] awhile, and therewith unafraid,
As I beheld and cast mine eyne a-law,[6]
　From bough to bough they hoppit[7] and they
　　played,
　And freshly in their birdis kind arrayed
Their featheris new, and fret them[8] in the sun,
And thankit love, that had their makis[9] won.

This was the plainë ditee of their note,
　And therewithal unto myself I thought,
'What life is this, that makis birdis dote?
　What may this be, how cometh it of ought?[10]
　What needeth it to be so dear ybought?
It is nothing, trow I, but feignit cheer,
And that men list to counterfeiten cheer.'

---

[1] rung.　　[2] with.　　[3] verse, stanza.　　[4] time.　　[5] stopped.
[6] down.　　[7] hopped.　　[8] adorned themselves.　　[9] mates.
　　　　　　　　　[10] aught.

Eft[1] wold I think: 'O Lord, what may this be,
   That Love is of so noble might and kind,
Loving his folk: and such prosperitee,
   Is it of him, as we in bookis find?
   May he our hertis setten and unbind?
Hath he upon our hertis such maistrye?
Or is all this but feignit fantasye?

For gif he be of so great excellence,
   That he of every wight has cure and charge,
What have I guilt to him[2] or done offence?
   That I am thrall, and birdis gone[3] at large,
   Sen him to serve he might set my corage?[4]
And gif he be noght so, than may I seyne,[5]
What makis folk to jangle of him in vain?

Can I nought ellis find, but gif that he
   Be lord, and as a lord may live and reign,
To bind and loose, and maken thrallis free,
   Than wold I pray his blissful grace benign
   To able me unto[6] his service digne;
And evermore for to be one of tho[7]
Him truly for to serve in weill and woe.

And therewith cast I doun mine eye again,
   Where as I saw, walking under the tour,
Full secretly, new cummyn her to playne,[8]
   The fairest and the freshest youngë flour
   That ever I saw, methought, before that hour,
For which sudden abate,[9] anon astert[10]
The blude of all my body to my hert.

And though I stood abasid tho a-lyte,
   No wonder was; for-why,[11] my wittis all

---

[1] again.   [2] How have I sinned against him.   [3] go.
[4] heart.   [5] say.   [6] qualify me for.   [7] those.   [8] play.
        [9] surprise.   [10] started.   [11] because.

Were so owre-come with pleasance and delight,
  Only through latting of mine eyen fall,
  That suddenly my hert became her thrall,
For ever, of free will; for of menace,
There was no token in her sweetë face.

And in my head I drew right hastily,
  And eft-soonës I leant it forth again,
And saw her walk that very womanly,
  With no wight mo but only women twain.
  Than gan I study in myself and seyne:
'Ah sweet! are ye a warldly creature,
Or heavenly thing in likeness of nature?

Or are ye God Cupidis owin princess,
  And cummyn are to loose me out of band?
Or are ye very Nature the goddess,
  That have depainted with your heavenly hand
  This garden full of flouris, as they stand?
What sall I think, alas! what reverence
Sall I minister to your excellence?

Gif ye a goddess be, and that ye like
  To do me pain, I may it naught astert;[1]
Gif ye be warldly wight that doth me sike,[2]
  Why list[3] God mak you so, my dearest hert,
  To do a silly prisoner thus smert
That loves you all,[4] and wot of naught but woe?
And therefore mercy, sweet, sen it is so?'

When I a little thraw had made my moan,
  Bewailing mine infortune and my chance,
Unknowing how or what was best to doon,
  So far I fallen was in lovis dance,
  That suddenly my wit, my countenance,

---

  [1] escape. [2] causes me to sigh. [3] pleased. [4] wholly.

My hert, my will, my nature, and my mind,
Was changit right clean in another kind. . . .

(stanzas 30–45.)

(ii)

To reckon of every thing the circumstance,
　　As happnit me when lessen gan my sore
Of my rancour and all my woeful chance,
　　It war too long; I lat it be therefore.
　　And thus this Flour, I can say you no more,
So heartly has unto my help attendit,
That from the death her man she has defendit.

And eke[1] the goddis merciful wirking,
　　For my long pain and true service in love,
That has me given halely[2] mine asking,
　　Which has my heart for ever set above
　　In perfect joy, that never may remove,
But only death: of whom, in laud and prise[3]
With thankful heart I say richt in this wise:—

Blissit mot[4] be the heyë goddis all,
　　So fair that glittern in the firmament!
And blissit be their might celestial,
　　That have convoyit hale, with one assent,
　　My love, and to so glad a consequent!
And thankit be Fortunys axletree
And wheel, that thus so weel has whirlit me.

Thankit mot be, and fair and love befall
　　The nichtingale, that with so good intent,
Sang there of love the notis sweet and small
　　Where my fair hertis lady was present,
　　Her with to glad, or that she further went!
And thou, geraflour![5] mot y-thankit be
All other flouris for the love of thee.

---

[1] also.　　[2] wholly.　　[3] praise.　　[4] may.　　[5] gilly flower.

'And thankit be the fairë castle wall,
  Where as I whilom lookit further and lent!
Thankit mot be the sanctis Marciall,[1]
  That me first causit hath this accident!
  Thankit mot be the greenë bewis bent,
Through whom, and under, first fortunit me
My heartis heal,[2] and my confort to be!'

For to the presence sweet and delitable,
  Richt of this flour that full is of pleasance,
By process and by meanis favourable,
  First of the blissful goddis purveyance,
  And syne through long and true continuance
Of very faith in love and true service,
I come am, and yet further in this wise.

Unworthy, lo, but only of her grace,
  In Loves yoke, that easy is and sure,
In guerdon of all my lovis space,
  She hath me tak, her humble creature.
  And thus befell my blissful aventure,
In youth of love, that now, from day to day,
Flourith aye new; and yet further, I say

Go, little treatise, naked of eloquence,
  Causing simples and poverty to wit;[3]
And pray the reader to have patience
  Of thy default, and to supporten it,
  Of his goodness thy brukleness[4] to knit,
And his tongue for to rulen and to steer,
That thy defaultis healit may been here.

Alas! and gif thou comest in presence,
  Whereas of blame fainest thou wald be quit,

---

[1] of the month of March (the month in which he was captured).
[2] healing.   [3] making known your simplicity and poverty.
[4] feebleness.

To hear thy rude and crooked eloquence,
　　Who sall be there to pray for thy remit?[1]
　　No wicht, but gif her mercy will admit
Thee for good will, that is thy guide and steer,[2]
To wham for me thou pitousely requere.

And thus endeth the fatal influence,
　　Causit from Heaven, where power is commit
Of governance, by the magnificence
　　Of him that hiest is in the Heaven sitt;
　　To Wham we thank that all our life hath writ,
Who couth it read, agone syne mony a year,
'Hich in the heavens' figure circulere.'[3]

Unto the impis[4] of my maisteris dear,
　　Gower and Chaucer, that on the steppis sat
Of rhetoric, while they were livand here,
　　Superlative as poets laureate
　　In moralitee and eloquence ornate,
I recommend my book in linis seven,
And eke their saulis unto the bliss of Heaven.

(The Kingis Quair, stanzas 187–97.)

ROBERT HENRYSON

1425?–1506?

Robene and Makyne

Robene sat on gude green hill,
Keepand a flock of fe:[5]
Merry Makyne said him till
'Robene, thou rue[6] on me;

---

[1] remission.　　[2] control.
[3] a repetition of the opening line of the poem.　　[4] hymns, poems.
[5] sheep.　　[6] have pity.

I have thee lovit loud and still[1]
Thir yearis two or three;
My dule in dern but gif thou dill,[2]
Doubtless but dreid[3] I dee.'

Robene answerit, 'By the Rood,
Nathing of love I knaw,
But keepis my sheep under yon wood,[4]
Lo where they rake on raw![5]
What has marrit[6] thee in thy mood,[7]
Makyne, to me thou shaw;
Or what is love, or to be lo'ed?
Fain wald I lear that law.'

'At lovis lair gif thou will lear
Tak there ane A B C:
Be heynd,[8] courteous, and fair of feir,[9]
Wise, hardy, and free;
So that no danger do thee deir,[10]
What dule in dern thou dree;[11]
Press thou with pain at all power,[12]
Be patient and privie.'[13]

Robene answerit her again,
'I wat nocht what is love;
But I have marvel in certain
What makis thee thus wanrufe:[14]
The weddir is fair, and I am fain,
My sheep gois haill abufe;
An[15] we wald play us in this plain,
They wald us baith reprufe.

---

[1] openly and secretly.   [2] unless thou assuagest my secret sorrow.
[3] without doubt.   [4] wood.   [5] wander in a row.   [6] marred.
[7] mind.   [8] gentle.   [9] demeanour.   [10] disdain harm thee.
[11] whatever sorrow thou sufferest in secret.
[12] strive earnestly to the best of your ability.
[13] discreet.   [14] unhappy.   [15] if.

'Robene, tak tent unto my tale,
And work all as I rede,[1]
And thou sall have my hairt all haill,
Eke and my maidenheid.
Sen God sendis boot for bale,[2]
And for mourning remeid,
In dern with thee but gif I deal,[3]
Doubtless I am but deid.'

'Makene, to-morn this ilka tide,[4]
An[5] ye will meet me here,
Peraventure my sheep may gang beside,[6]
Till we have liggit[7] full near;
But maugre have I, and I bide,
Fra they being to steir;[8]
What lyis on hairt I will nocht hide;
Makyne, than mak gude cheer.'

'Robene, thou reivis my roif[9] and rest;
I love but thee alane.'
'Makyne, adieu, the sun gois west,
The day is near hand gane.'
'Robene, in dule I am so drest,
That love will be my bane.'[10]
'Ga love, Makyne, wherever thou list,
For leman[11] I loe nane.'

'Robene, I stand in sic a styll;[12]
I sich,[13] and that full sair.'
'Makyne, I have been here this while;
At hame God gif I were!'

---

[1] counsel.   [2] comfort for sorrow.
[3] unless I deal with thee in secret.   [4] at this same time.
[5] if.   [6] stay near.   [7] lain.
[8] But I shall be ill at ease if I stay after they begin to move.
[9] deprivest me of ease.   [10] bane.   [11] mistress.   [12] plight.
[13] sigh.

'My honey, Robene, talk ane while,
Gif thou will do na mair.'
'Makyne, some other man beguile,
For hameward I will fare.'

Robene on his wayis went,
As licht as leaf on tree;
Makyne mournit in her intent,[1]
And trow'd him never to see.
Robene braid attour the bent;[2]
Than Makyne cryit on hie,
'Now may thou sing, for I am shent![3]
What ailis love at me?'

Makyne went hame withoutin fail,
Full weary efter couth[4] weep:
Than Robene in a full fair dale
Assemblit all his sheep.
By that some pairt of Makynis ail
Outthrow his hairt could creep;
He fallowit her fast her till assail,
And till her took gude keep.[5]

'Abide, abide, thou fair Makyne,
A word for ony thing!
For all my love it sall be thine,
Withoutin depairting.[6]
All haill thy hairt for till have mine[7]
Is all my coveting;
My sheep to-morn till houris nine
Will need of no keeping.'

'Robene, thou has heard sung and say,
In gestis[8] and storeis auld,

---

[1] thought.   [2] hurried over the heath.   [3] undone.   [4] she did.
[5] heed.   [6] division.   [7] to have thy heart wholly mine.   [8] tales.

The man that will nocht when he may
Sall have nocht when he wald.
I pray to Jesu every day
Mot eke[1] their cairis cauld,
That first pressis with thee to play,
Be firth,[2] forest, or fauld.'[3]

'Makyne, the nicht is soft and dry,
The weddir is warm and fair,
And the green wood richt near us by
To walk attour all where;
There may na janglour[4] us espy,
That is to love contrair;
Therein, Makyne, baith ye and I
Unseen we may repair.'

'Robene, that warld is all away
And quite brocht till ane end,
And never again thereto, perfay
Sall it be as thou wend;[5]
For of my pain thou made it play,[6]
And all in vain I spend;[7]
As thou has done, sa sall I say,
Mourn on, I think to mend.'

'Makyne, the hope of all my heal,
My hairt on thee is set,
And evermair to thee be leal,
While I may live but let;[8]
Never to fail, as otheris feill,[9]
What grace that ever I get.'
'Robene, with thee I will nocht deal;
Adieu, for thus we met.'

---

[1] may increase.   [2] coppice.   [3] enclosed field, enclosure.
[4] tell-tale.   [5] thoughtest.   [6] made game.   [7] spent.
[8] without hindrance.   [9] as many others.

Makyne went hame blithe aneuch,
Attour the holtis hair;[1]
Robene murnit, and Makyne leuch:[2]
She sang, he sichit sair;
And so left him, baith woe and wreuch,[3]
In dolour and in care,
Keepand his herd under a heuch,[4]
Amangis the holtis hair.

The Abbey Walk

Alone as I went up and doun,
In ane abbey was fair to see,
Thinkand what consolatioun
Was best into adversitie,
On case[5] I kest on side mine ee,
And saw this written upon a wall:
'Of what estate, man, that thou be,
Obey, and thank thy God of[6] all

'Thy kingdom and thy great empire,
Thy royalty, nor rich array,
Sall nocht endure at thy desire,
But as the wind will wend away;
Thy gold and all thy gudis gay,
When fortune list will fra thee fall;
Sen[7] thou sic[8] samples sees ilk[9] day,
Obey, and thank thy God of all.

'Job was maist rich in Writ we find,
Tobie[10] maist full of cheritie:
Job wox puir, and Tobie blind,
Baith temptit with adversitie.
Sen blindness was infirmitie,

---

[1] gray thickets. [2] laughed. [3] woeful and wretched. [4] cliff.
[5] by chance. [6] for. [7] since. [8] such. [9] every. [10] Tobit.

And poverty was natural,
Therefore richt patiently baith he and he[1]
Obeyit and thankit God of all.

'Though thou be blind, or have ane halt,
Or in thy face deformit ill,
Sa it come nocht through thy default,
Na man suld thee repreif by skill[2]
Blame nocht thy Lord, sa is his will;
Spurn nocht thy foot aganis the wall;
But with meek heart and prayer still
Obey, and thank thy God of all.

'God of his justice mon correct,
And of his mercy pity haif;
He is ane Judge to nane suspect.
To punish sinful man and saif.
Though thou be lord attour the laif[3]
And efterward made bound and thrall,
Ane puir beggar, with scrip and staff,
Obey, and thank thy God of all.

'This changing and great variance
Of erdly[4] statis up and doun
Is nocht but casualty and chance,
As some men sayis, without reasoun,[5]
But by the great provisioun
Of God above that rule thee sall;
Therefore ever thou mak thee boun[6]
To obey, and thank thy God of all.

---

[1] the one and the other.   [2] with reason,   [3] above the rest.
[4] earthly.
[5] i.e. is not, as some men say without reason, merely casualty
and chance.
[6] ready.

'In wealth be meek, heich[1] nocht thy self;
Be glad in woeful povertie;
Thy power and thy warldis pelf
Is nocht but very vanitie.
Remember Him that deit on tree,
For thy sake tastit the bitter gall;
Wha heis law hairtis and lawis hie[2]
Obey and thank thy God of all.'

The Taill of the Uponlandis Mous and the Burges Mous

Aesop, mine Author, makis mentioun
Of twa myis, and they were sisteris dear,
Of wham the eldest dwelt in ane boroughis toun,[3]
The other wynnit uponland,[4] weill near,
Solitar, while under busk,[5] while under breir,
Whilis in the corn, in other mennis skaith,[6]
As outlawis does and livis on their waith.[7]

This rural mous into the winter tide
Had hunger, cauld, and tholit[8] great distress,
The other mous that in the burgh can bide
Was guild brother and made ane free burges;
Toll free als,[9] but custom mair or less,[10]
And freedom had to ga wherever sho list,
Among the cheese in ark,[11] and meal in kist.[12]

Ane time when sho was full and unfootsair,
Sho took in mind her sister uponland,
And langit for to hear of her weelfare,
To see what life sho had under the wand:[13]

---

[1] exalt.   [2] who raises the low and humbles the high.   [3] burgh.
[4] landward. [5] bush. [6] to other men's hurt. [7] hunting. [8] suffered.
[9] also.   [10] exempt from both the Great and the Petty Customs.
[11] box.   [12] chest.   [13] in the open.

Barefoot, alone, with pikestaff in her hand,
As puir pilgrim sho passit out of toun,
To seek her sister baith owre dale and doun.

Furth mony wilsome[1] wayis can sho walk,
Through moss and muir, through bankis, busk, and
　　　breir,
Sho ran cryand till sho come to ane balk:[2]
'Come furth to me, my awin sister dear;
Cry "peip" anis!' With that the mous cryit 'Here!'
And knew her voice, as kinnisman will do,
Be very kind;[3] and furth sho come her to.

The heartly joy, God, gif ye had seen,
Beis kith[4] when that thir sisteris met;
And great kindness was shawin them between,
For whiles they leuch,[5] and whiles for joy they gret,[6]
While kissit sweet, whilis in armis plet,[7]
And thus they fure,[8] till soberit was their mood
Syne foot for foot into the chalmer yude.[9]

As I heard say, it was ane sober wane,[10]
Of fog[11] and fern full febillie was made,
Ane silly shiel[12] under ane steadfast stane,
Of whilk the entres was not hie nor braid;
And in the samin they went but mair abade,[13]
Without fire or candle birnand bricht,
For commonly sic pickers loves not licht.

When they were lodgit thus, thir[14] silly mice,
The youngest sister in her buttery glide,
And brocht furth nuttis and candle instead of spice;
Gif this was gude fare, I do it on them beside.[15]

---

[1] wild.　[2] bank.　[3] nature, instinct.　[4] is shown.　[5] laughed.
[6] cried.　[7] folded.　[8] fared.　[9] went.　[10] dwelling.　[11] moss.
[12] poor hut.　[13] without more delay.　[14] these.　[15] leave it to them.

The burges mous prompit[1] furth in pride,
And said, 'Sister, is this your daily food?'
'Why not,' said she, 'is not this meat richt gude?'

'Na, be my saull, I think it but ane scorn.'
'Madam,' quod sho, 'ye be the more to blame;
My mother said, sister, when we were born,
That I and ye lay baith within ane wame[2]:
I keep the rate and custom of my dame,
And of my living into poverty,
For landis have we nane in property.'

'My fair sister,' quod sho, 'have me excusit,
This rude diet and I can not accord;
To tender meat my stomach is aye usit,
For whiles I fare as weel as ony lord;
Thir widderit peas and nuttis, or they be bored,
Will brek my teeth and mak my wame[3] full sklender,
Whilk was before usit to meatis tender.'

'Weel, weel, sister,' quod the rural mous,
'Gif it please you, sic thingis as ye see here,
Baith meat and drink, harberie[4] and house,
Sall be your awin, will ye remain all year;
Ye sall it have with blithe and merry cheer,
And that suld mak the maissis[5] that are rude,
Amang freindis, richt tender and wonder gude.

'What pleasure is in the feastis delicate,
The whilkis are gevin with ane glowmand[6] brow?
Ane gentle heart is better recreate
With blithe courage, than seith to him ane cow:
Ane modicum is mair for till allow,
Swa that gude will be carver at the dais,
Than thrawit[7] will and mony spicit mais.'

---

[1] moved. [2] womb. [3] stomach. [4] lodging. [5] foods.
[6] frowning. [7] distorted.

For all her merry exhortatioun,
This burges mous had little will to sing,
But heavily sho cast her browis doun,
For all the dainties that sho could her bring.
Yet at the last sho said, half in hething,[1]
'Sister, this victual and your royal feast
May weel suffice unto ane rural beast.

'Lat be this hole, and come unto my place;
I sall to you shaw by experience
My Gude Friday is better nor your Pace[2];
My dish lickingis is worth your hail expence;
I have houses enow of great defence;
Of cat nor fall-trap I have na dreid.'
'I grant,' quod sho, and on togidder they yeid.

In stubbill array[3] throw gers and corn,
And under buskis privily couth[4] they creep,
The eldest was the guide and went beforn,
The younger to her wayis took gude keep.
On nicht they ran, and on the day can sleep;
Till in the morning, or[5] the laverock sang,
They fand the toun, and in blithly could gang.

Not far fra thine[6] unto ane worthy wane
This burges brocht them soon where they suld be;
Without 'God speed' their herberie was tane,
Into ane spence[7] with victual great plentie;
Baith cheese and butter upon their skelfis[8] hie,
And flesh and fish aneuch, baith fresh and salt,
And sackis full of meal and eke of malt.

Efter when they disposit were to dine,
Withouten grace they wesh and went to meat,
With all coursis that cookis could divine,

---

[1] derision.   [2] Easter.   [3] by secret ways.   [4] did.
    [5] before.   [6] thence.   [7] larder.   [8] shelves.

Mutton and beef, stricken in tailyeis[1] great;
Ane lordis fare thus couth they counterfeit,
Except ane thing, they drank the water clear
Instead of wine, but yet they made gude cheer.

With blithe upcast and merry countenance,
The eldest sister speirit at[2] her guest,
Gif that sho be reason[3] fand difference
Betwix that chalmer[4] and her sarie[5] nest.
'Yea, dame,' quod sho, 'how lang will this lest?'[6]
'For evermair, I wait, and langer too.'
'Gif it be swa,[7] ye are at ease,' quod sho.

Till eke their cheer ane subcharge[8] furth sho brocht,
Ane plate of groatis,[9] and ane dish full of meal;
Thraf[10] cakis als I trow sho sparit nocht,
Abundantly about her for to deal;
And mane[11] full fine sho brocht instead of geill,[12]
And ane white candle out of ane coffer stall,[13]
Instead of spice to gust[14] their mouth withal.

Thus made they merry till they micht na mair,
And 'Hail, Yule, hail!' cryit upon hie.
Yet after joy ofttimes cumis care,
And trouble after great prosperitie.
Thus as they sat in all their jollitie,
The spenser[15] come with keyis in his hand,
Openit the door, and them at denner fand.

They tarryit not to wesh, as I suppose,
But on to ga wha that micht foremost win.
The burges has ane hole, and in sho goes;
Her sister had na hole to hide her in:

---

[1] cuts, portions. [2] asked. [3] for good reason. [4] chamber.
[5] sorry. [6] last. [7] so. [8] additional cause. [9] grain.
[10] unleavened. [11] fine bread. [12] jelly. [13] stole.
[14] give relish to. [15] steward.

To see that silly mous it was great sin,[1]
So desolate and will of ane gude reid;[2]
For very dreid sho fell in swoon near deid.

But, as God wald, it fell ane happy case;
The spenser had na leisure for to bide,
Neither to seek nor search, nor scare nor chase,
But on he went, and left the door up wide.
The bauld burges his passing weel has spied;
Out of her hole sho come and cryit on hie,
'How fare ye, sister? Cry peip, wherever ye be!'

This rural mous lay flatling on the ground,
And for the death sho was full sair dredand,
For till her heart straik[3] mony woeful stound,
As in ane fever sho trimbillit fute and hand;
And whan her sister in sic ply her fand,
For very pity sho began to greet,
Syne confort her with wordis humble and sweet.

'Why lie ye thus? Rise up, my sister dear,
Come to your meat, this peril is overpast.'
The other answerit her with heavy cheer,
'I may not eat, sa sair I am aghast:
I had lever[4] thir forty dayis fast,
With water kail[5] and to gnaw beanis and peis,
Than all your feast in this dread and disease.'

With fair treaty yet sho gart her[6] uprise,
And to the burde they went and togidder sat,
And scantly had they drunken aince or twice,
When in come Gib Hunter, our jolly cat,
And bade God speed; the burges up with that,
And till the hole sho went as fire on flint:
Baudrons the other be the back has hint.[7]

---

[1] pity.   [2] at a loss for what to do.   [3] struck.   [4] rather.
[5] broth made without meat.   [6] caused her to.   [7] caught.

Fra foot to foot he kest her to and fra,
Whiles up, whiles doun, as cant[1] as ony kid;
Whiles wald her rin under the stra,
Whiles wald he wink, and play with her buk heid.[2]
Thus to the silly mous great pain he did,
Till at the last, through fortune and gude hap,
Betwix ane burde and the wall sho crap.

And up in haste behind ane parraling[3]
Sho clam so hie, that Gilbert micht not get her,
Syne be the cluke[4] there craftily can hing,
Till he was gane, her cheer was all the better.
Syne doun sho lap when there was nane to let[5] her,
And to the burges mous loud can sho cry:
'Farewell, sister, thy feast here I defy!

'Thy mangerie is mingit[6] all with care,
Thy goose is gude, thy gansell[7] sour as gall;
The subcharge of thy service is but sair,
Sa sal thou find hereefterwart may fall.
I thank yon curtain and yon perpall[8] wall
Of my defence now fra ane cruel beast.
Almichty God, keep me fra sic ane feast.

'Were I into the kith[9] that I come fra,
For weal nor woe suld I never come again.'
With that sho took her leave and furth can ga,
Whiles through the corn, and whilis through the
        plain;
When sho was furth and free, sho was full fain,
And merrily markit[10] unto the muir:
I cannot tell how weel therefter sho fure.

---

[1] lively.   [2] hide and seek.   [3] partition.   [4] claw.   [5] prevent.
[6] feast is mingled.   [7] garlic sauce.   [8] partition.   [9] country.
            [10] found her way.

But I heard say sho passit to her den,
As warm as wool, suppose it was not great
Full beinly[1] stuffit, baith but and ben,[2]
Of beanis and nuttis, peis, rye, and wheat;
Whenever sho list, sho had aneuch to eat;
In quiet and ease, withouten ony dreid,
But to her sisteris feast na mair sho yeid.

Moralitas

Freindis, ye may find, and[3] ye will tak heed,
Into this fable ane gude moralitie;
As fitchis[4] myngit are with noble seed,
Swa interminglit is adversitie
With eirdlie joy; swa that na estate is free,
Without trouble and some vexatioun:
As namely[5] they whilk clymmis up maist hie,
That are not content with small possessioun.

Blissit be simple life withouten dreid;
Blissit be sober feist in quietie:
Wha has aneuch, of na mair has he need,
Though it be little into quantitie.
Great abundance and blind prosperitie
Oftimes makis ane evil conclusioun;
The sweetest life, therefore, in this countrie
Is sickerness,[6] with small possessioun.

O wanton man! That usis for to feed
Thy wame, and makis it ane god to be,
Look to thyself: I warn thee weel, but dreid,
The cat cumis, and to the mous has ee:
What vaillis than thy feast and royaltie,
With dreidful heart, and tribulatioun?

---

[1] well.   [2] both in the outer and in the inner room.   [3] if.
[4] vetch.   [5] especially.   [6] security.

Best thing in eird therefore, I say, for me,
Is blitheness in heart, with small possessioun.

Thy awin fire, my freind, sa it be but ane gleid,[1]
It warmis weel, and is worth gold to thee;
And Solomon says, gif that thou will read,
'Under the heaven there can no better be,
Than aye to be blithe and live in honestie.'
Wherefore I may conclude by this reasoun:[2]
Of eirdlie joy it bearis maist degree,
Blitheness in heart, with small possessioun.

From *The Testament of Cresseid*

(i) *Prologue*

Ane doolie[3] season to ane careful dyte[4]
Suld correspond, and be equivalent.
Richt sa it wes when I began to write
This tragedy; the wedder richt fervent,
When Aries, in middis of the Lent,
Showeris of hail can fra the north descend,[5]
That scantly fra the cauld I micht defend.

Yet, nevertheless, within mine oratur[6]
I stood, when Titan had his beamis bricht
Withdrawin doun, and sylit[7] under cure,[8]
And fair Venus, the beauty of the nicht,
Upraise, and set unto the west full richt
Her golden face, in oppositioun
Of God Phoebus, direct descending doun.

Through out the glass her beamis brast[9] sa fair
That I micht see on every side me by.
The northin wind had purifyit the air,

---

[1] ember.   [2] declaration.   [3] dull.   [4] sorrowful poem.
[5] did bring down from the north.   [6] oratory.   [7] hidden.
[8] cover.   [9] pierced.

And shed[1] the misty cloudis fra the sky;
The frost freisit, the blastis bitterly
Fra Pole Arctic come whistling loud and schill,[2]
And causit me remove aganis my will.

For I traistit that Venus, Lovis Queen,
To whom some time I hecht[3] obedience,
My faded heart of love sho wald mak green;
And thereupon, with humble reverence,
I thocht to pray her hie magnificence;
But for great cauld as than I lattit[4] was,
And to my chalmer to the fire can pass.

Though love be hait,[5] yet in ane man of age
It kindles nocht sa soon as in youthheid,
Of whom the blude is flowing in ane rage,
And in the auld the corage doif[6] and deid,
Of whilk the fire outward is best remeid;
To help by physic where that nature failit,
I am expert—for baith I have assailit.[7]

I mend the fire, and beikit[8] me about,
Than took ane drink my spreitis to comfort,
And armit me weel fra the cauld thereout
To cut the winter nicht, and mak it short,
I took ane quair,[9] and left all other sport,
Written by worthy Chaucer glorious,
Of fair Cresseid and worthy Troilus. . . .

(ll. 1–42.)

*(The Gods have assembled in Council and pronounced
sentence on Cressida)*

(ii)

This duleful sentence Saturn took on hand,
And passit doun where careful[10] Cresseid lay,

[1] swept.   [2] shrill.   [3] promised.   [4] prevented.   [5] hot.
[6] dull.   [7] tried.   [8] warmed.   [9] book.   [10] sorrowful.

And on her heid he laid ane frosty wand;
Than lawfully on this wise can he say:
'Thy great fairness, and all thy beauty gay,
Thy wanton blude, and eek thy golden hair,
Here I exclude fra thee for evermair.

'I change thy mirth into melancholy,
Whilk is the mother of all pensiveness;
Thy moisture and thy heat in cauld and dry;
Thine insolence, thy play and wantonness
To great disease[1]; thy pomp and thy riches
In mortal need; and great penurity
Thou suffer sall, and as ane beggar die.'

O cruel Saturn! fraward[2] and angry,
Hard is thy doom, and too malicious:
On fair Cresseid why hes thou na mercy,
Whilk was sa sweet, gentle, and amorous?
Withdraw thy sentence, and be gracious
As thou was never; so shawis thou thy deed,
Ane wraikful[3] sentence given on fair Cresseid.

Than Cynthia, when Saturn passed away,
Out of her sait[4] descended down belyve,[5]
And read ane bill on Cresseid where sho lay,
Containing this sentence definitive:
'Fra heat of body I thee now deprive,
And to thy seikness sall be na recure,[6]
But in dolour thy dayis to endure.

'Thy crystal een minglit with blude I mak;
Thy voice sa clear, unpleasand, hoir and hace;[7]
Thy lusty lyre[8] owre spread with spottis black,
And lumpis haw[9] appeirand in thy face;

---

[1] discomfort.   [2] froward.   [3] vindictive.   [4] seat.
[5] straightway.   [6] recovery.   [7] rough and hoarse.
[8] complexion.   [9] livid.

Where thou cummis, ilk man sall flee the place;
Thus sall thou go begging fra house to house
With cup and clapper like ane lazarous.'[1]

This doolie dream, this ugly vision
Brocht to ane end, Cresseid fra it awoke,
And all that court and convocatioun
Vanished away; than raise sho up and took
Ane poleist glass, and her shadow could look;[2]
And when sho saw her face sa deformait,
Gif sho in heart was woe aneuch, God wait![3]

Weeping full sair, 'Lo, what it is,' quod she,
'With fraward langage for to move and steer
Our crabbit Goddis, and sa is seen on me!
My blaspheming now have I bocht full dear;
All eirdlie[4] joy and mirth I set arear[5]
Alas, this day! alas, this woeful tide!
When I began with my Goddis for to chide.'

Be this was said, ane child come fra the hall,
To warn Cresseid the supper was ready;
First knockit at the door, and syne could[6] call,
'Madam, your father bids you come in hy,
He has marvel sa lang on grouf[7] ye lie,
And says your prayers been too lang some deal,[8]
The Goddis wait[9] all your intent full weel.'

Quod sho, 'Fair child, ga to my father dear
And pray him come to speak to me anon.'
And sa he did, and said, 'Douchter, what cheer?'
'Alas!' quod sho, 'Father, my mirth is gone.'
'How sa?' quod sho, and sho can all expone,[10]

---

[1] leper.   [2] did look at.   [3] God knows if she was sad enough.
[4] earthly.   [5] away.   [6] then did.   [7] grovelling.
[8] are somewhat too long.   [9] know.   [10] explain.

As I have tauld, the vengeance and the wrack,[1]
For her trespass, Cupid on her could tak.

He lookit on her ugly lipper[2] face,
The whilk before was white as lily flower;
Wringand his hands, ofttimes he said, alas,
That he had levit to see that woeful hour;
For he knew weel that there was na succour
To her seikness, and that doublit his pain;
Thus was there care aneuch betwix tham twain.

When they togidder mournit had full lang,
Quod Cresseid, 'Father, I wald not be kenned;
Therefore in secret wise ye let me gang
Unto yon hospital at the tounis end;
And thidder some meat for cheritie me send,
To live upon; for all mirth in this eird
Is fra me gane—sic is my wicked weird.[3]

Then in ane mantle and ane bawer[4] hat,
With cup and clapper, wonder privily
He opnit ane secret yett, and out thereat
Convoyit her, that na man suld espy,
Unto ane village half ane mile thereby;
Deliverit her in at the spittal hous,[5]
And daily sent her part of her almous.[6]

Some knew her weel, and some had na knawledge
Of her, because she was so deformait
With bylis[7] black owrespread in her visage,
And her fair colour faidit and alterait.
Yet they presumit for her hie regrait,[8]
And still murning, sho was of noble kin:
With better will therefore they took her in.

---

[1] punishment. [2] leper. [3] fate. [4] beaver. [5] hospital.
[6] alms. [7] boils. [8] great sorrow.

The day passit, and Phoebus went to rest,
The cloudis black owrewhelmit all the sky:
God wait gif Cresseid was ane sorrowful guest,
Seeing that uncouth fare and harbery![1]
But[2] meat or drink sho dressit her to lie
In ane dark corner of the house alone;
And on this wise, weeping, sho made her moan.

The Complaint of Cresseid

'O sop of sorrow, sunken into care!
O catiff Cresseid! for now and evermair
Gane is thy joy, and all thy mirth in eird;
Of all blitheness now art thou blaiknit bare;[3]
There is na salve may save thee of thy sair.[4]
Fell is thy Fortune, wicked is thy weird;
Thy bliss is banished, and thy bale on breird;[5]
Under the earth God gif I graven were,[6]
Where nane of Greece nor yet of Troy might heird.[7]

'Where is thy chalmer wantonly beseen,
With burely bed and bankouris browderit bene,[8]
Spicis and wine in thy collatioun,
The cupis all of gold and silver sheen,
The sweet meatis, servit in plaittis clean,
With saipheron[9] sauce of ane gude seasoun,
Thy gay garmentis with mony gudely goun,
Thy pleasand lawn prinnit[10] with golden preen?[11]
All is arear, thy great royal renown.

'Where is thy garden with thir greissis gay,
And fresh flowris, whilk the Queen Floray

---

[1] lodging.   [2] without.   [3] blackened without hope.
[4] heal thee of thy disease.   [5] increasing.   [6] were laid in my grave.
                    [7] hear it.
[8] with handsome bed and tapestries embroidered beautifully.
          [9] saffron.   [10] pinned.   [11] pin.

Had painted pleasantly in every pane,
Where thou was wont full merrily in May
To walk and take the dew be it was day,
And hear the merle and mavis[1] mony ane,
With ladies fair in carolling to gane,[2]
And see the royal rinkis[3] in their array,
In garmentis gay, garnished on every grain.[4]

'Thy great triumphand fame and hie honour,
Where thou was callit of eirdlie wichtis flour—
All is decayit, thy weird is welterit[5] so,
Thy hie estait is turnit in darkness dour.
This lipper lodge[6] tak for thy burely bour,[7]
And for thy bed tak now ane bunch of stro;
For waillit[8] wine and meatis thou had tho,
Tak mowlit[9] breid, perry, and cider sour;
But cup and clapper, now is all ago.

'My clear voice and courtly carolling,
Where I was wont with ladies for to sing,
Is rawk[10] as rook, full hideous, hoir and hace;
My pleasand port, all otheris precelling[11]—
Of lustiness[12] I was hald[13] maist conding[14]—
Now is deformit the figure of my face—
To look on it na leid[15] now liking hes:
Sowpit in syte,[16] I say with sair siching,[17]
Lodgeit amang the lipper leid, alas!

'O ladies fair of Troy and Greece attend
My misery, whilk nane may comprehend,
My frivoll fortoun, my infelicity,

---

[1] blackbird and thrush.   [2] go.   [3] folk.   [4] in every colour.
[5] fortune is reversed.   [6] leper lodging.   [7] handsome bower.
[8] choice.   [9] mouldy.   [10] raucous.   [11] excelling.
[12] amorousness.   [13] held.   [14] excellent.   [15] person.
[16] drenched in sorrow.   [17] sighing.

My greit mischief, whilk na man can amend;
Be war in time, approachis near the end,
And in your mind a mirror mak of me;
As I am now, peradventure that ye,
For all your micht, may come to the same end,
Or ellis war,[1] gif ony war may be.

'Nocht is your fairness but ane fading flower,
Nocht is your famous laud and hie honour
But wind inflat[2] in other mennis earis;
Your roseing[3] red to rotting sall retour.[4]
Exempill mak of me in your memour,
Whilk of sic thingis woeful witness bearis,
All wealth in eird away as wind it weiris;[5]
Be war, therefore, approachis near the hour:
Fortune is fickle, when sho beginnis and steiris.'

Thus chydand with her dreary destiny,
Weeping, sho woke the nicht fra end to end;
But all in vain; her dule, her careful cry,
Micht not remeid, nor yet her mourning mend.
Ane lipper lady raise, and till her wend,
And said, 'Why spurnis thou aganis the wall,
To slay thyself, and mend nathing at all.

'Sen thy weeping doubillis but thy woe,
I counsel thee mak virtue of ane need;
Go leir[6] to clap thy clapper to and fro,
And live efter the law of lipper leid.'
There was na boot, but furth with them she yeid,[7]
Fra place to place, till cauld and hunger sair
Compellit her to be ane rank beggair.

That samin time of Troy the garnisoun,
Whilk had to chieftain worthy Troilus,

---

[1] worse. [2] blown. [3] rosy. [4] return. [5] wastes.
[6] learn. [7] went.

Through jeopardy of weir[1] had stricken doun
Knichtis of Greece in number marvellous:
With great triumph and laud victorious
Again to Troy richt royally they rade,
The way where Cresseid with the lipper bade.

Seeing that company, they come all with ane stevin;[2]
They gave ane cry, and shook cuppis gude speed;
Said, 'Worthy lords, for Goddis love of heaven,
To us lipper part of your almous deed!'[3]
Than to their cry noble Troilus took heed,
Having pity, near by the place can pass
Where Cresseid sat, not witting what sho was.

Than upon him sho cast up baith her een,
And with ane blenk it come into his thocht
That he sometime her face before had seen;
But sho was in sic plye[4] he knew her nocht;
Yet than her look into his mind it brocht
The sweet visage and amorous blenking[5]
Of fair Cresseid, sometime his awin darling.

Na wonder was, suppose in mind that he
Took her figure sa soon, and lo! Now why!
The idole of ane thing in case may be
Sa deep imprentit in the fantasy,
That it deludes the wittis outwardly
And so appearis in form and like estate
Within the mind as it was figurait.

Ane spark of love than till his heart could spring,
And kindlit all his body in ane fire,
With het fever ane sweit and trimbling
Him took, till he was ready to expire;
To bear his shield his breist began to tire;

[1] war.   [2] cry.   [3] give of your charity.   [4] plight.   [5] glances.

Within ane while he changit mony hue,
And, nevertheless, not ane another knew.

For knichtlie pity and memorial
Of fair Cresseid, a girdle can he tak,
Ane purse of gold, and mony gay jowall,
And in the skirt of Cresseid doun can swak:[1]
Than raid away, and not ane word he spak,
Pensive in heart, till he come to the toun,
And for greit care oft syis[2] almaist fell doun.

The lipper folk to Cresseid than can draw,
To see the equal distribution
Of the almous; but when the gold they saw,
Ilk ane to other privily can roun,[3]
And said, 'Yon lord has mair affectioun,
However it be, unto yon lazarous
Than to us all; we knaw by his almous.'

'What lord is yon,' quod sho, 'have ye na feill,[4]
Has done to us so greit humanitie?'
'Yes,' quod a lipper man, 'I knaw him weill;
Sir Troilus it is, gentle and free.'
When Cresseid understood that it was he,
Stiffer than steel there stert ane bitter stound
Throughout her heart, and fell doun to the ground.

When sho, owrecome with sighing sair and sad,
With mony careful cry and cauld 'Ochane!
Now is my breist with stormy stoundis stad,[5]
Wrappit in woe, ane wretch full will of wane.'[6]
Than swoonit sho oft or sho could refrain,
And ever in her swooning cryit sho thus:
'O false Cresseid! and true knicht Troilus!

---

[1] throw.   [2] often.   [3] whisper.   [4] knowledge.   [5] beset.
[6] devoid of hope.

'Thy love, thy lawtie,[1] and thy gentleness,
I countit small in my prosperity,
Sa elevat I was in wantonness,
And clam[2] upon the fickle wheel sa hie;
All faith and love I promissit to thee
Was in the self[3] fickle and frivolous;
O, false Cresseid! and true knicht Troilus!

'For love of me thou kept gude continence,
Honest and chaste in conversatioun,
Of all wemen protector and defence
Thou was, and helpit their opinioun:[4]
My mind in fleshly foul affectioun
Was inclinit to lustis lecherous:
Fie, false Cresseid! O, true knicht Troilus!

'Lovers, beware, and tak gude heed about
Whom that ye love, for whom ye suffer pain;
I lat you wit, there is richt few thereout
Whom ye may trust to have true love again;
Preve when ye will, your labour is in vain;
Therefore, I rede ye tak them as ye find,
For they are sad[5] as widdercock in wind,

'Because I know the great unstableness,
Bruckle[6] as glass, into myself I say,
Trusting in other as great unfaithfulness,
As unconstant, and as untrue of fay;[7]
Thoch some be true, I wait richt few are they;
Wha findis truth, lat him his lady ruse:[8]
Nane but myself, as now, I will accuse.'

When this was said, with paper sho sat doun,
And on this manner made her testament:
'Here I beteiche[9] my corpse and carrioun

---

[1] loyalty.   [2] climbed.   [3] in itself.   [4] aided their reputation.
[5] steadfast.   [6] brittle.   [7] faith.   [8] extol.   [9] deliver.

With wormis and with taidis[1] to be rent;
My cup and clapper, and mine ornament,
And all my gold, the lipper folk sall have,
When I am deid, to bury me in grave.

'This royal ring, set with this ruby reid,
Whilk Troilus in drowrie[2] to me send,
To him again I leave it when I am deid,
To mak my careful deid[3] unto him kend:
Thus I conclude shortly, and mak ane end;
My spreit I leave to Diane, where sho dwells,
To walk with her in waste woodis and wellis.[4]

'O Diomede! Thou has baith brooch and belt,
Whilk Troilus gave me in takning[5]
Of his true love'—and with that word sho swelt;[6]
And soon ane lipper man took off the ring,
Syne buryit her withouten tarrying:
To Troilus forthwith the ring he bare,
And of Cresseid the death he can declare.

When he had heard her great infirmitie,
Her legacie and lamentatioun,
And how sho endit in sic povertie,
He swelt[7] for woe, and fell doun in ane swoun;
For great sorrow his heart to brist was boun:[8]
Siching full sadly, said, 'I can no more;
Sho was untrue, and woe is me therefore.'

Some said he made ane tomb of marble gray,
And wrait her name and superscriptioun,
And laid it on her grave, where that sho lay,
In golden letteris, containing this reasoun:[9]

---

[1] toads.   [2] courtship.   [3] sorrowful death.   [4] fountains.
[5] token.   [6] died.   [7] fainted.   [8] was ready to break.
[9] declaration.

'Lo, fair ladies, Cresseid of Troyis toun,
Sometime countit the flower of womanheid,
Under this stane, late lipper, lyis deid.'

(ll. 309–616.)

The Praise of Age

Wythin a garth, under a reid rosere,[1]
Ane auld man, and decrepit, heard I sing;
Gay was the note, sweet was the voice and clear:
It was great joy to hear of sic a thing.
'And to my doom',[2] he said in his ditting,[3]
'For to be young I wald nocht, for my wis [4]
Of all this warld to mak me lord and king:
The more of age the nearer heavenis bliss.

'False is this warld, and full of variance,
Owreset with syn[5] and other sytis mo;
Truth is all tint,[6] guile has the governance,
Wrechitness has wrocht all wealthis weal to woe;
Freedom is tynt, and flemyt[7] the lordis fro,
And covetice is all the cause of this;
I am content that youthheid is ago[8]:
The more of age the nearer heavenis bliss.

'The state of youth I repute for na gude,
For in that state great peril now I see;
Bot full small grace, the raging of his blood
Can nane gainstand[9] while that he aged be;
Syne of the thing that tofore joyit he
Nothing remains for to be callit his;
For-why[10] it was but very vanitie:
The more of age the nearer heavenis bliss.

[1] rose-tree.   [2] in my opinion.   [3] singing.   [4] wish.
[5] overwhelmed with sorrow.   [6] lost.   [7] put to flight.
[8] gone.   [9] withstand.   [10] because.

'No man suld traist this wrechit warld, for why
Of erdly joy aye sorrow is the end;
The state of it can no man certify,
The day a king; the morn na gude to spend.
What have we here but grace us to defend?
The whilk God grant us till amend our miss,
That to his glore he may our saulis send;
The more of age the nearer heavenis bliss.'

WILLIAM DUNBAR
1460?–1520?

From *The Twa Mariit Wemen and the Wedo*
(i)

Upon the midsummer even, merriest of nichtis,
I movit furth alane, near as midnicht was past,
Beside ane goodlie green garth, full of gay flouris,
Hedgeit, of ane huge hicht, with hawthorn trees;
Whereon ane bird, on ane branch, so birst out her notis
That never ane blithefuller bird was on the beuch
    heard:
What through the sugarit sound of her sang glaid,
And through the savour sanative[1] of the sweet flouris,
I drew in dern[2] to the dyke to dirken efter mirthis;[3]
The dew donkit[4] the dale, and dynnit[5] the foulis.
I heard, under ane hollyn[6] heavenly green hewit,
Ane hie speech, at my hand, with hautand[7] wordis;
With that in haste to the hedge so hard I inthrang[8]
That I was heildit[9] with hawthorn, and with heynd[10]
    leavis:
Through pykis[11] of the plet thorn I presandlie luikit,

---

[1] health-giving. [2] secret. [3] to lie still in search of amusements.
[4] made dank. [5] made a din. [6] holly. [7] proud. [8] pressed.
[9] concealed. [10] sheltering. [11] prickles.

Gif ony person wald approach within that pleasand
    garden.
I saw three gay ladies sit in ane green arbour,
All graithit[1] into garlandis of fresh gudlie flouris;
So glitterit as the gold were their glorious gilt tresses,
While all the gressis did gleam of the glaid hewis;
Kemmit[2] was their clear hair, and curiously shed,[3]
Atour their shulders doun shyre,[4] shining full bricht;
With curches,[5] cassin[6] them abune, of kirsp[7] clear and
    thin:
Their mantles green were as the gress that grew in
    May seasoun,
Fetrit[8] with their white fingeris about their fair sidis:
Of ferliful[9] fine favour were their faces meek,
All full of flourist fairheid,[10] as flouris in June;
White, seemly, and soft, as the sweet lilies;
New upspread upon spray, as new spynist[11] rose,
Arrayit royally about with mony rich vardour,[12]
That Nature, full nobillie, enamelit with flouris
Of alkin[13] hewis under heaven, that ony heynd[14] knew;
Fragrant, all full of fresh odour finest of smell.
Ane cumlie table coverit was before thai clere[15] ladies,
With royal cuppis upon rawis full of rich wines:
And of thir fair wlonkes,[16] twa weddit war with lordis,
Ane was ane widow, I wist, wanton of laitis.[17]
And as they talkit at the table of mony tale sindry,
They wauchtit at[18] the wicht[19] wine, and waris out[20]
    wordis;
And syne they spak more speedily, and sparit no
    matteris.

(ll. 1–40.)

[1] arrayed.   [2] combed.   [3] parted.   [4] sheer, wholly.
[5] kerchiefs.   [6] cast.   [7] lawn.   [8] fastened.   [9] wonderful.
[10] beauty.   [11] blossoming.   [12] verdure.   [13] every kind of.
[14] person.   [15] beautiful.   [16] beauties.   [17] manners.   [18] quaffed.
[19] strong.   [20] dispense.

(ii)

Thus draif they out that dear night with dances full
    noble,
Till that the day did up daw, and dew donkit the
    flouris;
The morrow mild was and meek, the mavis[1] did sing,
And all removit the mist, and the mead smellit;
Silver shouris doun shook, as the sheen crystal,
And birds shouted in shaw,[2] with their schill notis;
The golden glitterand gleam so gladit their heartis,
They made a glorious glee amang the green bewis.
The soft souch[3] of the swyr,[4] and soun of the streamis,
The sweet savour of the sward, and singing of foulis
Micht confort ony creature of the kin of Adam;
And kindle again his courage though it were cauld
    slocknit.[5]
Than raise thir royal roses, in their rich weedis,
And rakit[6] hame to their rest, through the ryce
    bloomis;[7]
And I all privily passes to a pleasand arbour,
And with my pen did report their pastance[8] most
    merry.

(ll. 511–26.)

The Golden Targe[9]

Right as the stern of day[10] begouth[11] to shine,
When gone to bed were Vesper and Lucine,[12]
    I raise, and by a rosere[13] did me rest;
Up sprang the golden candle matutine,[14]

[1] thrush.   [2] grove.   [3] whisper of the wind.   [4] hollow.
[5] cold and extinguished.   [6] went.   [7] blossoms of the ticket.
[8] pastime.   [9] The golden shield of Reason.   [10] day star (sun).
[11] began.   [12] the morning star and the moon.   [13] rose-tree.
[14] of the morning.

With clear depurit beames crystalline,
  Glading the merry foulis in their nest;
    Or[1] Phoebus was in purpur cape revest[2]
Up raise the lark, the heaven's minstrel fine
  In May, in till a morrow mirthfullest.

Full angellike thir birdis sang their houris
Within their curtains green, into their bouris,
  Apparralit white and red, with bloomes sweet;
Enamelit was the field with all colouris,
The pearly droppis shake in silver shouris,
  Till all in balm did branch and leavis fleet[3];
    To part fra Phoebus did Aurora greet,[4]
Her crystal tearis I saw hing on the flouris,
  Whilk he for love all drank up with his heat.

For mirth of May, with skippis and with hoppis,
The birdis sang upon the tender croppis,
  With curious note, as Venus chapel clerkis:
The roses young, new spreading of their knoppis,[5]
War powderit bricht with heavenly berial[6] droppis,
  Through bemes red, birnand as ruby sparkis;
    The skyes rang for shouting of the larkis,
The purpur heaven owre skailit in silver sloppis[7]
  Owregilt[8] the treis, branchis leavis and barkis.

Doun through the ryce[9] a river ran with streamis,
So lustily again thai lykand leamis,[10]
  That all the lake[11] as lamp did leam of licht,
Whilk shadowit all about with twinkling gleamis;

---

[1] before.   [2] clad.   [3] float.   [4] weep.   [5] birds.   [6] beryl.
[7] the rosy sky covered over with silver clouds like scales, i.e. the mackerel sky.
[8] gilded over.   [9] bushes.
[10] So delightfully against these pleasing gleams.   [11] water.

That bewis bathit were in second beamis[1]
  Through the reflex of Phoebus visage bricht;
  On every side the hedges raise on hicht,
The bank was green, the brook was full of breamis,[2]
  The stanneris[3] clear as stern in frosty nicht.

The crystal air, the sapphire firmament,
The ruby skyes of the orient,
  Kest berial beamis on emerant bewis green;
The rosy garth[4] depaint and redolent,
With purpur, azure, gold, and gulis gent
  Arrayed was, by dame Flora the queen;
  So nobily, that joy was for to seen;
The roch[5] again the river resplendent
  As lowe[6] enlumynit all the leaves sheen.

What through the merry foulis harmony,
And through the riveris soun richt ran me by,[7]
  On Flora's mantle I sleepit as I lay,
Where soon in to my dreames fantasy
I saw approach again the orient sky,
  A sail, as white as blossom upon spray,
  With merse[8] of gold, bricht as the stern of day;
Whilk tendit to the land full lustily,
  As falcon swift desirous of her prey.

And hard on board unto the bloomit meads,
Amang the greene rispis[9] and the reedis,
  Arrivit she, whar fro anon there landis
Ane hundred ladies, lusty into weedis,[10]
As fresh as flouris that in May upspreadis,
  In kirtillis grene, withouten kell[11] or bandis:

[1] That the bows were bathed in secondary beams from the reflection of the bright visage of Phoebus.
[2] little rapids. [3] pebbles. [4] rose garden. [5] rock. [6] flame.
[7] the sound of the river (which) ran past me. [8] top.
[9] coarse grass. [10] pleasant to look upon in their garments. [11] cap.

Their bricht hairis hang glittering on the strandis
In tressis clear, wyppit[1] with golden threadis;
   With pappis white, and middlis small as wandis.

Discrive[2] I wald, but who could weel endite
How all the fieldis with thai lilies white
   Depaint were bricht, whilk to the heaven did
      glete?[3]
Nocht thou, Homer, as fair as thou could write,
For all thine ornate stylis so perfyte;
   Nor yet thou, Tullius, whose lippis sweet
   Of rhetoric did into termes fleet:
Your aureate tongis both been all too lyte,
   For to compile that paradise complete.

There saw I Nature and Venus, queen and queen,
The fresh Aurora, and lady Flora sheen,
   Juno, Apollo, and Proserpina,
Diane the goddess chaste of woodis green,
My lady Clio, that help of makaris[4] been,
   Thetis, Pallas, and prudent Minerva,
   Fair feignit Fortune, and leamand Lucina,
Thir michty queenis in crounis micht be seen,
   With beamis blithe, bricht as Lucifera.

There saw I May, of mirthful monethis queen,
Betwix Aprile and June, her sisteris sheen,
   Within the garden walking up and doun,
Wham of the foulis gladdith all bedene;[5]
Sho was full tender in her yearis green.
   There saw I Nature present her a goun,
   Rich to behald, and noble of renoun,
Of every hue under the heaven that been
   Depaint, and broud[6] be gude proportioun.

---

[1] bound.   [2] describe.   [3] glitter.   [4] poets.   [5] quickly.
            [6] embroidered.

Full lustily thir ladies all in fere[1]
Enterit within this park of most plesere,
  Where that I lay owre-helit[2] with leavis ronk;
The merry foulis, blissfullest of cheer,
Salust[3] Nature, me thocht, on their manere,
  And every bloom on branch, and eke[4] on bonk,
  Opnit and spread their balmy leavis donk,
Full low inclining to their queen so clear,
  Wham of their noble nourishing they thonk.

Syne to Dame Flora, on the samyn wise,
They saluse, and they thank a thousand syse;
  And to Dame Venus, loves michty queen,
They sang ballattis in love, as was the guise,
With armorous notis lusty to devise,[5]
  As they that had love in their heartis green;
  Their honey throatis, opnyt fro the spleen,
With warbles sweet did pierce the heavenly skies,
  Till loud resownyt the firmament serene.

Ane other court there saw I consequent,[6]
Cupid the king, with bow in hand ybent
  And dreadful arrowis grunden sharp and square:
There saw I Mars, the god armipotent,
Awful and sterne, strong and corpulent;[7]
  There saw I crabbit Saturn auld and hair,
  His look was like for to perturb the air;
There was Mercurius, wise and eloquent,
  Of rhetoric that fand the flouris fair;

There was the god of gardens, Priapus;
There was the god of wilderness, Phanus[8];
  And Janus, god of entree delightable;
There was the god of floodis Neptunus;

There was the god of windis Eolus,
  With variand look, richt like a lord unstable;
  There was Bacchus the gladder of the table;
There was Pluto, the eldritch incubus,
  In cloak of green, his court usit no sable.

And every one of thir, in green arrayit,
On harp or lute full merrily they playit,
  And sang ballettis with michty notis clear:
Ladies to dance full soberly assayit,
Endlang the lusty river so they mayit:
  Their observance richt heavenly was to hear;
  Than crap[1] I through the leavis, and drew near,
Where that I was richt suddenly affrayit,
  All through a look, whilk I have bocht full dear.

And shortly for to speak, be Lovis Queen
I was espiet, sho bade her archeris keen
  Go me arrest; and they no time delayit;
Than ladies fair let fall their mantles green,
With bowis big in tressit hairis sheen,[2]
  All suddenly they had a field arrayit;
  And yet richt greatly was I nocht affrayit,
The party was so pleasand for to seen;
  A wonder lusty bicker[3] me assayit.

And first of all, with bow in hand ybent
Come Dame Beauty, richt as sho wald me shent;[4]
  Syne followit all her damoselis yfere
With mony diverse awful instrument,
Unto the press, Fair Having with her went,
  Fine Portraiture, Pleasance, and Lusty Cheer.
  Than come Reason, with shield of gold so clear,
In plate and mail; as Mars armipotent
  Defendit me that noble chevalier.

---

[1] crept.   [2] The bows had bowstrings of bright plaited hair.
[3] attack.   [4] destroyed.

Syne tender Youth come with her virgins ying,
Green Innocence, and shameful Abaising,
  And quaking Dread, with humble Obedience;
The Golden Targe harmit they no thing;
Courage in them was nocht begun to spring;
  Full sore they dread to done a violence:
  Sweet Womanhood I saw come in presence,
Of artilye[1] a warld she did in bring,
  Servit with[2] ladies full of reverence.

Sho led with her Nurture and Lawliness,
Continuance, Patience, Gude Fame, and Steadfast-
    ness,
Discretion, Gentrice, and Considerance,
Leful Company, and Honest Business,
  Benign Look, Mild Cheer, and Soberness:
  All thir bure ganyeis[3] to do me grevance;
But Reasoun bure the Targe with sic constance,
Their sharp assayes micht do no duress
  To me, for all their awful ordinance.

Unto the press pursuït Hie Degree,
Her followit aye Estate and Dignitee,
  Comparisoun, Honour, and Noble Array,
Will, Wantonness, Renown, and Libertee,
Richesse, Freedom, and eke nobilitee,
  Wit ye they did their banner hie display;
  A cloud of arrowis as hail schour lowsit[4] they,
And shot, till wastit was their artilye,
  Syne went aback reboytit of[5] their prey.

When Venus had perceivit this rebute,[6]
Dissimilance[7] sho bade go mak pursuit,
  At all powere to pierce the Golden Targe;

[1] weapons.   [2] handled by.   [3] arrows.   [4] loosed.
    [5] driven back from.   [6] repulse.   [7] Dissimulation.

And sho that was of doubleness the root,
Askit her choice of archeris in refute.[1]
    Venus the best bade her go wale[2] at large;
    Sho took Presence, plicht anchor[3] of the barge,
And Fair Calling that weel a flayn[4] could shoot,
    And Cherishing for to complete her charge.

Dame Hameliness sho took in company,
That hardy was, and hend[5] in archery,
    And brocht Dame Beauty to the field again;
With all the choice of Venus' chivalry
They come, and bickerit unabaisitly:[6]
    The schour of arrowis rappit on as rain;
    Perilous Presence, that mony sire has slain,
The battle brocht on border hard me by,[7]
    The 'sault was all the sairer, sooth to sayn.

Thick was the shot of grunden[8] dartis keen;
But Reason with the Shield of Gold so sheen,
    Warly[9] defendit who so ever assayit;
The awful stour[10] he manly did sustain
Till Presence kest a powder in his een,
    And than as drunken man he all forvayit:[11]
When he was blind the fool with him they playit,
And banist him amang the bewis green;
    That sorry sicht me suddenly affrayit.

Than was I wounded to the death weel near,
And yolden[12] as a woeful prisonere
    To Lady Beauty; in a moment space:
Me thocht sho seemit lustier of cheer,[13]
Efter that Reason tint[14] had his een clear,

[1] defence.   [2] choose.   [3] sheet-anchor.   [4] arrow.   [5] skilful.
[6] battered without any fear.
[7] brought the battle to a frontier close beside me.
[8] sharpened.   [9] cautiously.   [10] conflict.   [11] went astray.
[12] yielded.   [13] more pleasant of countenance.   [14] lost.

Than of before, and lovelier of face:
Why was thou blindit, Reason? Why, alas!
And gert[1] ane hell my paradise appear,
    And mercy seem, where that I fand no grace?

Dissimulance was busy me to sile,[2]
And Fair Calling did oft upon me smile,
    And Cherishing me fed with wordis fair;
New Acquaintance embracit me a while,
And favourite me, while men micht go a mile,
    Syne took her leave; I saw her nevermair:
    Than saw I Danger toward me repair,
I could eschew her presence by no wile,
    On side[3] sho lookit with ane fremyt fare.[4]

And at the last, Departing could her dress,[5]
And me deliverit unto Heaviness
    For to remain, and sho in cure[6] me took;
By this the Lord of Windis, with wodeness,[7]
God Aeolus, his bugle blew, I guess;
    That with the blast the leavis all to-shook,
    And suddenly, in the space of a look,
All was hine went,[8] there was but wilderness,
    There was no more but birdis, bank, and brook.

In twinkling of ane ee to ship they went,
And swyth[9] up sail unto the top they stent,[10]
    And with swift course atour the flood they frak;[11]
They firit guns with powder violent,
Till that the reek[12] raise to the firmament,
    The rochis all resounit with the rack,[13]
    For reird[14] it seemit that the rainbow brak;

[1] made.   [2] beguile.   [3] askance.   [4] strange behaviour.
[5] did make herself ready.   [6] keeping.   [7] madness.
[8] gone hence.   [9] quickly.   [10] stretch.   [11] move quickly.
[12] smoke.   [13] noise.   [14] roar.

With spirit afraid upon my feet I sprent[1]
Amang the clewis,[2] so careful was the crack.

And as I did awake of my sweving,[3]
The joyful birdis merrily did sing
For mirth of Phoebus tender beames sheen;
Sweet were the vapouris, soft the morrowing,
Halesome the vale, depaint with flouris ying;[4]
The air attemperit, sober, and amene;[5]
In white and red was all the field beseen,[6]
Through Naturis noble fresh enamelling,
In mirthful May, of every moneth queen.

O reverend Chaucer, rose of rethoris[7] all,
As in our tongue ane flour imperiall,
That raise in Britain ever, who readis richt,
Thou bearis of makaris the triumph riall;
Thy fresh enamellit termes celicall[8]
This matter could illuminit have full bricht:
Was thou nocht of our English all the licht,
Surmounting every tongue terrestrial,
As far as Mayis morrow does midnicht?

O moral Gower, and Lydgate laureate,[9]
Your sugarit lippis and toungis aureate,
Been to our earis cause of great delight;
Your angel mouthis most mellifluate[10]
Our rude langage has clear illuminate,
And fair owre-gilt our speech, that imperfyte
Stood, or your golden pennis shupe to write;
This isle before was bare, and desolate
Of rhetoric, or lusty fresh indite.[11]

---

[1] sprung.   [2] clefts in the rock.   [3] dream.   [4] young.   [5] mild.
[6] arrayed.   [7] eloquent writers.   [8] heavenly.
[9] crowned with laurel.   [10] flowing with honey.   [11] writing.

Thou little quair, be ever obedient,
Humble, subject, and simple of entent,[1]
   Before the face of every cunning wicht:
I knaw what thou of rhetoric has spent;
Of all her lusty roses redolent
   Is none in to thy garland set on hicht;
   Eshame[2] thereof and draw thee out of sicht.
Rude is thy weed, disteynit,[3] bare, and rent,
   Weel aucht thou be affeirit[4] of the licht.

To a Lady

Sweet rose of virtue and of gentleness,
Delightsome lily of every lustiness,[5]
   Richest in bounty, and in beauty clear,
   And every virtue that is held maist dear,
Except only that ye are merciless.

Into your garth this day I did pursue,
There saw I flowris that fresche were of hue;
   Baith white and reid most lusty were to seen,
   And hailsome herbis upon stalkis green;
Yet leaf nor flour find could I nane of rue.

I dout that Merch, with his cauld blastis keen,
Has slain this gentle herb, that I of mene,[6]
   Whose piteous death dois to my heart sic pain
   That I wald mak to plant his root again,
So confortand his leavis unto me been.

The Dance of the Seven Deadly Sins

Of Februar the fifteen nicht,
Full lang before the dayis licht,
   I lay into a trance;

[1] mind. [2] be ashamed. [3] stained. [4] well mayest thou be afraid.
[5] pleasure. [6] complain of.

And then I saw baith Heaven and Hell:
Methocht, amangis the feindis fell,
    Mahoun[1] gart cry ane dance
Of shrewis[2] that were never shriven,
Aganis the feast of Fastern's even,[3]
    To mak their observance:
He bad gallandis ga graith a gyiss,[4]
And cast up gamountis[5] to the skyis,
    That last came out of France.

'Lat see,' quod he, 'now wha beginnis?'
With that the foul Seven Deadly Sinnis
    Begouth to leip at anis.
And first of all in dance was Pride,
With hair wild[6] back and bonnet on side,
    Like to make wastie wanis;[7]
And round about him, as a wheel,
Hang all in rumpillis[8] to the heel
    His kethat[9] for the nanis;
Mony proud trumpour[10] with him trippit
Through scaldand fire, aye as they skippit
    They girned with hiddous granis.

Hely harlottis on hautain wise[11]
Come in with mony sindrie guise,[12]
    But yet leuch never Mahoun:
Till priestis come in with bare shaven neckis;
Than all the fiendis leuch, and made geckis,
    Black Belly and Bawsy Broun.[13]

Than Ire come in with sturt and strife;
His hand was aye upon his knife,

---

[1] The Devil.   [2] wretches.   [3] Shrove Tuesday.
[4] He bade gallants go prepare a masque.   [5] gambols.
[6] combed.   [7] waste dwellings.   [8] folds.   [9] cassock.
[10] deceiver.   [11] proud harlots in haughty fashion.   [12] disguise.
[13] names of witches.

He brandeist[1] like a beir:[2]
Boasteris, braggeris, and bargaineris,[3]
Efter him passit into pairis,
    All bodin in feir of weir;[4]
In jackis,[5] stryppis[6] and bonnettis of steel,
Their leggis were chenyeit[7] to the heel,
    Frawart[8] was their affeir:[9]
Some upon other with brandis beft,[10]
Some jaggit[11] otheris to the heft,[12]
    With knyvis that sharp could shear.

Next in the dance followit Envy,
Filled full of feud and felony,
    Hid malice and despite;
For privy hatrent[13] that traitor trymlit.[14]
Him followit mony freik dissymlit,[15]
    With feigneit wirdis white;
And flattereris into mennis facis;
And backbiteris of sindry racis;
    To ley that had delight;
And rownaris[16] of false leasingis;[17]
Alas! that courtis of noble kingis
    Of them can never be quite.[18]

Next him in dance come Covetice,
Root of all evil and ground of vice,
    That never could be content;
Cativis, wretchis, and okkeraris,[19]
Hood-pickis,[20] hoardaris, and gadderaris,
    All with that warlo[21] went:

---

[1] swaggered.   [2] boar.
[3] wranglers.   [4] arrayed in accoutrements of war.
[5] quilted jackets.   [6] armour.   [7] covered with chain mail.
[8] froward. [9] bearing. [10] struck with swords. [11] stabbed. [12] haft.
[13] hatred.   [14] trembled.   [15] dissembling man.   [16] whisperers.
[17] lies.   [18] quit.   [19] usurers.   [20] misers.   [21] warlock.

Out of their throatis they shot on other
Het molten gold, methocht a fother,[1]
   As fire-flaucht[2] maist fervent;
Aye as they toomit them[3] of shot,
Fiendis filled them new up to the throat
   With gold of alkin prent.[4]

Syne Sweirness, at the second bidding,
Come like a sow out of a midding,
   Full sleepy was his grunye:[5]
Mony sweir bumbard belly huddron,[6]
Mony slut daw[7] and sleepy duddron,[8]
   Him servit aye with sounyie.[9]
He drew them furth in till a chainyie,[10]
And Belial, with a bridle reinyie,
   Ever lashed them on the lunyie:[11]
In dance they were so slaw of feet,
They gave them in the fire a heat,
   And made them quicker of counyie.[12]

Then Lechery, that laithly corse,
Come bearand[13] like a baggit horse,[14]
   And Idleness did him lead;
There was with him ane ugly sort,[15]
And mony stinkand foul tramort,[16]
   That had in sin been deid.
When they were entrit in the dance,
They were full strange of countenance,
   Like turkas birnand reid;[17]
All led they other by the tersis,[18]
Suppose they fuckit with their erses
   It micht be na remeid.

[1] abundance.   [2] lightning.   [3] emptied themselves.
[4] every kind of stamp. [5] snout, face. [6] lazy stupid greedy lump.
[7] dirty slut.   [8] sloven.   [9] excuse.   [10] chain.   [11] loin.
[12] motion.   [13] roaring.   [14] stallion.   [15] company.   [16] corpse.
       [17] like red-hot pincers.   [18] penis.

Then the foul monster Gluttony,
Of wame[1] unsatiable and greedy,
    To dance he did him dress:
Him followit mony foul drunkart,
With can and collop,[2] cup and quart
    In surfeit and excess.
Full mony a waistless wallydrag,[3]
With wamis unweildable[4] did furth wag,
    In creish[5] that did increase;
'Drink!' aye they cryit, with mony a gape,
The fiendis gave them het lead to lap,
    Their lovery[6] was na less.

Na menstrallis playit to them but doubt,
For gleemen there were halden[7] out,
    By day, and eke by nicht;
Except a menstrall that slew a man,
Swa till his heritage he wan,
    Entering by brief of richt.

Then cryd Mahoun for a Hieland padyane;[8]
Syne ran a fiend to fetch MacFadyen,
    Far northward in a nuke;
Be he the coronach had done shout
Erschemen[9] so gadderit him about,
    In Hell great room they took.
Thae tarmegantis, with tag and tatter,[10]
Full loud in Ersche[11] begouth to clatter,
    And roup[12] like raven and rook:
The Devil sa deavit[13] was with their yell,
That in the deepest pit of Hell
    He smoorit[14] them with smuke.[15]

---

[1] belly. [2] drinking-cup. [3] big-bellied person.
[4] unwieldy bellies. [5] fat. [6] allowance. [7] kept. [8] pageant.
[9] Gaelic speakers, Highlanders. [10] ragged termagants.
[11] Gaelic. [12] croak. [13] deafened. [14] smothered. [15] smoke.

Amends to the Tailors and Soutars

Betwix twell houris and eleven,
I dreamed ane angel came fra Heaven,
With pleasand stevin[1] sayand on hie,
'Tailyouris and Soutaris, blest be ye.

'In Heaven hie ordained is your place,
Above all sanctis in great solace,
Next God, greatest in dignitie:
Tailyouris and soutaris, blest be ye.

'The cause to you is nocht unkend,[2]
That[3] God mismaks ye do amend,
By craft and great agilitie:
Tailyouris and soutaris, blest be ye.

'Soutaris, with shoon weel made and meet,
Ye mend the faults of ill-made feet,
Wherefore to Heaven your saulis will flee:
Tailyouris and soutaris, blest be ye.

'Is nocht in all this fair a flyrok,[4]
That has upon his feet a wyrok,[5]
Knowll tais,[6] nor mowlis[7] in no degree,
But ye can hide them; blest be ye.

'And ye tailyouris, with weel-made clais
Can mend the worst made man that gais,
And mak him seemly for to see:
Tailyouris and soutaris, blest be ye.

'Though God mak ane misfashionit man,
Ye can him all shape new again,
And fashion him better be sic three:[8]
Tailyouris and soutaris, blest be ye.

---

[1] voice. [2] not unknown. [3] what. [4] light, insignificant **creature.**
[5] lump. [6] knotted toes. [7] chilblains. [8] three times **as well.**

'Though a man have a broken back,
Have he a gude crafty tailyour—what rack?[1]
That can it cover with craftis slie:
Tailyouris and soutaris, blest be ye.

'Of God great kindness may ye claim,
That helpis his people fra crook and lame,
Supportand faultis with your supple:[2]
Tailyouris and soutaris, blest be ye.

'In erd ye kith[3] sic mirakillis here,
In Heaven ye sall be sanctis full clear,
Though ye be knavis in this countree:
Tailyouris and soutaris, blest be ye.'

Meditation in Winter

In to thir dark and drublie[4] dayis,
When sable all the heavens arrayis,
   With misty vapouris, cloudis and skyis,[5]
   Nature all courage me denies
Of sangis ballattis and of playis.

When that the nicht does lengthen houris,
With wind, with hail, with heavy shouris,
   My dule spreit dois lurk for schoir;[6]
   My heart for languor dois forloir,[7]
For lack of simmer with his flouris.

I wake, I turn, sleep may I nocht,
I vexit am with heavy thocht;
   This warld all owre I cast about,
   And aye the mair I am in dout,
The mair that I remeid have socht.

[1] matter.   [2] assistance.   [3] show.   [4] dripping.   [5] shadows.
[6] hide for fear.   [7] is utterly lost.

I am assayit on every side,
Despair sayis aye, 'In time provide,
  And get some thing whereon to leif,[1]
  Or with great trouble and mischief,
Thou sall into this court abide.'

Then Patience says, 'Be nocht aghast:
Hald Hope and Truth within thee fast;
  And lat Fortune wirk furth her rage,
  Whan that no reasoun may assuage,
Till that her glass be run and past.'

And Prudence in my ear sayis aye,
'Why wald thou hald that will away?[2]
  Or crave that thou may have mo space,
  Thou tending to ane other place,
A journey going every day?'

And than sayis Age, 'My friend, come near,
And be nocht strange, I thee requeir:
  Come, brother, by the hand me tak,
  Remember thou has compt to mak
Of all thy time thou spendit here.'

Syne Deid castis up his yettis[3] wide,
Saying, 'Thir open sall ye abide;[4]
  Albeit that thou were never sa stout,
  Under this lintel sall thou lout:[5]
There is nane other way beside.'

For fear of this all day I droop;
No gold in kist, nor wine in cup
  No ladeis beauty, nor lovis bliss
  May lat me to remember[6] this:
How glad that ever I dine or sup.

---

[1] live.   [2] Why would you keep what will disappear?   [3] gates.
[4] you must endure these open.   [5] stoop.
[6] prevent my remembering.

Yet, when the nicht beginnis to short,
It dois my spreit some pairt confort,
   Of thocht oppressit with the shouris.
   Come, lusty summer! with thy flouris,
That I may live in some disport.

Lament for the Makaris

I that in heill[1] was and gladnèss
Am trublit now with great sickness
And feblit with infirmitie:—
   Timor Mortis conturbat me.

Our plesance here is all vain glory,
This fals world is but transitory,
The flesh is bruckle,[2] the Feynd is slee:—[3]
   Timor Mortis conturbat me.

The state of man does change and vary,
Now sound, now sick, now blyth, now sary,
Now dansand[4] mirry, now like to dee:—
   Timor Mortis conturbat me.

No state in Erd here standis sicker;[5]
As with the wynd wavis the wicker[6]
So wavis this world's vanitie:—
   Timor Mortis conturbat me.

Unto the deid gois all Estatis,
Princis, Prelatis, and Potestatis,
Baith rich and poor of all degree:—
   Timor Mortis conturbat me.

He takis the knichtis in to field
Enarmit under helm and scheild;
Victor he is at all mellie:—[7]
   Timor Mortis conturbat me.

[1] health.   [2] brittle, feeble.   [3] sly.   [4] dancing.   [5] sure.
[6] willow.   [7] mellay.

That strong unmerciful tyrand
Takis, on the motheris breast sowkand,[1]
The babe full of benignitie:—
Timor Mortis conturbat me.

He takis the campion[2] in the stour,[3]
The captain closit in the tour,
The lady in bour full of bewtie:—
Timor Mortis conturbat me.

He spairis no lord for his piscence,[4]
Na clerk for his intelligence;
His awful straik[5] may no man flee:—
Timor Mortis conturbat me.

Art-magicians and astrologgis,
Rethoris, logicianis, and theologgis,
Them helpis no conclusionis slee:—
Timor Mortis conturbat me.

In medecine the most practicianis,
Leechis, surrigianis, and physicianis,
Themself from Death may not supplee:—[6]
Timor Mortis conturbat me.

I see that makaris[7] amang the lave[8]
Playis here their padyanis,[9] syne gois to grave;
Sparit is nocht their facultie:—
Timor Mortis conturbat me.

He has done petuously devour
The noble Chaucer, of makaris flour,
The Monk of Bury, and Gower, all three:—
Timor Mortis conturbat me.

---

[1] sucking. [2] champion. [3] fight. [4] puissance. [5] stroke.
[6] save. [7] poets. [8] the leave, the rest. [9] pageants.

The good Sir Hew of Eglintoun,
And eik[1] Heriot, and Wyntoun,
He has tane out of this cuntrie:—
Timor Mortis conturbat me.

That scorpion fell has done infeck
Maister John Clerk, and James Afflek,
Fra ballat-making and tragedie:—
Timor Mortis conturbat me.

Holland and Barbour he has berevit;
Alas! that he nocht with us levit
Sir Mungo Lockart of the Lee:—
Timor Mortis conturbat me.

Clerk of Tranent eik he has tane,
That made the Anteris[2] of Gawaine;
Sir Gilbert Hay endit has he:—
Timor Mortis conturbat me.

He has Blind Harry and Sandy Traill
Slain with his schour[3] of mortal hail,
Whilk Patrick Johnstoun might nought flee:—
Timor Mortis conturbat me.

He has reft Merseir his endite,[4]
That did in love so lively write,
So short, so quick, of sentence hie:—
Timor Mortis conturbat me.

He has tane Roull of Aberdene,
And gentill Roull of Corstorphine;
Two better fallowis[5] did no man see:—
Timor Mortis conturbat me.

---

[1] also.   [2] adventures.   [3] shower.   [4] inditing.   [5] fellows.

In Dunfermline he has done roune[1]
With Maister Robert Henrysoun;
Sir John the Ross enbrast has he:—
Timor Mortis conturbat me.

And he has now tane, last of aa,
Good gentil Stobo and Quintin Shaw,
Of whom all wichtis[2] hes pitie:—
Timor Mortis conturbat me.

Good Maister Walter Kennedy
In point of deid lies verily;
Great ruth it were that so suld be:—
Timor Mortis conturbat me.

Sen he has all my brether tane,
He will naught lat me live alane;
On force I man[3] his next prey be:—
Timor Mortis conturbat me.

Sen for the deid remeid is none,
Best is that we for deid dispone,[4]
Efter our deid that live may we:—
Timor Mortis conturbat me.

O wretch, beware

O wretch, beware! this world will wend thee fro,
  Whilk has beguilit mony great estate;
Turn to thy friend, believe nocht on thy foe,
  Sen thou man go, be graithing to thy gait;[5]
  Remeid in time, and rue nocht all too late;
Provide thy place, for thou away man pass
  Out of this vale of trouble and dissait:
Vanitas Vanitatum, et omnia Vanitas.

---

[1] whispered.   [2] wights, persons.   [3] must.   [4] make disposition.
    [5] making ready for thy journey.

Walk furth, pilgrim, while thou has dayis licht,
   Dress fro desert,[1] draw to thy dwelling-place;
Speed home, for-why[2] anon comis the nicht
   Whilk does thee follow with ane ythand[3] chase!
   Bend up thy sail, and win thy port of grace;
For and the death owretak thee in trespass,
   Then may thou say thir wordis with alas!
Vanitas, Vanitatum, et omnia Vanitas.

Here nocht abidis, here standis no thing stable,
   For this false world aye flittis to and fro;
Now day up bricht, now nicht as black as sable,
   Now ebb, now flood, now friend, now cruel foe;
   Now glad, now sad, now weel, now into woe;
Now clad in gold, dissolvit now in ass;[4]
   So dois this warld transitory go:
Vanitas Vanitatum, et omnia Vanitas.

Rorate coeli desuper

Rorate coeli desuper![5]
Heavens distill your balmy shouris,
For now is risen the bricht day ster,[6]
Fro the rose Mary, flour of flouris:
The clear Sun, whom no cloud devouris,
Surmounting Phoebus in the east,
Is cumin of his heavenly touris;
Et nobis Puer natus est.[7]

Archangellis, angellis, and dompnationis,
Thronis, potestatis, and martyris seir,[8]
And all ye heavenly operationis,
Ster, planet, firmament, and sphere,

---

[1] go from the desert.   [2] because.   [3] busy.   [4] **ash.**
[5] send down dews, ye heavens.   [6] day star, i.e. sun.
       [7] And unto us is born a Child.   [8] various.

Fire, erd, air, and water clear,
To him give loving,[1] most and lest,
That come into so meek mannere;
Et nobis Puer natus est.

Sinneris be glaid, and penance do,
And thank your maker hairtfully;
For he that ye micht nocht come to,
To you is cumin full humbly,
Your saulis with his blood to buy,
And lowse you of the fiendis arrest,
And only of his awin mercy,
Pro nobis Puer natus est.[2]

All clergy do to him incline,
And bow unto this barne benign,
And do your observance divine
To him that is of kingis King;
Incense[3] his altar, read, and sing
In haly kirk, with mind digest,[4]
Him honouring attour[5] all thing,
Qui nobis Puer natus est.[6]

Celestial fowlis in the air
Sing with your notis upon hicht;
In firthis[7] and in forrestis fair
Be mirthful now, at all your micht,
For passit is your dully nicht;
Aurora hes the cloudis perst,
The sun is risen with glaidsome licht,
Et nobis Puer natus est.

Now spring up flouris fra the root,
Revert[8] you upward naturally,

[1] praise.   [2] Unto us is born a Child.   [3] burn incense about.
[4] well prepared.   [5] above.   [6] Who was born unto us a Child.
[7] coppices.   [8] turn.

In honour of the blissit fruit
That raise up fro the rose Mary;
Lay out your leavis lustily,
Fro deid tak life now at the lest[1]
In worship of that Prince worthy,
Qui nobis Puer natus est.

Sing heaven imperial, most of hicht,
Regions of air mak armony;
All fish in flood and fowl of flicht,
Be mirthful and mak melody:
All '*Gloria in Excelsis*' cry,
Heaven, erd, sea, man, bird, and best,[2]
He that is crownit abone the sky
Pro nobis Puer natus est.

Done is a battle on the dragon black

Done is a battle on the dragon black,
Our campion Christ confoundit has his force;
The yettis[3] of hell are broken with a crack,
The sign triumphal raisit is of the cross,
The devillis trymmillis[4] with hiddous voce,
The saulis are borrowit[5] and to the bliss can go,
Christ with his blood our ransonis dois indoce:[6]
Surrexit Dominus de sepulchro.[7]

Dungen[8] is the deidly dragon Lucifer,
The cruel serpent with the mortal stang;[9]
The auld keen tiger, with his teeth on char,[10]
Whilk in a wait has lyen for us so lang,
Thinking to grip us in his clawis strang;

---

[1] at last.　　[2] beast.　　[3] gates.　　[4] tremble.　　[5] ransomed.
[6] endorse.　　[7] The Lord has risen from the grave.
[8] struck down.　　[9] sting.　　[10] ajar.

The merciful Lord wald nocht that it were so,
He made him for to failye of that fang:[1]
Surrexit Dominus de sepulchro.

He for our sake that sufferit to be slain,
And like a lamb in sacrifice was dicht,[2]
Is like a lion risen up again,
And as gyane[3] raxit[4] him on hicht;
Sprungen is Aurora radious[5] and bricht,
On loft is gone the glorious Apollo,
The blissful day departit fro the nicht:
Surrexit Dominus de sepulchro.

The great victour again is risen on hicht,
That for our quarrel to the death was woundit;
The sun that wox all pale now shinis bricht,
And, darkness clearit, our faith is now refoundit;
The knell of mercy fra the heaven is soundit,
The Christian are deliverit of their woe,
The Jewis and their error are confoundit:
Surrexit Dominus de sepulchro.

The foe is chasit, the battle is done cease,
The prison broken, the jevellouris fleit and flemit;[6]
The weir is gone, confermit is the peace,
The fetteris lowsit and the dungeon temit,[7]
The ranson made, the prisoneris redeemit;
The field is won, owrecomen is the foe,
Despoilit of the treasure that he yemit:[8]
Surrexit Dominus de sepulchro.

The Ballad of Kynd Kittok

My gudame wes a gay wif, bot scho wes ryght gend,[9]
Scho dwelt furth far in to France, upon Falkland
Fell;

---

[1] prey.   [2] prepared   [3] giant.   [4] stretched.   [5] radiant.
[6] banished.   [7] emptied.   [8] kept.   [9] foolish.

Thay callit her Kynd Kittok, whasa hir weill kend;[1]
　　Scho wes like a caldrone cruke cler under kell;[2]
Thay threpit[3] that scho deit of thrist, and maid a
　　gude end.
　　Efter hir dede, scho dredit nought in hevin for to
　　　dwell,
And sa to hevin the hieway dreidles scho wend,
　　Yit scho wanderit and yeid by[4] to ane elriche[5] well.
　　　Scho met thar, as I wene,
　　　　Ane ask[6] rydand on a snaill,
　　　　And cryit, 'Ourtane fallow, haill!'
　　　　And raid ane inche behind the taill,
　　　Till it wes neir evin.

Sa scho had hap to be horsit to hir herbry[7]
　　At ane ailhous neir hevin, it nyghttit thaim thare;[8]
Scho deit of thrist in this warld, that gert[9] hir be so
　　dry,
　　Scho never eit, bot drank our mesur and mair.[10]
Scho slepit whill[11] the morne at noon, and rais airly;
　　And to the yettis of hevin fast can the wif fair,
And by Sanct Petir, in at the yett, scho stall prevely:
　　God lukit and saw hir lattin in and lewch his hert
　　　sair.
　　　And thar, yeris sevin
　　　　Scho levit a gud life,
　　　　And wes our Ladyis hen wife:
　　　　And held Sanct Petir at strife
　　　Ay whill scho wes in hevin.

[1] whoever knew her well.
[2] like a hook for a caldron, beautiful under her head-dress
　　(comic irony).
[3] said.　[4] went aside.　[5] supernatural.　[6] newt.　[7] hostelry.
[8] night came on them.　[9] caused.　[10] too much.　[11] while.

Scho lukit out on a day and thoght ryght lang
  To see the ailhous beside, in till ane evill hour;
And out of hevin the hie gait[1] cought[2] the wif gang
  For to get hir ane fresche drink, the aill of hevin
    wes sour.
Scho come againe to hevinnis yett, when the bell
    rang,
  Sanct Petir hat[3] hir with a club, whill a gret clour[4]
Rais in hir heid, becaus the wif yeid[5] wrang.
  Than to the ailhous agane scho ran the pycharis[6]
    to pour,
    And for to brew and baik.
      Frendis, I pray yow hertfully,
      Gif ye be thristy or dry,
      Drink with my Guddame, as ye ga by,
    Anys[7] for my saik.

GAVIN DOUGLAS

1475?–1522

An Evening and Morning in June

(i)

The licht begouth to quenschyng out and fail,
The day to dirken, decline, and devail;[8]
The gummis[9] risis, doun fallis the donk rime,[10]
Baith here and there skuggis[11] and shadows dim;
Up goes the bak with her peelit leddren flicht,[12]
The larkis descendis from the skyis hicht,[13]
Singand her compline sang eftir her guise,
To tak her rest, at matin hour to rise:

---

[1] the high road.   [2] 'could', did.   [3] hit.   [4] bump, swelling.
[5] went.   [6] pitchers.   [7] once.   [8] sink.   [9] vapours.   [10] mist.
[11] shades.   [12] bat flying with wings of peeled leather.   [13] height.

Out owre the swyre[1] swimmis the soppis of mist,
The nicht furthspread her cloak with sable lyst;[2]
That all the beauty of the fructuous field
Was with the earthis umbrage[3] clean owreheild:[4]
Baith man and beast, firth, flood, and woodis wild
Involvit in the shadows war insylde:[5]
Still war the fowlis fleis[6] in the air
All store[7] and cattle sesit[8] in their lair;
All creature where so them likis best
Bownis[9] to tak the halesome nichtis rest,
Eftir the dayis labour and the heat:
Close waren[10] all and at their soft quiet,
But steerage[11] or removing, he or she,
Outhir beast, bird, fish, fowl by land or sea.
And shortly every thing that doth repair
In firth or field, flood, forest, earth or air,
Or in the scroggis,[12] or in the buskis ronk,[13]
Lakis, maressis,[14] or their poolis donk,[15]
Astablit[16] lyggis[17] still to sleep and restis
Be[18] the small birdis sittand on their nestis,
The little midges and the urisome fleis,[19]
As weel the wild as the tame bestial,
And every other thingis great and small,—
Out tak[20] the merry nichtingale Philomene,
That on the thorn sat singand fro the spleen.
Whais mirthful nottis langand[21] for to hear,
Until ane garth under ane green laurere[22]
I walk anon, and in a siege[23] doun sat
Now musing upon this, and now on that.
I see the Pole,[24] and eek the Ursas bricht

---

[1] valley.   [2] border.   [3] shadow.   [4] covered over.   [5] enfolded.
[6] birds that fly.   [7] stock.   [8] tethered.   [9] prepares.   [10] were.
[11] movement.   [12] thickets.   [13] rank.   [14] marshes.   [15] dank.
[16] settled.   [17] lies.   [18] from.   [19] troublesome flies.   [20] except.
[21] longing.   [22] laurel.   [23] seat.   [24] Pole Star.

And hornyt Lucine castand bot dim licht,
Because the summer skyës shane so clear. . . .

(*Prologue to the Thirteenth Book of the Aeneid*, ll. 33–73.)

(ii)

Yonder doun dwynis[1] the even sky away,
And up springis the bricht dawning of the day
In till ane other place, not fer in sunder,
That to behald was plesance, and half wonder.
Furth quenching gan the sternes ane be ane
That now is left bot Lucifer alane.
And furthermore, to blazon this new day,
Wha micht discryve the birdis blissful lay?
Belyve[2] on wing the busy lark upsprang
To salus the blythe morrow with her sang;
Soon owre the fieldis shinis the licht clere,
Welcome to pilgrim baith and labourere.
Tyte[3] on his hindis[4] gaif the grieve ane cry,
'Awake! On foot! Go till our husbandry!'
And the herd callis furth upon his page
To drive the cattle to their pasturage;
The hindis wife clepis[5] up Katherine and Jill;
'Yea, dame,' said they, God wat, with ane good
      will.
The dewy green powderit with daisies gay
Shew on the sward ane colour dapple gray;
The misty vapours springand up full sweet
Maist comfortable to glaid all mannis sprete;
Thereto thir birdis singis in their shawis[6]
As menstralis playis 'The jolly day now dawis'.

(*Prologue to the Thirteenth Book of the Aeneid*, ll. 163–86.)

[1] sinks.   [2] straightway.   [3] quickly.   [4] hinds.   [5] calls.
[6] copses.

An Evening and Morning in Winter

In this congealit season sharp and chill,
The caller air, penetrative and pure,
Dazing the blude in every creature,
Made seek warm stovis and bene[1] fyris hot.
In double garment cled and wyliecoat,[2]
With michty drink, and meatis confortive,
Aganis the stormy winter for to strive,
Recreate weel, and by the chimney bekit[3]
At even betime doun on ane bed me strekit,[4]
Warpit[5] my hede, kest on claithis thrynfald
For to expel the perilous piercand cauld.
I crossit me, syne bownit[6] for to sleep,
Where, lemand[7] through the glass, I did tak keep[8]
Latonia the lang irksome nicht
Her subtle blenkis[9] shed and watery licht;
Full high up whirlit in her regioun,
Till[10] Phoebus richt in oppositioun,
Into the Crab her proper mansion draw
Haldand the hicht although the sun went law.
Hornit Hebawd, whilk we clepe the nicht owl
Within her cavern hard I shout and yowl
Laithly of form, with crooked camscho[11] beak,
Ugsome[12] to hear was her wild elrische[13] skreik.
The wild geese eek clacking by nichtis tide[14]
Atour[15] the city fleand[16] hard I glide.
On slummer I slade[17] full sad, and slepyt sound
Till the horizon upward can rebound.
Phoebus crownit bird, the nichtis orloger,[18]
Clappand his wingis thrice had crawin clear,

[1] comfortable.   [2] short jacket.   [3] warmed.   [4] stretched.
[5] wrapped.   [6] prepared.   [7] gleaming.   [8] observed.
[9] glances.   [10] to.   [11] bent.   [12] horrible.   [13] eldritch.   [14] time.
[15] above.   [16] flying.   [17] slid.   [18] hour-teller.

Approaching near the breaking of the day—
Within my bed I wakynnit whare I lay,
Sa fast declynnys Cynthia the moon.
And kayis keklys[1] on the roof abune;
Palamedes birdis[2] crowpand[3] in the sky,
Fleand on randoun, shapen like ane Y,
And as ane trumpet rang their vocis soun,
Whais cryis been prognosticacioun
Of windy blastis and ventositeis
Fast by my chalmer, in high wisnit[4] trees,
The soir gled[5] whissllis with mony ane pew,
Wharby the day was dawing weel I knew,
Bade beat[6] the fire, and the candle alicht;
Syne blissit me, and in my weedis dicht;[7]
Ane shot window[8] unshut ane little on char[9]
Persavit the morning bla,[10] wan and har,[11]
With cloudy gum[12] and rack owrewhelmyt the air,
The sowlye[13] stythlie,[14] hasard,[15] rouch and hare.[16]
Branches brattlyng,[17] and blaiknyt[18] shew the brays[19]
With hirstis[20] harsk[21] of waggand wyndil strayis;[22]
The dew droppis congealit on stibble and rind,[23]
And sharp hailstanis mortfundit of kind,[24]
Hoppand on the thack[25] and on the causay[26] by.
The shot I closit, and drew inward in hy,[27]
Shiverand for cald, the season was sa snell,[28]
Shupe[29] with hait flambis[30] to stem the freezing
    fell.[31]

(*Prologue to the Seventh Book of the Aeneid*, ll. 91–145.)

[1] jackdaws cackle.   [2] cranes.   [3] croaking.   [4] withered.
[5] red kite. [6] kindle. [7] clothed. [8] window that can be opened.
[9] ajar.   [10] bleak.   [11] grey.   [12] vapour.   [13] soil.   [14] stiff.
[15] ashen.   [16] grey.   [17] rattling.   [18] blackened.   [19] slopes.
[20] clumps.   [21] harsh.   [22] coarse grass.   [23] hide.   [24] cold as death.
[25] thatch.   [26] street.   [27] hastily.   [28] sharp.   [29] set about.
    [30] flames.   [31] biting frost.

SIR DAVID LYNDSAY

1490–1555

The Pardoner's Sermon

My patent pardouns, ye may see,
Cum fra the Cane of Tartarie,
　Weill seald with oster-schellis.
Thocht ye have no contritioun,
Ye sall have full remission,
　With help of buiks and bellis.
Here is ane relict, lang and braid,
Of Finn Macoull the richt chaft-blaid,
　With teith and all togidder;
Of Colling's cow here is ane horne,
For eating of Mackonnal's corne
　Was slaine into Balquhidder.
Here is ane cord, baith great and lang,
Whilk hangit Johne the Armistrang,
　Of gude hemp saft and sound:
Gude halie peopill, I stand for'd
Wha ever beis hangit with this cord
　Neids never to be dround.
The culum[1] of Sanct Bridis cow,
The gruntill[2] of Sanct Antoni's sow,
　Whilk buir his haly bell:
Wha ever he be hears this bell clinck,
Gif me ane ducat for til drink,
　He sall never gang to hell,
Without he be of Beliell borne:
Maisters, trow ye that this be scorne?
　Cum win this pardoun, cum.
Wha luifis thair wyfis nocht with thair hart,
I have power them for till part.

　　　　[1] backside.　　[2] snout.

Me think yow deif and dum!
Hes nane of yow curst wickit wyfis,
That halds yow into sturt and stryfis,
    Cum tak my dispensatioun:
Of that cummer I sall mak yow quyte,
Howbeit your selfis be in the wyte,[1]
    And mak ane fals narratioun.
Cum win the pardoun, now let see,
For meill, for malt, or for monie,
    For cok, hen, guse, or gryse.[2]
Of relicts heir I haif ane hunder;
Why cum ye nocht? this is ane wonder:
    I trow ye be nocht wyse.

(From *Ane Satyre of the Thrie Estaitis.*)

Complaint of the Common Weill of Scotland

And thus as we were talking to and fro
We saw a busteous berne[3] come owre the bent,[4]
But horse, on fute, as fast as he micht go,
Whose raiment was all raggit, riven and rent,
With visage lean, as he had fastit Lent:
And forwart fast his wayis he did advance,
With ane richt malancolious countenance.

With scrip on hip,[5] and pykestaff in his hand,
As he had purposit to pass fra hame.
Quod I: 'Gude man, I wald fain understand,
Gif that ye plesit, to wit what were your name?'
Quod he: 'My son, of that I think great shame;
Bot sen thou wald of my name have ane feill,[6]
Forsooth, they call me John the Common weill.'

---

[1] wrong.   [2] young pig.   [3] vigorous fellow.   [4] heath.
    [5] with a wallet at his side.   [6] knowledge.

'Schir Common weill, who has you so disguisit?'
Quod I: 'or what makis you so miserabill?
I have marvel to see you so supprysit,
The whilk that I have seen so honorabill.
To all the warld ye have been profitable,
And weill honorit in everilk natioun:
How happenis, now, your tribulatioun?'

'Allace!' quod he, 'thou sees how it does stand
With me, and how I am disherisit
Of all my grace, and mon pass of Scotland,
And go, afore whare I was cherisit.
Remain I here, I am bot perisit;
For there is few to me that takis tent,
That garris me go so raggit, riven and rent.

'My tender friendis are all put to flycht;
For Policy is fled again to France.
My sister, Justice, almost hath tint[1] her sicht,
That she can nocht hold evenly the balance.
Plain wrang is clene[2] capitane of Ordinance,
The whilk debarris Lawtie and Reason,
And small remeid is found for open treason.

'Into the South, allace, I was near slain:
Owre all the land I culd find no relief;
Almost betwixt the Merse and Lochmabane[3]
I culd nocht knaw ane leill[4] man be ane thief.
To schaw their reif,[5] thift,[6] murder, and mischief,
And vicious werkis, it wald infect the air:
And als langsum to me for to declare.

'Into the Highland I culd find no remeid,
Bot suddenly I was put to exile.

---

[1] lost. [2] complete. [3] Berwickshire and Lochmaben, Dumfriesshire.
                [4] true.   [5] cattle-stealing.   [6] theft.

Tha sweir swyngeoris[1] they took of me none heed,
Nor amangs them let me remain ane while.
Als, in the out Ilis[2] and in Argyle,
Unthrift, sweirness,[3] falset, poverty and strife
Put Policy in danger of her life.

'In the Lawland I come to seek refuge,
And purposit there to mak my residence;
Bot singular profit gart me soon disluge,
And did me great injuries and offence,
And said to me: "Swith, harlot, hie thee hence:
And in this country see thou tak no curis,[4]
Sa lang as my auctoritie enduris.

' "Therefore, adieu, I may no langer tarry." '
'Fare weill,' quod I, and with Sanct John to borrow
Bot wit ye weill my heart was wonder sarye,
When Common weill so sopit was in sorrow.
Yit after the nicht comis the glad morrow;
'Wharefore, I pray you, shaw me in certain,
When that ye purpose for to come again.'

'That questioun, it sall be soon decidit,'
Quod he: 'thare sall na Scot have conforting
Of me, till that I see the country guidit
By wisdom of ane gude, auld prudent king,
Whilk sall delight him maist abune all thing,
To put justice till execution,
And on strang traitouris mak punitioun.

'Als yet to thee I say ane other thing:
I see richt weill that proverb is full true.
Woe to the realm that has owre young a king.'
With that he turnit his back and said 'adieu'.
Over firth and fell richt fast fra me he flew,

[1] lazy sluggards. [2] Hebrides. [3] laziness. [4] charge, governing.

Whose departing to me was displesand.
With that, Remembrance took me by the hand.

And soon, me thocht, she brocht me to the roche,[1]
And to the cove where I began to sleep.
With that ane ship did speedily approach,
Full plesandlie sailing upon the deep;
And syne did slack her sailis, and gan to creep
Towart the land, anent where that I lay:
Bot, wit you weill, I gat ane felloun fray.[2]

All her cannounis she let crack off at onis:
Down shook the streameris from the top-castell;
They sparit nocht the poulder nor the stonis;
They shot their boltis and doun their anchoris fell;
The marineris they did so youte and yell,
That hastily I stert out of my dream,
Half in ane fray, and speedily past hame.

And lichtly dinit, with lyste[3] and appetite,
Syne efter, past intil ane oritore,
And took my pen, and than began to write
All the visioun that I have shawin before.
Sir, of my dream as now thou gettis no more,
Bot I beseik God for to send thee grace
To rule thy realm in unity and peace.

SIR RICHARD MAITLAND

1496–1586

Against the Thieves of Liddesdale

Of Liddesdale the common thieves
Sa pertly stealis now and reives
That nane may keep,

---

[1] rock.   [2] cruel fright.   [3] pleasure.

Horse, nolt,[1] or sheep,
Nor yet daur sleep for their mischieves.

They plainly through the country rides;
I trow the meikle deil them guides.
Where they on set
Aye in their gate,
There is na yett[2] nor door them bides.

They leave richt nocht; wherever they gae;
There can na thing be hid them frae,
For, gif men wald
Their houses hald,
Then wax they bauld to burn and slay.

Thae thieves have nearhand herreit haill
Ettrick Forest and Lauderdale;
Now are they gane
In Lothiane,
And sparis nane that they will wale.

Thae landis are with stouth[3] sa socht
To extreme poverty are brocht,
Thae wicked shrewis
Has laid the plewis
That nane or few is that are left ocht.

By common taking of blackmail
They that had flesh, gude bread and ale,
Now are sa wrackit,
Made puir and nakit
Fain to be stakit[4] with water kale.

Thae thieves that steals and tursis[5] hame
Ilk ane[6] of them has ane to-name;[7]

---

[1] cattle.   [2] barred gate.   [3] stealing.   [4] supplied.   [5] carry.
[6] each.   [7] nickname.

Will of the Laws,
Hab of the Shaws;
To make bare wa's they think na shame.

They spuilye puir men of their packs;
They leave them nocht on bed nor backs;
Baith hen and cock,
With reel and rock,[1]
The Lairdis Jock, all with him taks.

They leave not spindle, spoon, nor spit,
Bed, bouster, blanket, sark, nor sheet;
John of the Park
Ripes kist and ark,[2]
For all sic wark he is richt meet.

He is weel kenned John of the Side,
A greater thief did never ride;
He never tires
For to break byres;
Owre muir and mires owre guid ane guide.

There is ane, callit Clement's Hob,
Fra ilk puir wife reivis her wob;[3]
And all the lave,
Whatever they have
The deil receive therefor his gob.[4]

To see sa grit stouth wha wald trow it,
Bot gif some grit man it allowit,
Richt sair I rue,
Though it be true,
There is sa few that dare avow it.

Of some grit men they have sic gate[5]
That ready are them to debate,[6]

---

[1] distaff.   [2] chest.   [3] web.   [4] mouth.   [5] influence.   [6] champion.

And will upweir[1]
Their stollen gear
That nane daur steir them, air nor late.

What causes thevis us owregang[2]
But want of justice us amang;
Nane takis care,
Though all forfare:[3]
Na man will spare now to do wrang.

Of stouth thoch now they come guid speed
That neither of God nor man has dreid,
Yet, or I dee
Some sall them see
Hing on a tree till they be deid.

ALEXANDER SCOTT

fl. 1547–84

A Rondel of Love

Lo! what it is to love,
  Learn ye, that list to prove
Be me, I say, that no ways may
  The ground of grief remove,
But still decay, both nicht and day:
  Lo! what it is to love.

  Love is ane fervent fire,
  Kindilit without desire:
Short pleasure, lang displeasure;
  Repentance is the hire;
Ane poor treasure without measure:[4]
  Love is ane fervent fire.

[1] defend. [2] oppress. [3] perish. [4] a treasure poor beyond measure.

To love and to be wise,
  To rage with good advice,[1]
Now thus, now than,[2] so goes the game.
  Incertain is the dice.
There is no man, I say that can
  Both love and to be wise.

Flee always from the snare;
  Learn at me to beware;
It is ane pain and double train
  Of endless woe and care;
For to refrain that danger plain,
  Flee always from the snare.

Hence, hairt, with her that must depairt

Hence, hairt, with her that must depairt,
  And hald thee with thy sovereign,
For I had lever[3] want ane hairt
  Nor have the hairt that does me pain;
  Therefore go, with thy love remain,
And let me live thus unmolest;
  And see that thou come not again,
But bide with her thou lovis best.

Sen sho that I have servit lang
  Is to depart so suddenly,
Address thee now, for thou sall gang
  And bear thy lady company.
  Fra sho be gone, hairtless am I,
For why[4] thou art with her possest;
  Therefore, my hairt, go hence in hy,[5]
And bide with her thou lovis best.

---

[1] to be mad and yet rational.   [2] otherwise.   [3] rather.
          [4] because.   [5] haste.

Though this belappit[1] body here
  Be bound to servitude and thrall,
My faithful hairt is free inteir[2]
  And mind to serve my lady at all.
  Wald God that I were perigall,[3]
Under that redolent rose to rest!
  Yet at the least, my hairt, thou sall
Abide with her thou lovis best.

Sen in your garth the lily white
  May not remain among the lave,[4]
Adieu the flower of haill delight!
  Adieu the succour that may me save!
  Adieu the fragrant balm suave,
And lamp of ladies lustiest!
  My faithful hairt sho sall it have,
To bide with her it lovis best.

Deplore, ye ladies clear of hue,
  Her absence, sen sho must depart,
And specially, ye lovers true,
  That wounded been with lovis dart:
  For some of you sall want ane hairt
Alsweill as I: therefore at last
  Do go with mine, with mind inwart,[5]
And bide with her thou lovis best.

Return thee, hairt

Return thee, hairt, hameward again,
  And bide where thou was wont to be;
Thou art ane fool to suffer pain
  For love of her that loves not thee.
  My hairt, lat be sic fantasy;

[1] beleaguered.   [2] entirely.   [3] worthy.   [4] remainder.   [5] sincere.

Love nane but as they mak thee cause;
　And lat her seek ane hairt for thee,
For fiend a crumb of thee sho faws.[1]

To what effect sould thou be thrall
　But[2] thank, sen thou has thy free will?
My hairt, be not sa bestial,
　But knaw who does thee good or ill;
　Remain with me and tarry still,
And see wha playis best their pawis,[3]
　And lat fillok[4] ga fling her fill,
For fiend a crumb of thee sho faws.

Though sho be fair I will not fenyie;[5]
　Sho is the kind of others ma;[6]
For why there is a fellone menye,[7]
　That semis good, and are not sa.
　My hairt, tak neither pain nor wa,[8]
For Meg, for Marjory, or yet Mause,
　But be thou glad and lat her ga,
For fiend a crumb of thee sho faws.

Because I find sho took in ill,[9]
　At her departing thou mak na care;
But all beguiled, go where sho will,
　Beshrew the hairt that mane[10] maks mair.
　My hairt, be merry late and air,
This is the final end and clause,
　And lat her follow ane filly fair,[11]
For feind a crumb of thee sho faws.

---

[1] possesses.　　　[2] without.　　　[3] part.　　　[4] the filly.
　[5] feign fondness.　　　[6] she is more like others.
　[7] a great number.　　　[8] woe.　　[9] took it amiss.
　　　　[10] moan.　　　[11] foppish youth.

Lament of the Master of Erskine

Depairt, depairt, depairt,
Alas! I must depairt
From her that has my hairt,
  With hairt full sore,
Aganis my will indeed,
And can find no remeid:
I wait[1] the pains of deid
  Can do no more.

Now must I go, alas!
From sicht of her sweet face,
The ground of all my grace,
  And sovereign;
What chance that may fall me,
Sall I never merry be,
Unto the time I see
  My sweet again.

I go, and wat not where,
I wander here and there,
I weep and sichis sair
  With painis smart;
Now must I pass away, away,
In wilderness and wilsome[2] way,
Alas! this woeful day
  We suld depairt!

My spreit does quake for dread,
My thirlit[3] hairt does bleed,
My painis does exceed—
  What suld I say?
I, woeful wicht, alone,

[1] know.   [2] dreary.   [3] pierced.

Makand ane piteous moan,
Alas! my hairt is gone
    For ever and aye.

Through languor of my sweet
So thirlit is my spreit,
My days are most complete[1]
    Through her absence:
Christ sen[2] sho knew my smart,
Ingravit in my hairt,
Because I must depairt,
    From her presence.

Adieu, my awin[3] sweet thing,
My joy and comforting,
My mirth and solacing
    Of erdly gloir:
Fair weel, my lady bricht,
And my remembrance richt;
Fare weel and have gude nicht:
    I say no more.

To love unlovit

To love unlovit is ane pain;
For she that is my sovereign,
    Some wanton man so hie has set her,
That I can get no love again,
    But breks my hairt, and nocht the better.

When that I went with that sweet may,[4]
To dance, to sing, to sport and play,
    And oft times in my armis plet[5] her;
I do now murne both nicht and day,
    And breks my hairt, and nocht the better.

[1] ended.   [2] send.   [3] own.   [4] maid.   [5] embrace.

Where I was wont to see her go
Richt trimly passand to and fro,
 With comely smiles when that I met her;
And now I live in pain and woe,
 And breks my hairt, and nocht the better.

Whattan ane glaikit[1] fool am I
To slay myself with melancholy,
 Sen weel I ken I may not get her!
Or what suld be the cause, and why,
 To brek my hairt, and nocht the better?

My hairt, sen thou may not her please,
Adieu, as good love comes as gaes,
 Go choose ane other and forget her;
God give him dolour and disease,
 That breks their hairt, and nocht the better.

ALEXANDER MONTGOMERIE

1540?–1610?

The Nicht is Neir Gane

Hey! now the day dawis;
The jolly cock crawis;
Now shroudis[2] the shawis[3]
 Thro' Nature anon.
The throstle cock cryis
On lovers wha lyis:
Now skaillis[4] the skyis;
 The nicht is neir gone.

The fieldis ouerflowis
With gowans[5] that growis,

---

[1] silly. [2] dress themselves. [3] woods. [4] clears. [5] daisies.

Quhair lilies like lowe[1] is
  As red as the ro'an.[2]
The turtle that true is,
With notes that renewis,
Her pairty[3] pursuis:
    The nicht is neir gone.

Now hairtis with hindis
Conform to their kindis,
Hie tursis[4] their tyndis[5]
    On ground whair they grone.[6]
Now hurchonis,[7] with hairis,
Aye passis in pairis;
Whilk duly declaris
    The nicht is neir gone.

The season excellis
Through sweetness that smellis;
Now Cupid compellis
    Our hairtis each one
On Venus wha waikis,
To muse on our maikis,[8]
Syne sing, for their saikis:
    'The nicht is neir gone!'

All courageous knichtis
Aganis the day dichtis
The breist-plate that bricht is,
    To fecht with their fone.[9]
The stonèd steed[10] stampis
Through courage, and crampis,[11]
Syne on the land lampis:[12]
    The nicht is neir gone.

---

[1] flame.   [2] rowan.   [3] partner, mate.   [4] carry.   [5] antlers.
[6] groan, bell.   [7] hedgehogs, 'urchins'.   [8] mates.   [9] foes.
    [10] stallion.   [11] prances.   [12] gallops.

The freikis[1] on feildis
That wight wapins[2] weildis
With shyning bright shieldis
    At Titan in trone;[3]
Stiff speiris in reistis
Ouer corseris crestis
Are broke on their breistis:
    The nicht is neir gone.

So hard are their hittis,
Some sweyis, some sittis,
And some perforce flittis[4]
    On ground quhile they grone.
Syne groomis that gay is
On blonkis[5] that brayis
With swordis assayis:—
    The nicht is neir gone.

An Admonition to Young Lassies

A bonnie 'No' with smiling looks again
    I wald ye learned, sen they so comely are.
As touching 'Yes', if ye suld speak so plain,
    I might reprove you to have said so far.
    Nocht that your grant, in ony ways micht gar[6]
Me loathe the fruit that courage ocht to choose;
    But I wald only have you seem to skar,[7]
And let me tak it, feigning to refuse;

And warsle, as it war against your will,
    Appearing angry, though ye have no ire:
For have, ye hear, is halden half a fill.[8]

---

[1] men, warriors.   [2] stout weapons.
[3] over against Titan (the sun), or read 'as'.   [4] are cast.
[5] white palfreys.   [6] make.   [7] discourage.
[8] possession, you hear, is held to halve desire.

I speak not this, as trowing for to tire:
But as the forger when he feeds his fire
With sparks of water maks it burn more bauld;
So, sweet denial doubles but desire,
And quickens courage fra becoming cauld.

Wald ye be made of, ye maun mak it nice;
For dainties here are delicate and dear,
But plenty things are prized to little price;[1]
Then though ye hearken, let no wit ye hear,
But look away, and len them aye your ear:
For, follow love, they say, and it will flee.
Wald ye be loved, this lesson maun ye leir:[2]
Flee whilom love, and it will follow thee.

Sweethairt, rejoice in mind

Sweethairt, rejoice in mind,
    With comfort day and nicht,
Ye have ane love as kind
    As ever loved wicht;
Though I be out of sicht,
    Lat nocht your courage fall,
My joyful hairt and licht,
    Ye have and ever sall.

My bonnie burd,[3] be blithe,
    And ye sall find me so
Imprent to you, I kyth,[4]
    To lat you nocht be woe;
Wherever I ride or go,
    Ye sall nocht sorry be,
My leal love, hairt, and jo,[5]
    Nane has my hairt but thee.

---

[1] things that are plentiful are little valued.   [2] must you learn.
[3] maid.   [4] constant to you, I declare.   [5] sweetheart.

And ye, my true love sweet,
  This do ye nocht gang stand,[1]
My blitheness for to beit,[2]
  As I serve at your hand;
To think me nocht constand,
  My bonnie burd, lat be:
My constant hairt sall stand
  To you till that I die.

I bid[3] no mair of you,
  But God grant you his bliss:
God be as blithe of you
  As I wald be of this,
Your lily lips to kiss,
  Thinkand that mind of yours,
My awn true love she is,
  That loves her paramours.[4]

Adieu to his Mistress

Adieu, O daisy of delight;
Adieu, most pleasant and perfite;
  Adieu, and have gude nicht:
Adieu, thou lustiest on live;
Adieu, sweet thing superlative;
  Adieu, my lamp of licht!
Like as the lizard does indeed
  Live by the manis face,
Thy beauty likewise suld me feed,
  If we had time and space.
    Adieu now; be true now
      Sen that we must depairt.
    Forget not, and set not
      At licht my constant hairt.

[1] gainsay.   [2] kindle.   [3] pray.   [4] *par amour.*

Albeit my body be absent,
My faithful hairt is vigilent
  To do you service true;
Bot when I haunt into the place
Where I was wont to see that face,
  My dolour does renew.
Then all my pleasure is bot pain,
  My cares they do incress;
Until I see your face again
  I live in heaviness.
    Sair weeping, but sleeping,
      The nichtis I ourdrive;
    Whiles murning, whiles turning,
      With thoughtis pensitive.

Sometime Good Hope did me comfort,
Saying, the time suld be bot short
  Of absence to endure.
Then courage quickens so my spreit,
When I think on my lady sweet,
  I hald my service sure.
I can not plaint of my estate,
  I thank the gods above;
For I am first in her conceit,
  Whom both I serve and love.
    Her friendis ay wendis
      To cause her to revoke;
    She bidis, and slidis
      No more than does a rock.

O lady, for thy constancie,
A faithful servant sall I be:
  Thine honour to defend;
And I sall surely, for thy sake,
As doth the turtle for her make,
  Love to my livis end.

No pain nor travail, fear nor dreid,
　　Sall cause me to desist.
Then ay when ye this letter read,
　　Remember how we kiss'd;
　　　　Embracing with lacing,
　　　　　　With other's tearis sweet,
　　　　Sic blissing in kissing
　　　　　　I quit till we twa meet.

JOHN STEWART OF BALDYNNIS

1550?–1605?

Medoro's Inscription for a Cave

O herbis green, and pretty plants formois,[1]
O limpid watter springing suave and clear,
O cave obscure agreeable to those
Who wold tham cool in thy fresch umber dear,
Whair Angelique maist beutifull but peer,
In vaine desyrd be uthers monie mo,
Oft nakit lay betwix my armis here,
I, Medor puir, whom ye have easit so,
May not requyt yow moir, bot whair I go
Your praise sall ever stedfastlie endure.
Lords, ladies, knychts, and lustie lovers tho,
And every gentle heart I will procure
To wiss yow weill and free of dainger sure.
Both sone and mone and nymphs yow saif from tort,
And nevir pastor with his troup injure
Your verduir rich, O seimlie fair resort.
　　But aye about yow birdis blythlie sing,
　　And unmolestit be your silver spring.

(From *Roland Furious*, Canto X, ll. 233–50.)

[1] beautiful.

JAMES MELVILLE
1556–1614

Robin at My Window

The air was cleart with white and sable clouds,
Hard froist, with frequent schours of hail and snaw,
Into the nicht the stormie wind with thouds
And balefull billows on the sea did blaw;
Men, beastis, and foulis unto their beilds[1] did draw,
Fain than to find the fruct of summer thrift,
Whan clad with snaw was sand, wood, crag and
    clift.

I satt at fyre weill guyrdit in my gown;
The starving sparrows at my window cheiped;
To reid ane whyle I to my book was bown.
In at ane pane the pretty progne[2] peipped,
And moved me, for fear I should have sleiped,
To ryse and sett ane keasement oppen wyd,
To see gif robein wald cum in and byde.

Puir progne, sueitlie I have hard ye sing
Thair at my window on the simmer day;
And now sen winter hidder dois ye bring
I pray ye enter in my hous and stay
Till it be fair, and than thous go thy way,
For trowlie thous be treated courteouslie
And nothing thralled in thy libertie.

Cum in, sueit robein, welcum verrilie,
Said I, and down I satt me by the fire:
Then in cums robein reidbreist mirrelie,
And suppis and lodgis at my hartis desire:

       [1] homes.   [2] robin (properly swallow, Procne).

But on ye morn, I him perceived to tyre,
For Phoebus schyning sueitlie him allurd,
I gave him leif, and furth guid robein furd.

> (From *The Black Bastill, or a Lamentation of
> the Kirk of Scotland*, as quoted in Thomas
> M'Crie's *Life of Andrew Melville*.)

ALEXANDER HUME

1557?–1609

Of the Day Estivall[1]

O Perfect Light, whilk shed away,
  The darkness from the light,
And set a ruler o'er the day,
  Ane other o'er the night.

Thy glory when the day forth flies,
  Mair vively[2] does appear,
Nor[3] at midday unto our eyes,
  The shining sun is clear.

The shadow of the earth anon,
  Removes and drawes by,
Syne in the east, when it is gone,
  Appears a clearer sky.

Whilk sun perceives the little larks,[4]
  The lapwing and the snipe,
And tunes their sangs like Nature's clerks,
  O'er meadow, muir, and stryp.[5]

But every bais'd[6] nocturnal beast,
  Na langer may abide,

---

[1] summer.   [2] vividly.   [3] than.
[4] which sun the little larks, &c. perceive.   [5] rill.   [6] abased.

They hie away baith maist and least
    Themselves in howes[1] to hide.

They dread the day fra they it see,
    And from the sight of men,
To saits and covers[2] fast they flee,
    As lions to their den.

Our hemisphere is polished clear,
    And lightened more and more,
While every thing be clearly seen,
    Whilk seemed dim before.

Except the glistering astres bright,
    Which all the night were clear,
Offusked[3] with a greater light,
    Na langer does appear.

For joy the birds with boulden[4] throats,
    Agains his visage sheen,
Takes up their kindly[5] music notes,
    In woods and gardens green.

Up braids[6] the careful husbandman,
    His corns and vines to see,
And every timeous[7] artizan
    In booth work busily.

The pastor quits the slothful sleep,
    And passes forth with speed,
His little camow[8]-nosed sheep,
    And routing[9] kye to feed.

The passenger from perils sure,
    Gangs gladly forth the way:
Brief, every living creature,
    Takes comfort of the day.

---

[1] hollows. [2] retreats and coverts. [3] obscured. [4] swollen.
[5] natural. [6] hastens. [7] early rising. [8] crooked. [9] lowing.

The subtle mottie rayons[1] light,
  At rifts they are in wonne,[2]
The glancing thains,[3] and vitre[4] bright,
  Resplends against the sun.

The dew upon the tender crops,
  Like pearles white and round,
Or like to melted silver drops,
  Refreshes all the ground.

The misty rock,[5] the clouds of rain,
  From tops of mountains skails,[6]
Clear are the highest hills and plain,
  The vapour takes the vales.

Begaried[7] is the sapphire pend,[8]
  With spraigns[9] of scarlet hue,
And preciously from end to end,
  Damasked white and blue.

The ample heaven of fabric sure
  In cleanness doth surpass,
The crystal and the silver pure,
  Or clearest poleist glass.

The time sa tranquil is and still,
  That na where sall ye find,
Save on ane high and barren hill,
  Ane air of peeping[10] wind.

All trees and simples[11] great and small,
  That balmy leaf do bear,
Nor they were painted in a wall,
  Na mair they move or steer.

[1] rays full of motes.   [2] have entered.   [3] vanes.   [4] glass.
[5] vapour.   [6] melts.   [7] variegated.   [8] vault (of the sky).
[9] streaks.   [10] whispering.   [11] herbs.

Calm is the deep and purpour sea,
  Yea, smoother nor the sand,
The waves that woltring wont to be,
  Are stable like the land.

So silent is the cessile[1] air,
  That every cry and call,
The hills, and dales, and forest fair,
  Again repeats them all.

The rivers fresh, the caller[2] streams,
  O'er rocks can softly rin;
The water clear like crystal seems,
  And makes a pleasant din.

The fields, and earthly superfice,[3]
  With verdure green is spread,
And naturally, but[4] artifice,
  In party colours cled.

The flourishes[5] and fragrant flowers,
  Through Phoebus' fost'ring heat
Refreshed with dew and silver showers,
  Casts up ane odour sweet.

The clogged busy humming bees,
  That never thinks to drown,
On flowers and flourishes of trees
  Collects their liquor brown.

The sun maist like a speedy post,
  With ardent course ascends;
The beauty of the heavenly host
  Up to the zenith tends.

---

[1] yielding.   [2] cool.   [3] surface of the earth.   [4] without.
[5] blossom on trees or shrubs.

Nocht guided by na Phaeton,
  Nor trained in a chyre,[1]
But by the high and haly One,
  Whilk does all where empire.

The burning beams down from his face
  Sa fervently can beat,
That man and beast now seeks a place
  To save them fra the heat.

The breathless flocks draws to the shade,
  And fraicheur of their fauld;
The startling nolt[2] as they were mad
  Runs to the rivers cauld.

The herds beneath some leafy tree
  Amids the flowers they lie;
The stable ships upon the sea
  Tends up their sails to dry.

The hart, the hind, and fallow deer,
  Are tapisht[3] at their rest;
The fowls and birds that made the beir[4]
  Prepares their pretty nest.

The rayons dour[5] descending down
  All kindles in a gleid;[6]
In city nor in boroughstown[7]
  May nane set forth their heid.

Back from the blue paymented whun,[8]
  And from ilk plaister wall,
The hot reflexing of the sun
  Inflames the air and all.

---

[1] drawn in a chariot.   [2] cattle.   [3] crouching.
[4] sound.   [5] keen.   [6] flame.   [7] burgh.
[8] whinstone used for a pavement.

The labourers that timely raise,[1]
All weary, faint, and weak,
For heat down to their houses gais,
Noon-meat and sleep to take.

The caller wine in cave[2] is sought,
Men's brothing[3] breasts to cool;
The water cauld and clear is brought,
The sallets[4] steept in ule.[5]

Some plucks the honey plum and pear,
The cherry and the pêche;
Some likes the reamand[6] London beer,
The body to refresh.

Forth of their skeps[7] some raging bees
Lies out and will not cast;[8]
Some other swarms hives on the trees
In knots togidder fast.

The corbies[9] and the keckling kais[10]
May scarce the heat abide;
Hawks prunyeis[11] on the sunny braes,
And wedders, back and side.

With gilted eyes and open wings,
The cock his courage shaws;
With claps of joy his breast he dings,[12]
And twenty times he craws.

The doo[13] with whistling wings sa blue,
The winds can fast collect,
Her purpour pens[14] turns mony hue
Against the sun direct.

---

[1] rose early.   [2] cellar.   [3] steaming.   [4] salads.   [5] oil.
[6] foaming.   [7] hives.   [8] swarm.   [9] crows.   [10] jackdaws.
[11] preen themselves.   [12] strikes.   [13] dove.   [14] wings.

Now noon is went; gane is midday;
   The heat does slake at last;
The sun descends down west away,
   Fra three o'clock be past.

A little cool of braithing wind
   Now softly can arise;
The warks through heat that lay behind
   Now men may enterprise.

Furth fares the flocks to seek their food
   On every hill and plain;
Ilk[1] labourer as he thinks good
   Steps to his turn again.

The rayons of the sun we see
   Diminish in their strength;
The shade of every tower and tree
   Extended is in length.

Great is the calm, for everywhere
   The wind is sitten down;
The reek[2] thraws[3] right up in the air
   From every tower and town.

Their firdoning[4] the bonnie birds
   In banks they do begin;
With pipes of reeds the jolly herds
   Halds up the merry din.

The mavis and the philomene,[5]
   The starling whistles loud;
The cushats[6] on the branches green
   Full quietly they crowd.[7]

---

[1] each.   [2] smoke.   [3] rises in a spiral.   [4] piping.
[5] nightingale.   [6] wood pigeons.   [7] coo.

The gloaming comes; the day is spent;
    The sun goes out of sight;
And painted is the occident
    With purpour sanguine bright.

The scarlet nor the golden thread,
    Who would their beauty try,
Are nothing like the colour red
    And beauty of the sky.

Our west horizon circular,
    Fra time the sun be set,
Is all with rubies, as it were,
    Or roses red o'erfret.

What pleasure were to walk and see,
    Endlang a river clear,
The perfect form of every tree
    Within the deep appear.

The salmon out of cruives and creels[1]
    Up hailed into skowts;[2]
The bells, and circles on the weills,[3]
    Through louping[4] of the trouts.

O then it were a seemly thing,
    While all is still and calm,
The praise of God to play and sing,
    With cornet and with shalm.

But now the herds with mony shout
    Calls other by their name;
'Ga, Billie, turn our good about.
    Now time is to go hame.'

---

[1] osier-traps for fish.   [2] boats.   [3] pools.   [4] leaping.

With belly fu' the beasts belyve[1]
  Are turned fra the corn,
Whilk soberly they hameward drive,
  With pipe and lilting horn.

Through all the land great is the gild[2]
  Of rustic folks that cry,
Of bleating sheep fra they be filled,
  Of calves and routing kye.

All labourers draws hame at even,
  And can till other say,
Thanks to the gracious God of heaven
  Whilk sent this summer day.

MARK ALEXANDER BOYD

1563–1601

Sonnet

Fra bank to bank, fra wood to wood I rin,
  Ourhailit[3] with my feeble fantasie;
    Like til a leaf that fallis from a tree,
Or til a reed ourblawin with the win.

Two gods guides me: the ane of tham is blin,
  Yea and a bairn brocht up in vanitie;
    The next a wife ingenrit of the sea,
And lichter nor a dauphin with her fin.

Unhappy is the man for evermair
  That tills the sand and sawis in the air;
    But twice unhappier is he, I lairn,
That feidis in his hairt a mad desire,
And follows on a woman throw the fire,
  Led by a blind and teachit by a bairn.

[1] straightway.   [2] noise.   [3] overwhelmed.

ANON.

(From *The Gude and Godlie Ballatis*, 1567.)

Go, heart, unto the lamp of licht

Go, heart, unto the lamp of licht,
    Go, heart, do service and honour,
Go, heart, and serve him day and nicht,
    Go, heart, unto thy Saviour.

Go, heart, to thy only remeid[1]
    Descending from the heavenly tour:
Thee to deliver from pyne and deide,[2]
    Go, heart, unto thy Saviour.

Go, heart, but[3] dissimulatioun,
    To Christ, that took our vile nature,
For thee to suffer passioun,
    Go, heart, unto thy Saviour.

Go, heart, richt humill and meek,
    Go, heart, as leal and true servitour,
To him that heill[4] is for all seek,[5]
    Go, heart, unto thy Saviour.

Go, heart, with true and haill intent,
    To Christ thy help and haill succour,
Thee to redeem he was all rent,
    Go, heart, unto thy Saviour.

To Christ, that raise from death to live,[6]
    Go, heart, unto thy latter hour,
Whais great mercy can nane discrive,[7]
    Go, heart, unto thy Saviour.

---

[1] remedy.   [2] pain and death.   [3] without.   [4] health.
[5] sick.   [6] life.   [7] describe.

Ane Sang of the Birth of Christ, with the Tune of Baw Lula Low

My saul and life stand up and see
Wha lyis in ane crib of tree.
What Babe is that, sa gude and fair?
It is Christ, Goddis son and heir.

Welcome now, gracious God of micht,
To sinners vile, puir, and unricht.
Thou come to save us from distress;
How can we thank thy gentleness?

O God that made all creature,
How art thou now becumit sa puir,
That on the hay and stray will lie,
Amang the asses, oxen, and kye!

And war the warld ten time sa wide,
Cled owre with gold and stanes of pride,
Unworthy it war, yet to thee,
Under thy feet ane stool to be.

The silk and sandell[1] thee to ease,
Are hay, and simple sweilling[2] claes,
Wherein thou glories, greatest King,
As thou in heaven war in thy Ring.[3]

Thou took sic painis temporal,
To make me rich perpetual,
For all this warldis wealth and gude
Can nathing rich thy celsitude.

O my dear heart, young Jesus sweet,
Prepare thy cradle for my spreit,
And I sall rock thee in my heart,
And never mair fra thee depart.

[1] sendal, rich silk.   [2] swaddling.   [3] kingdom.

But I sall praise thee evermore
With sangis sweet unto thy gloir;
The knees of my heart sall I bow,
And sing this richt Balulalow.

Gloir be to God eternallie,
Whilk gave his only Son for me:
The angellis joyis for to hear
The gracious gift of this New Year.

> (A translation of Luther's hymn for Christmas
> Eve *Vom himel hoch da kom ich her.*
> The first six stanzas are omitted.)

Welcome, Fortune

Welcome, Fortune, welcome again,
The day and hour I may weel bliss,[1]
Thou has exilit all my pain,
Whilk to my heart great pleasure is.

For I may say, that few men may,
Seeing of pain I am drest,[2]
I have obtainit all my pay,—
The love of her that I love best.

I knaw nane sic as sho is one,
Sa true, sa kind, sa lovandly,
What suld I do, an sho war gone?
Alas! yet had I lever[3] die.

To me sho is baith true and kind,
Worthy it war sho had the praise,
For na disdain in her I find,
I pray to God I may her please.

[1] bless.   [2] redressed.   [3] rather.

When that I hear her name exprest,
My heart for joy does loup[1] therefor.
Above all other I love her best,
Until I die, what wald sho more?

All my love, leave me not

All my love, leave me not,
Leave me not, leave me not,
All my love, leave me not,
   Thus mine alone.
With ane burden on my back
I may not bear it I am sa waik,
Luve, this burden fra me tak
   Or ellis I am gone.

With sinnis I am laden sore,
Leave me not, leave me not,
With sinnis I am laden sore,
   Leave me not alone.
I pray Thee, Lord, therefore,
Keep not my sinnis in store,
Lowse[2] me or I be forlore,
   And hear my moan.

With Thy handis Thou has me wrocht,
Leave me not, leave me not,
With Thy handis Thou has me wrocht,
   Leave me not alone.
I was sauld and Thou me bocht,
With Thy blude Thou has me coft[3]
Now am I hither socht
   To Thee, Lord, alone.

[1] leap.   [2] loose.   [3] bought.

I cry and I call to Thee,
To leave me not, to leave me not,
I cry and I call to Thee
To leave me not alone.
　All they that laden be
Thou biddis come to Thee
Then sall they savit be
　Through Thy mercy alone.

ANON.

(From the Banatyne Manuscript, 1568.)

The Wife of Auchtermuchty

In Auchtermuchty there dwelt ane man,
Ane husband, as I heard it tauld,
Wha weil could tipple out a can,
And neither luvit hunger nor cauld.
Till anis it fell upon a day,
He yokit his pleuch upon the plain;
Gif it be true as I heard say,
The day was foul for wind and rain.

He lousit[1] the pleuch at the landis en',
And draif his oxen hame at even;
When he come in he lookit ben,
And saw the wife baith dry and clean,
And sittand at ane fire beikand[2] bauld,
With ane fat soup as I heard say:
The man being very weet and cauld,
Between thae twa it was na play.

Quoth he, 'Where is my horses' corn?
My ox has neither hay nor strae;

---

[1] loosened.　　[2] basking.

Dame, ye maun to the pleuch to-morne,
I sall be hussy,¹ gif I may.'
'Husband,' quod she, 'content am I
To tak the pleuch my day about,
Sa ye will rule baith calvis and kye,
And all the house baith in and out.

'Bot sen that ye will hussif-skep² ken,
First ye sall sift, and syne sall knead;
And ay as ye gang but and ben,
Luik that the bairnis dryt not the bed.
Ye'se lay ane soft wisp to the kiln,
We haif ane dear farm on our heid;
And ay as ye gang furth and in,
Keep weil the gaislingis fra the gled.'³

The wife was up richt late at even,
I pray God gif her evil to fare,
She kirn'd the kirn, and scum'd it clean,
And left the gudeman bot the bledoch⁴ bare.
Than in the morning up she gat,
And on her hairt laid her disjeune,⁵
She put as meikle in her lap,
As micht haif ser'd them baith at noon.

Sayis, 'Jock, will thou be maister of wark,
And thou sall haud and I sall call;
I'se promise thee ane gude new sark,
Either of round claith or of small.'
She lousit oxen aucht or nine,
And hynt⁶ ane gadstaff⁷ in her hand;
And the gudeman raise eftir syne,
And saw the wife had done command.

---

¹ housewife.   ² housewifery.   ³ kite.   ⁴ buttermilk.
    ⁵ breakfast (*déjeuner*).   ⁶ took.   ⁷ goad.

And ca'd the gaislingis furth to feed,
There was bot seven-some of them all,
And by there comis the greedy gled,
And lickit up five, left him bot twa.
Than out he ran in all his main,
How sune he heard the gaislingis cry;
Bot than or he come in again,
The calvis brak louse and soukit the kye.

The calvis and kye being met in the loan,
The man ran with ane rung[1] to red;
Than by their comis ane ill-willy cow,
And brodit his buttock whill that it bled.
Than hame he ran to ane rock[2] of tow,
And he sat doun to 'say the spinning;
I trow he loutit[3] owre near the lowe,[4]
Quod he, 'This wark has ill beginning.'

Than to the kirn that he did stoure,
And jumlit at it whill he swat,
When he had jumlit a full lang hour,
The sorrow crap of butter he gat.
Albeit na butter he could get,
Yit he was cummerit with the kirn,
And syne he het the milk owre het,
And sorrow spark of it wald yirn.[5]

Than ben there come ane greedy sow,
I trow he cun'd her little thank,
And in she shot her meikle mou',
And ay she winkit and she drank.
He cleikit up ane crukit club,
And thocht to hit the sow ane rout;
The twa gaislingis the gled had left,
That straik dang baith their harnis out.

[1] cudgel.　　[2] distaff.　　[3] leant.　　[4] flame.　　[5] curdle.

Than he bure kindling to the kiln,
Bot she start all up in ane lowe,
Whatever he heard, whatever he saw,
That day he had na will to mow.
Than he yeid to take up the bairnis,
Thocht to haif fund them fair and clean;
The first that he gat in his armis
Was all bedirtin to the een.

The first that he gat in his armis
It was all dirt up to the een.
'The divil cut off their handis,' quod he,
'That fild yow all sa fow this strene.'
He trailit the foul sheets doun the gait,
Thocht to have washed thame on ane stane;
The burn, was risen grit of spait,
Away fra him the sheets hes tane.

Than up he gat on ane knowe-heid,
On her to cry, on her to shout,
She heard him, and she heard him not,
Bot stoutly steer'd the stottis about.
She draif the day unto the nicht,
She lousit the pleuch and syne come hame;
She fand all wrang that sould been richt,
I trow the man thocht richt great shame.

Quod he, 'My office I forsake
For all the dayis of my life,
For I wald put ane house to wraik,
Had I been twenty dayis gudewife.'
Quod she, 'Weil mot ye bruik the place,
For truly I will never accep' it.'
Quod he, 'Fiend fall the liaris face,
Bot yit ye may be blyth to get it.'

Than up she gat an meikle rung,
And the gudeman made to the door;
Quod he, 'Dame, I sall hald my tongue,
For an we fecht I'll get the waur.'
Quod he, 'When I forsook my pleuch,
I trow I bot forsook my seill,[1]
And I will to my pleuch again,
For I and this house will never do weil.'

The Bewteis of the Fute-ball

Brissit brawnis and broken banis,
Strife, discord, and waistis wanis,[2]
Crookit in eild,[3] syne halt withal—
Thir are the bewteis of the fute-ball.

The Reeds in the Loch Sayis

Though raging stormes movis us to shake,
And wind makis waters overflow;
We yield thereto bot dois not break
And in the calm bent up we grow.

So baneist men, though princes rage,
And prisoners, be not despairit.
Abide the calm, whill that it 'suage,
For time sic causis has repairit.

My heart is heich above

My heart is heich above,
My body is full of bliss,
For I am set in luve,
As weil as I wald wiss;

---

[1] happiness.   [2] children.   [3] old-age.

I luve my lady pure,
  And she luvis me again;
I am her serviture,
  She is my soverane.

She is my very heart,
  I am her hope and heal;
She is my joy inwart,
  I am her luvar leal;
I am her bound and thrall,
  She is at my command;
I am perpetual
  Her man, both fute and hand.

The thing that may her please
  My body sall fulfil;
Whatever her disease,
  It dois my body ill.
My bird, my bonnie ane,
  My tender babe venust,[1]
My luve, my life alane,
  My liking and my lust.

We interchange our hairtis
  In otheris armis soft;
Spreitless we twa depairtis
  Usand our luvis oft;
We murne when licht day dawis,
  We plain the nicht is short,
We curse the cock that crawis,
  That hinderis our disport.

I glowffin[2] up agast,
  When I her miss on nicht,

---

[1] beautiful.   [2] start.

And in my oxter fast
   I find the bowster richt;
Then languor on me lies,
   Like Morpheus the mair,
Whilk causis me uprise
   And to my sweet repair:

And then is all the sorrow
   Furth of remembrance,
That ever I had aforrow
   In luvis observance.
Thus never I do rest,
   So lusty a life I lead,
When that I list to test
   The well of womanheid.

Luvaris in pain, I pray
   God send you sic remead
As I have nicht and day,
   You to defend from deid;
Therefore be ever true
   Unto your ladies free,
And they will on you rue,
   As mine has done on me.

Blest, blest and happy he

Blest, blest and happy he
Whose eyes behold her face,
But blessed more whose ears hath heard
The speeches framed with grace.

And he is half a god
That these thy lips may kiss,
Yet god all whole that may enjoy
   Thy body as it is.

WILLIAM FOWLER

1560–1612

Ship-broken men whom stormy seas sore toss

Ship-broken men whom stormy seas sore toss
Protests with oaths not to adventure more;
Bot all their perils, promises, and loss
They quite forget when they come to the shore:
Even so, fair dame, whiles sadly I deplore
The shipwreck of my wits procured by you,
Your looks rekindleth love as of before,
And dois revive which I did disavow;
So all my former vows I disallow,
And buries in oblivion's grave, but groans;
Yea, I forgive, hereafter, even as now
My fears, my tears, my cares, my sobs, and moans,
In hope if anes I be to shipwreck driven,
Ye will me thole to anchor in your heaven.

ANON.

Old Ballads

Sir Patrick Spens

The King sits in Dunfermline town,
　　Drinking the blude-red wine;
'O whare will I get a skeely skipper,
　　To sail this new ship of mine?'—

O up and spake an eldern knight,
　　Sat at the King's right knee,—
'Sir Patrick Spens is the best sailor,
　　That ever sailed the sea.'—

Our King has written a braid letter,
  And seal'd it with his hand,
And sent it to Sir Patrick Spens,
  Was walking on the strand.

'To Noroway, to Noroway,
  To Noroway o'er the faem;
The King's daughter of Noroway,
  'Tis thou maun bring her hame.'

The first word that Sir Patrick read,
  Sae loud loud laughed he;
The neist word that Sir Patrick read,
  The tear blinded his ee.

'O wha is this has done this deed,
  And tauld the King o' me,
To send us out, at this time of the year,
  To sail upon the sea?

'Be it wind, be it weet, be it hail, be it sleet,
  Our ship must sail the faem;
The King's daughter of Noroway,
  'Tis we must fetch her hame.'—

They hoysed their sails on Monenday morn,
  Wi' a' the speed they may;
They hae landed in Noroway,
  Upon a Wodensday.

They hadna been a week, a week,
  In Noroway, but twae,
When that the lords o' Noroway
  Began aloud to say,—

'Ye Scottishmen spend a' our King's gowd,
  And a' our Queenis fee.'—
'Ye lie, ye lie, ye liars loud!
  Fu' loud I hear ye lie;

'For I brought as much white monie,
    As gane my men and me,
And I brought a half-fou[1] of gude red gowd,
    Out o'er the sea wi' me.

'Make ready, make ready, my merrymen a'!
    Our gude ship sails the morn.'—
'Now, ever alake, my master dear,
    I fear a deadly storm!

'I saw the new moon, late yestreen,
    Wi' the auld moon in her arm;
And, if we gang to sea, master,
    I fear we'll come to harm.'

They hadna sail'd a league, a league,
    A league but barely three,
When the lift grew dark, and the wind blew
      loud,
    And gurly[2] grew the sea.

The ankers brak, and the topmasts lap,
    It was sic a deadly storm;
And the waves cam o'er the broken ship,
    Till a' her sides were torn.

'O where will I get a gude sailor,
    To take my helm in hand,
Till I get up to the tall top-mast,
    To see if I can spy land?'—

'O here am I, a sailor gude,
    To take the helm in hand,
Till you go up to the tall top-mast;
    But I fear you'll ne'er spy land.'—

    [1] eighth of a peck.   [2] boisterous.

He hadna gane a step, a step,
    A step but barely ane,
When a bout[1] flew out of our goodly ship,
    And the salt sea it came in.

'Gae, fetch a web o' the silken claith,
    Another o' the twine,
And wap[2] them into our ship's side,
    And let nae the sea come in.'—

They fetch'd a web o' the silken claith,
    Another o' the twine,
And they wapp'd them round that gude ship's
        side,
    But still the sea cam in.

O laith, laith, were out gude Scots lords
    To weet their cork-heel'd shoon!
But lang or a' the play was play'd,
    They wat their hats aboon.

And mony was the feather bed,
    That flatter'd on the faem;
And mony was the gude lord's son,
    That never mair cam hame.

The ladyes wrang their fingers white,
    The maidens tore their hair,
A' for the sake of their true loves;
    For them they'll see nae mair.

O lang, lang, may the ladyes sit,
    Wi' their fans into their hand,
Before they see Sir Patrick Spens
    Come sailing to the strand!

[1] bolt.   [2] wrap.

And lang, lang, may the maidens sit,
  With their gowd kaims in their hair,
A' waiting for their ain dear loves!
  For them they'll see nae mair.

Half-owre, half-owre to Aberdour,
  'Tis fifty fathoms deep,
And there lies gude Sir Patrick Spens,
  Wi' the Scots lords at his feet.

The Battle of Otterbourne

It fell about the Lammas tide,
  When the muir-men win their hay,
The doughty Douglas bound him to ride
  Into England, to drive a prey.

He chose the Gordons and the Græmes,
  With them the Lindesays, light and gay
But the Jardines wald not with him ride,
  And they rue it to this day.

And he has burn'd the dales of Tyne,
  And part of Bambrough shire;
And three good towers on Reidswire fells,
  He left them all on fire.

And he march'd up to Newcastle,
  And rode it round about;
'O wha 's the lord of this castle,
  Or wha 's the lady o't?'—

But up spake proud Lord Percy, then,
  And O but he spake hie!
'I am the lord of this castle,
  My wife's the lady gay.'

'If thou'rt the lord of this castle,
    Sae weel it pleases me!
For, ere I cross the Border fells,
    The tane of us shall die.'—

He took a lang spear in his hand,
    Shod with the metal free,
And for to meet the Douglas there,
    He rode right furiouslie.

But O how pale his lady look'd,
    Frae aff the castle wa',
When down before the Scottish spear
    She saw proud Percy fa'.

'Had we twa been upon the green,
    And never an eye to see,
I wad hae had you, flesh and fell;
    But your sword sall gae wi' me.'—

'But gae ye up to Otterbourne,
    And wait there dayis three;
And, if I come not ere three dayis end,
    A fause knight ca' ye me.'—

'The Otterbourne's a bonnie burn;
    'Tis pleasant there to be;
But there is nought at Otterbourne,
    To feed my men and me.

'The deer rins wild on hill and dale,
    The birds fly wild from tree to tree;
But there is neither bread nor kale,
    To fend my men and me.

'Yet I will stay at Otterbourne,
    Where you shall welcome be;
And, if ye come not at three dayis end,
    A fause lord I'll ca' thee.'—

'Thither will I come,' proud Percy said,
 'By the might of Our Ladye!'—
'There will I bide thee,' said the Douglas,
 'My troth I plight to thee.'

They lighted high on Otterbourne,
 Upon the bent sae brown;
They lighted high on Otterbourne,
 And threw their pallions down.

And he that had a bonnie boy,
 Sent out his horse to grass;
And he that had not a bonnie boy,
 His ain servant he was.

But up then spake a little page,
 Before the peep of dawn—
'O waken ye, waken ye, my good lord,
 For Percy's hard at hand.—

'Ye lie, ye lie, ye liar loud!
 Sae loud I hear ye lie:
For Percy had not men yestreen
 To dight my men and me.

'But I have dream'd a dreary dream,
 Beyond the Isle of Skye;
I saw a dead man win a fight,
 And I think that man was I.'

He belted on his guid braid sword,
 And to the field he ran;
But he forgot the helmet good,
 That should have kept his brain.

When Percy wi' the Douglas met,
 I wat he was fu' fain!
They swakked their swords, till sair they swat,
 And the blood ran down like rain.

But Percy with his good broad sword,
    That could so sharply wound,
Has wounded Douglas on the brow,
    Till he fell to the ground.

Then he call'd on his little foot-page,
    And said—'Run speedilie,
And fetch my ain dear sister's son,
    Sir Hugh Montgomery.

'My nephew good,' the Douglas said,
    'What recks the death of ane!
Last night I dream'd a dreary dream,
    And I ken the day's thy ain.

'My wound is deep; I fain would sleep;
    Take thou the vanguard of the three,
And hide me by the braken bush,
    That grows on yonder lilye lee.

'O bury me by the braken bush,
    Beneath the blooming brier,
Let never living mortal ken,
    That ere a kindly Scot lies here.'

He lifted up that noble lord,
    Wi' the saut tear in his ee;
He hid him in the braken bush,
    That his merrie-men might not see.

The moon was clear, the day drew near,
    The spears in flinders flew,
But mony a gallant Englishman
    Ere day the Scotsmen slew.

The Gordons good, in English blood,
    They steep'd their hose and shoon;
The Lindsays flew like fire about,
    Till all the fray was done.

The Percy and Montgomery met,
  That either of other were fain;
They swapped swords, and they twa swat,
  And aye the blood ran down between.

'Now yield thee, yield thee, Percy,' he said,
  'Or else I vow I'll lay thee low!'—
'To whom must I yield,' quoth Earl Percy,
  'Now that I see it must be so?'—

'Thou shalt not yield to lord nor loun,
  Nor yet shalt thou yield to me;
But yield thee to the braken bush,
  That grows upon yon lilye lee!'—

'I will not yield to a braken bush,
  Nor yet will I yield to a brier;
But I would yield to Earl Douglas,
  Or Sir Hugh the Montgomery, if he were here.'

As soon as he knew it was Montgomery,
  He struck his sword's point in the gronde;
The Montgomery was a courteous knight,
  And quickly took him by the honde.

This deed was done at the Otterbourne
  About the breaking of the day;
Earl Douglas was buried at the braken bush,
  And the Percy led captive away.

The Border Widow's Lament

My love he built me a bonny bower,
  And cled it a' wi' lilye flour;
A brawer bower ye ne'er did see,
  Than my true love he built to me.

There came a man by middle day,
He spied his sport, and went away;
And brought the King that very night,
Who brak my bower, and slew my knight.

He slew my knight, to me sae dear;
He slew my knight, and poin'd[1] his gear;
My servants all for life did flee,
And left me in extremitie.

I sew'd his sheet, making my mane;
I watch'd the corpse, myself alane;
I watch'd his body, night and day;
No living creature came that way.

I took his body on my back,
And whiles I gaed, and whiles I sat;
I digg'd a grave, and laid him in,
And happ'd him with the sod sae green.

But think na ye my heart was sair,
When I laid the mool on his yellow hair;
O think na ye my heart was wae,
When I turn'd about away to gae?

Nae living man I'll love again,
Since that my lovely knight is slain;
Wi' ae lock of his yellow hair
I'll chain my heart for evermair.

Kinmont Willie

O have ye na heard o' the fause Sakelde?
  O have ye na heard o' the keen Lord Scroope?
How they hae ta'en bauld Kinmont Willie,
  On Haribee to hang him up?

[1] made forfeit.

Had Willie had but twenty men,
  But twenty men as stout as he,
Fause Sakelde had never the Kinmont ta'en,
  Wi' eight score in his companie.

They band his legs beneath the steed,
  They tied his hands behind his back;
They guarded him, fivesome on each side,
  And they brought him ower the Liddel-rack.[1]

They led him thro' the Liddel-rack,
  And also thro' the Carlisle sands;
They brought him in to Carlisle castell,
  To be at my Lord Scroope's commands.

'My hands are tied, but my tongue is free,
  And whae will dare this deed avow?
Or answer by the Border law?
  Or answer to the bauld Buccleuch?'—

'Now haud thy tongue, thou rank reiver!
  There's never a Scot shall set thee free:
Before ye cross my castle yate,
  I trow ye shall take farewell o' me.'

'Fear na ye that, my lord,' quo' Willie:
  'By the faith o' my body, Lord Scroope,' he said,
'I never yet lodged in a hostelrie
  But I paid my lawing[2] before I gaed.'

Now word is gane to the bauld Keeper,
  In Branksome Ha', where that he lay,
That Lord Scroope has ta'en the Kinmont Willie,
  Between the hours of night and day.

He has ta'en the table wi' his hand,
  He garr'd the red wine spring on hie—

---

  [1] a ford on the Liddel.   [2] reckoning.

'Now Christ's curse on my head,' he said,
   'But avengèd of Lord Scroope I'll be!

'O is my basnet a widow's curch?[1]
   Or my lance a wand of the willow-tree?
Or my arm a ladye's lilye hand,
   That an English lord should lightly[2] me!

'And have they ta'en him, Kinmont Willie,
   Against the truce of Border tide?
And forgotten that the bauld Buccleuch
   Is Keeper here on the Scottish side?

'And have they e'en ta'en him, Kinmont Willie,
   Withouten either dread or fear?
And forgotten that the bauld Buccleuch
   Can back a steed, or shake a spear?

'O were there war between the lands,
   As well I wot that there is nane,
I would slight Carlisle castell high,
   Though it were builded of marble stane.

'I would set that castell in a low,[3]
   And sloken it with English blood!
There's never a man in Cumberland
   Should ken where Carlisle castell stood.

'But since nae war's between the lands,
   And there is peace, and peace should be;
I'll neither harm English lad or lass,
   And yet the Kinmont freed shall be!'

He has call'd him forty Marchmen bauld,
   I trow they were of his ain name,
Except Sir Gilbert Elliot, call'd
   The Laird of Stobs, I mean the same.

---

[1] kerchief, coif.   [2] treat disrespectfully.   [3] flame.

He has call'd him forty Marchmen bauld,
  Were kinsmen to the bauld Buccleuch;
With spur on heel, and splent[1] on spauld,[2]
  And gleuves of green, and feathers blue.

There were five and five before them a',
  Wi' hunting-horns and bugles bright:
And five and five came wi' Buccleuch,
  Like Warden's men, array'd for fight.

And five and five, like a mason-gang,
  That carried the ladders lang and hie;
And five and five, like broken men;
  And so they reach'd the Woodhouselee.

And as we cross'd the Bateable Land,[3]
  When to the English side we held,
The first o' men that we met wi',
  Whae sould it be but fause Sakelde?

'Where be ye gaun, ye hunters keen?'
  Quo' fause Sakelde; 'come tell to me!'—
'We go to hunt an English stag,
  Has trespass'd on the Scots countrie.'

'Where be ye gaun, ye marshal men?'
  Quo' fause Sakelde; 'come tell me true!'—
'We go to catch a rank reiver,
  Has broken faith wi' the bauld Buccleuch.'

'Where be ye gaun, ye mason lads,
  Wi' a' your ladders, lang and hie?'—
'We gang to herry a corbie's nest,
  That wons not far frae Woodhouselee.'—

---

[1] split, or overlapping armour.   [2] shoulder, *épaule*.
[3] debatable land; a stretch of frontier between the Solway Firth
  and Scots Dyke, claimed by both nations.

'Where be ye gaun, ye broken men?'
　　Quo' fause Sakelde; 'come tell to me!'—
Now Dickie of Dryhope led that band,
　　And the never a word of lear[1] had he.

'Why trespass ye on the English side?
　　Row-footed[2] outlaws, stand!' quo' he;
The never a word had Dickie to say,
　　Sae he thrust the lance through his fause bodie.

Then on we held for Carlisle toun,
　　And at Staneshaw-bank the Eden we cross'd;
The water was great and meikle of spate,
　　But the never a horse nor man we lost

And when we reach'd the Staneshaw-bank,
　　The wind was rising loud and hie;
And there the Laird gar'd leave our steeds,
　　For fear that they should stamp and neigh.

And when we left the Staneshaw-bank,
　　The wind began fu' loud to blaw;
But 'twas wind and weet, and fire and sleet,
　　When we came beneath the castle wa'.

We crept on knees, and held our breath,
　　Till we placed the ladders against the wa';
And sae ready was Buccleuch himsell
　　To mount the first before us a'.

He has ta'en the watchman by the throat,
　　He flung him down upon the lead—
'Had there not been peace between our lands,
　　Upon the other side thou hadst gaed!—

'Now sound out, trumpets!' quo' Buccleuch;
　　'Let's waken Lord Scroope right merrilie!'

[1] lore.　　[2] rough-footed.

Then loud the Warden's trumpet blew—
O wha dare meddle wi' me?

Then speedilie to wark we gaed,
　And raised the slogan ane and a',
And cut a hole through a sheet of lead,
　And so we wan to the castle ha'.

They thought King James and a' his men
　Had won the house wi' bow and spear;
It was but twenty Scots and ten,
　That put a thousand in sic a stear![1]

Wi' coulters, and wi' forehammers,[2]
　We gar'd the bars bang merrilie,
Until we came to the inner prison.
　Where Willie o' Kinmont he did lie.

And when we cam to the lower prison,
　Where Willie o' Kinmont he did lie—
'O sleep ye, wake ye, Kinmont Willie,
　Upon the morn that thou's to die?'—

'O I sleep saft, and I wake aft;
　It's lang since sleeping was fley'd[3] frae me!
Gie my service back to my wife and bairns,
　And a' gude fellows that spier[4] for me.'

The Red Rowan has hente him up,
　The starkest man in Teviotdale—
'Abide, abide now, Red Rowan,
　Till of my Lord Scroope I take farewell.

'Farewell, farewell, my gude Lord Scroope!
　My gude Lord Scroope, farewell!' he cried;
'I'll pay you for my lodging mail,[5]
　When first we meet on the Border side.'—

---

[1] stir, commotion. 　　[2] sledge-hammers. 　　[3] scared.
　　　　[4] inquire. 　　[5] rent.

Then shoulder high, with shout and cry,
    We bore him down the ladder lang;
At every stride Red Rowan made,
    I wot the Kinmont's airns play'd clang!

'O mony a time,' quo' Kinmont Willie,
    'I have ridden horse baith wild and wood;[1]
But a rougher beast than Red Rowan
    I ween my legs have ne'er bestrode.

And mony a time,' quo' Kinmont Willie,
    'I've prick'd a horse out oure the furs;[2]
But since the day I back'd a steed,
    I never wore sic cumbrous spurs!'

We scarce had won the Staneshaw-bank
    When a' the Carlisle bells were rung,
And a thousand men on horse and foot
    Cam wi' the keen Lord Scroope along.

Buccleuch has turn'd to Eden Water,
    Even where it flow'd frae bank to brim,
And he has plunged in wi' a' his band,
    And safely swam them through the stream.

He turn'd him on the other side,
    And at Lord Scroope his glove flung he;
'If ye like na my visit in merry England,
    In fair Scotland come visit me!'

All sore astonish'd stood Lord Scroope,
    He stood as still as rock of stane;
He scarcely dared to trew[3] his eyes,
    When through the water they had gane.

[1] mad.   [2] furrows.   [3] trust.

'He is either himsell a devil frae hell,
  Or else his mother a witch maun be;
I wadna have ridden that wan water
  For a' the gowd in Christentie.'

Jamie Telfer of the Fair Dodhead

It fell about the Martinmas tyde,
  When our Border steeds get corn and hay,
The Captain of Bewcastle bound him to ryde,
  And he's ower to Tividale to drive a prey.

The first ae guide that they met wi',
  It was high up in Hardhaughswire;
The second guide that they met wi',
  It was laigh[1] down in Borthwick water.

'What tidings, what tidings, my trusty guide?'—
  'Nae tidings, nae tidings, I hae to thee;
But gin ye'll gae to the fair Dodhead,
  Mony a cow's cauf I'll let thee see.'

And when they cam to the fair Dodhead,
  Right hastily they clam the peel;[2]
They loosed the kye out, ane and a',
  And ranshackled the house right weel.

Now Jamie Telfer's heart was sair,
  The tear aye rowing[3] in his ee;
He pled wi' the Captain to hae his gear,
  Or else revengèd he wad be.

The Captain turned him round and leugh;
  Said—'Man, there's naething in thy house,
But ae auld sword without a sheath,
  That hardly now would fell a mouse.'

---

[1] low.   [2] stockade or wall.   [3] rolling.

The sun wasna up, but the moon was down,
　It was the gryming[1] of a new-fa'n snaw,
Jamie Telfer has run ten myles a-foot,
　Between the Dodhead and the Stobs's Ha'.

And when he cam to the fair tower-yate,
　He shouted loud, and cried weel hie,
Till out bespak auld Gibby Elliot—
　'Whae's this that brings the fraye[2] to me?'—

'It's I, Jamie Telfer of the fair Dodhead,
　And a harried man I think I be!
There's naething left at the fair Dodhead,
　But a waefu' wife and bairnies three.'

'Gae seek your succour at Branksome Ha',
　For succour ye'se get nane frae me!
Gae seek your succour where ye paid black-mail,
　For, man, ye ne'er paid money to me.'—

Jamie has turned him round about,
　I wat the tear blinded his ee—
'I'll ne'er pay mail to Elliot again,
　And the fair Dodhead I'll never see.

'My hounds may a' rin masterless,
　My hawks may fly frae tree to tree,
My lord may grip my vassal lands,
　For there again maun I never be!'—

He has turn'd him to the Tiviot-side,
　E'en as fast as he could drie,
Till he cam to the Coultart Cleugh,
　And there he shouted baith loud and hie.

---

[1] sprinkling.　　[2] fright, alarm.

Then up bespak him auld Jock Grieve,
  'Whae's this that brings the fraye to me?'—
'It's I, Jamie Telfer in the fair Dodhead,
  A harried man I trow I be.

'There's naething left in the fair Dodhead.
  But a greeting wife and bairnies three,
And sax poor ca's[1] stand in the sta',
  A' routing loud for their minnie.'[2]—

'Alack a wae!' quo' auld Jock Grieve,
  'Alack! my heart is sair for thee!
For I was married on the elder sister,
  And you on the youngest of a' the three.'

Then he has ta'en out a bonny black,
  Was right weel fed with corn and hay,
And he's set Jamie Telfer on his back,
  To the Catslockhill to tak the fraye.

And whan he cam to the Catslockhill,
  He shouted loud, and cried weel hie,
Till out and spak him William's Wat,
  'O whae's this brings the fraye to me?'—

'It's I, Jamie Telfer of the fair Dodhead,
  A harried man I think I be!
The Captain of Bewcastle has driven my gear;
  For God's sake rise, and succour me!'—

'Alas for wae!' quoth William's Wat,
  'Alack, for thee my heart is sair!
I never cam by the fair Dodhead,
  That ever I fand thy basket bare.'

---

[1] calves.   [2] mother.

He's set his twa sons on coal-black steeds,
   Himsell upon a freckled gray,
And they are on wi' Jamie Telfer,
   To Branksome Ha' to tak the fraye.

And when they cam to Branksome Ha',
   They shouted a' baith loud and hie,
Till up and spak him auld Buccleuch,
   Said, 'Whae's this brings the fraye to me?'—

'It's I, Jamie Telfer of the fair Dodhead,
   And a harried man I think I be!
There's nought left in the fair Dodhead,
   But a greeting wife and bairnies three.'—

'Alack for wae!' quoth the gude auld lord,
   'And ever my heart is wae for thee!
But fye gar cry on Willie, my son,
   And see that he come to me speedilie!

'Gar warn the water,[1] braid and wide,
   Gar warn it sune and hastilie!
They that winna ride for Telfer's kye,
   Let them never look in the face o' me!

'Warn Wat o' Harden, and his sons,
   Wi' them will Borthwick Water ride;
Warn Gaudilands, and Allanhaugh,
   And Gilmanscleugh, and Commonside.

'Ride by the gate at Priesthaughswire,
   And warn the Currors o' the Lee;
As ye cum down the Hermitage Slack,
   Warn doughty Willie o' Gorrinberry.'

[1] raise the cry along the waterside.

The Scotts they rade, the Scotts they ran,
    Sae starkly and sae steadilie!
And aye the ower-word o' the thrang
    Was—'Rise for Branksome readilie!'

The gear was driven the Frostylee up,
    Frae the Frostylee unto the plain,
Whan Willie has look'd his men before,
    And saw the kye right fast drivand.

'Whae drives thir kye?' 'gan Willie say,
    'To make an outspeckle¹ o' me?'—
'It's I, the Captain o' Bewcastle, Willie;
    I winna layne² my name for thee.'—

'O will ye let Telfer's kye gae back?
    Or will ye do aught for regard o' me?
Or, by the faith of my body,' quo' Willie Scott,
    'I'se ware³ my dame's cauf skin on thee!'—

'I winna let the kye gae back,
    Neither for thy love, nor yet thy fear;
But I will drive Jamie Telfer's kye,
    In spite of every Scott that's here.'—

'Set on them, lads!' quo' Willie than;
    'Fye, lads, set on them cruellie!
For ere they win to the Ritterford,
    Mony a toom⁴ saddle there sall be!'

Then till't⁵ they gaed wi' heart and hand,
    The blows fell thick as bickering hail;
And mony a horse ran masterless,
    And mony a comely cheek was pale.

---

¹ laughing-stock.   ² lie, falsen.
³ spend, use my mother's calf-skin whip.   ⁴ empty.   ⁵ to it.

But Willie was stricken ower the head,
    And thro' the knapscap[1] the sword has gane;
And Harden grat[2] for very rage,
    Whan Willie on the grund lay slane.

But he's ta'en aff his gude steel cap,
    And thrice he's waved it in the air—
The Dinlay snaw was ne'er mair white
    Nor the lyart[3] locks of Harden's hair.

'Revenge! revenge!' auld Wat 'gan cry;
    'Fye, lads, lay on them cruellie!
We'll ne'er see Tiviot-side again,
    Or Willie's death revenged sall be.'

O mony a horse ran masterless,
    The splinter'd lances flew on hie;
But or they wan to the Kershope ford,
    The Scotts had gotten the victory.

John o' Brigham there was slane,
    And John o' Barlow, as I heard say;
And thirty mae o' the Captain's men
    Lay bleeding on the grund that day.

The Captain was run through the thick of the thigh,
    And broken was his right leg-bane;
If he had lived this hundred years,
    He had never been loved by woman again.

'Hae back the kye!' the Captain said;
    'Dear kye, I trow, to some they be!
For gin I suld live a hundred years,
    There will ne'er fair lady smile on me.'

---

[1] headpiece.   [2] wept.   [3] grizzled.

Then word is gane to the Captain's bride,
   Even in the bower where that she lay,
That her lord was prisoner in enemy's land,
   Since into Tividale he had led the way.

'I wad lourd[1] have had a winding-sheet,
   And helped to put it ower his head,
Ere he had been disgraced by the Border Scot,
   Whan he ower Liddel his men did lead!'

There was a wild gallant amang us a',
   His name was Watty wi' the Wudspurs,[2]
Cried—'On for his house in Stanegirthside,
   If ony man will ride with us!'

When they cam to the Stanegirthside,
   They dang wi' trees, and burst the door;
They loosed out a' the Captain's kye,
   And set them forth our lads before.

There was an auld wyfe ayont the fire,
   A wee bit o' the Captain's kin—
'Whae dar loose out the Captain's kye,
   Or answer to him and his men?'—

'It's I, Watty Wudspurs, loose the kye,
   I winna layne my name frae thee!
And I will loose out the Captain's kye,
   In scorn of a' his men and he.'

Whan they cam to the fair Dodhead,
   They were a wellcum sight to see!
For instead of his ain ten milk kye,
   Jamie Telfer has gotten thirty and three.

---

[1] liefer, rather. [2] hotspur, or madspur.

And he has paid the rescue shot,
  Baith wi' gowd and white monie;
And at the burial o' Willie Scott,
  I wat was mony a weeping e'e.

Bonny George Campbell

Hie upon Hielands,
  And laigh[1] upon Tay,
Bonny George Campbell
  Rade out on a day:
Saddled and bridled,
  Sae gallant to see,
Hame cam' his gude horse,
  But never cam' he.

Down ran his auld mither,
  Greetin'[2] fu' sair;
Out ran his bonny bride,
  Reaving[3] her hair;
'My meadow lies green,
  And my corn is unshorn,
My barn is to bigg,[4]
  And my babe is unborn.'

Saddled and bridled
  And booted rade he;
A plume in his helmet,
  A sword at his knee;
But toom[5] cam' his saddle
  A' bluidy to see,
O hame cam' his gude horse,
  But never cam' he!

---

[1] low.   [2] crying, lamenting.   [3] tearing.   [4] build.   [5] empty.

Edom o' Gordon

It fell about the Martinmas,
　　When the wind blew shrill and cauld,
Said Edom o' Gordon to his men,
　　'We maun draw to a hauld.[1]

'And what a hauld sall we draw to,
　　My merry men and me?
We will gae to the house o' the Rodes,
　　To see that fair ladye.'

The lady stood on her castle wa',
　　Beheld baith dale and down;
There she was 'ware of a host of men
　　Cam' riding towards the town.[2]

'O see ye not, my merry men a',
　　O see ye not what I see?
Methinks I see a host of men;
　　I marvel wha they be.'

She ween'd it had been her lovely lord,
　　As he cam riding hame;
It was the traitor, Edom o' Gordon,
　　Wha reck'd nae sin nor shame.

She had nae sooner buskit[3] hersell,
　　And putten on her gown,
But Edom o' Gordon an' his men
　　Were round about the town.

They had nae sooner supper set,
　　Nae sooner said the grace,
But Edom o' Gordon an' his men
　　Were lighted about the place.

　　　[1] place of shelter.　　　[2] stead.　　　[3] attired.

The lady ran up to her tower-head,
  Sae fast as she could hie,
To see if by her fair speeches
  She could wi' him agree.

'Come doun to me, ye lady gay,
  Come doun, come doun to me;
This night sall ye lig within mine arms,
  To-morrow my bride sall be.'—

'I winna come down, ye fals Gordon,
  I winna come down to thee;
I winna forsake my ain dear lord,
  That is sae far frae me.'—

'Gie owre your house, ye lady fair,
  Gie owre your house to me;
Or I sall brenn yoursel therein,
  But and your babies three.'—

'I winna gie owre, ye fals Gordon,
  To nae sic traitor as ye;
And if ye brenn my ain dear babes,
  My lord shall mak ye dree.[1]

'Now reach my pistol, Glaud, my man,
  And charge ye weel my gun;
For, but an I pierce that bluidy butcher,
  My babes, we been undone!'

She stood upon her castle wa',
  And let twa bullets flee:
She miss'd that bluidy butcher's heart,
  And only razed his knee.

[1] suffer.

'Set fire to the house!' quo' fals Gordon,
  All wud[1] wi' dule and ire:
'Fals lady, ye sall rue this deid
  As ye brenn in the fire!'—

'Wae worth, wae worth ye, Jock, my man!
  I paid ye weel your fee;
Why pu' ye out the grund-wa' stane,[2]
  Lets in the reek to me?

'And e'en wae worth ye, Jock, my man!
  I paid ye weel your hire;
Why pu' ye out the grund-wa' stane,
  To me lets in the fire?'—

'Ye paid me weel my hire, ladye,
  Ye paid me weel my fee:
But now I'm Edom o' Gordon's man,
  Maun either do or dee.'

O then bespake her little son,
  Sat on the nurse's knee:
Says, 'Mither dear, gie owre this house,
  For the reek it smithers me.'—

'I wad gie a' my gowd, my bairn,
  Sae was I a' my fee,
For ae blast o' the western wind,
  To blaw the reek frae thee.'

O then bespake her dochter dear—
  She was baith jimp[3] and sma':
'O row me in a pair o' sheets,
  And tow me owre the wa'!'

---

[1] mad. [2] stone closing a garderobe flue. [3] slender, trim.

They row'd[1] her in a pair o' sheets,
    And tow'd her owre the wa';
But on the point o' Gordon's spear
    She gat a deadly fa'.

O bonnie, bonnie was her mouth,
    And cherry were her cheiks,
And clear, clear was her yellow hair,
    Whereon the red blood dreips.

Then wi' his spear he turn'd her owre;
    O gin her face was wane!
He said, 'Ye are the first that e'er
    I wish'd alive again.'

He turn'd her owre and owre again;
    O gin her skin was white!
'I might hae spared that bonnie face
    To hae been some man's delight.

'Busk and boun,[2] my merry men a',
    For ill dooms I do guess;
I canna look in that bonnie face
    As it lies on the grass.'—

'Wha looks to freits,[3] my master dear,
    It's freits will follow them;
Let it ne'er be said that Edom o' Gordon
    Was daunted by a dame.'

But when the lady saw the fire
    Come flaming owre her head,
She wept, and kiss'd her children twain,
    Says, 'Bairns, we been but dead.'

---

[1] wrapped.   [2] trim up and prepare to go.   [3] ill omens.

The Gordon then his bugle blew,
    And said, 'Awa', awa'!
This house o' the Rodes is a' in a flame;
    I hauld it time to ga'.'

And this way lookit her ain dear lord,
    As he cam owre the lea;
He saw his castle a' in a lowe,[1]
    As far as he could see.

Then sair, O sair, his mind misgave,
    And all his heart was wae:
'Put on, put on, my wighty[2] men,
    Sae fast as ye can gae.

'Put on, put on, my wighty men,
    Sae fast as ye can drie!
For he that's hindmost o' the thrang
    Sall ne'er get good o' me.'

Then some they rade, and some they ran,
    Out-owre the grass and bent;
But ere the foremost could win up,
    Baith lady and babes were brent.

And after the Gordon he is gane,
    Sae fast as he might drie;
And soon i' the Gordon's foul heart's blude
    He's wroken[3] his dear ladye.

The Bonny Earl o' Moray

Ye Highlands and ye Lawlands,
    O where hae ye been?
They hae slain the Earl o' Moray,
    And hae laid him on the green.

---

[1] flame.   [2] sturdy, active.   [3] avenged.

Now wae be to thee, Huntley!
  And whairfore did ye sae!
I bade you bring him wi' you,
  But forbade you him to slay.

He was a braw gallant,
  And he rid at the ring;
And the bonny Earl o' Moray,
  O he might hae been a king!

He was a braw gallant,
  And he play'd at the ba';
And the bonny Earl o' Moray
  Was the flower amang them a'!

He was a braw gallant,
  And he play'd at the gluve;
And the bonny Earl o' Moray,
  O he was the Queen's luve!

O lang will his Lady
  Look owre the Castle Doune,
Ere she see the Earl o' Moray
  Come sounding through the toun!

The Twa Corbies[1]

As I was walking all alane,
I heard twa corbies making a mane:
The tane unto the tither did say,
'Whar sall we gang and dine the day?'

'—In behint yon auld fail[2] dyke
I wot there lies a new-slain knight;
And naebody kens that he lies there
But his hawk, his hound, and his lady fair.

[1] ravens.   [2] turf.

'His hound is to the hunting gane,
His hawk to fetch the wild-fowl hame,
His lady's ta'en anither mate,
So we may mak' our dinner sweet.

'Ye'll sit on his white hause[1]-bane,
And I'll pike out his bonny blue e'en:
Wi' ae lock o' his gowden hair
We'll theek[2] our nest when it grows bare.

'Mony a one for him maks mane,
But nane sall ken whar he is gane:
O'er his white banes, when they are bare,
The wind sall blaw for evermair.'

Lord Randal

'O where ha ye been, Lord Randal, my son?
And where hae ye been, my handsome young man?'
'I hae been at the greenwood; mother, mak my bed
    soon,
For I'm wearied wi' hunting, and fain wad lie down.'

'And wha met ye there, Lord Randal, my son?
And wha met you there, my handsome young man?'
'O I met wi' my true-love; mother, mak my bed
    soon,
For I'm wearied wi' hunting, an fain wad lie down.'

'And what did she give you, Lord Randal, my son?
And what did she give you, my handsome young
    man?'
'Eels fried in a pan; mother, mak my bed soon,
For I'm wearied wi' hunting, and fain wad lie down.'

[1] neck.   [2] thatch.

'And wha gat your leavins, Lord Randal, my son?
And wha gat your leavins, my handsome young
    man?'
'My hawks and my hounds; mother, mak my bed
    soon,
For I'm wearied wi' hunting, and fain wad lie down.'

'And what becam of them, Lord Randal, my son?
And what becam of them, my handsome young
    man?'
'They stretched their legs out and died; mother, mak
    my bed soon,
For I'm wearied wi' hunting, and fain wad lie down.'

'O I fear you are poisoned, Lord Randal, my son!
I fear you are poisoned, my handsome young man!'
'O yes, I am poisoned; mother, mak my bed soon,
For I'm sick at the heart, and I fain wad lie down.'

'What d'ye leave to your mother, Lord Randal, my
    son?
What d'ye leave to your mother, my handsome young
    man?'
'Four and twenty milk kye; mother, mak my bed
    soon,
For I'm sick at the heart, and I fain wad lie down.'

'What d'ye leave to your sister, Lord Randal, my
    son?
What d'ye leave to your sister, my handsome young
    man?'
'My gold and my silver; mother, mak my bed soon,
For I'm sick at the heart, and I fain wad lie down.'

'What d'ye leave to your brother, Lord Randal, my
  son?
What d'ye leave to your brother, my handsome
  young man?'
'My houses and my lands; mother, mak my bed
  soon,
For I'm sick at the heart, and I fain wad lie down.'

'What d'ye leave to your true-love, Lord Randal, my
  son?
What d'ye leave to your true-love, my handsome
  young man?'
'I leave her hell and fire; mother, mak my bed soon,
For I'm sick at the heart, and I fain wad lie down.'

Edward

'Why does your brand sae drop wi' blude,
    Edward, Edward?
Why does your brand sae drop wi' blude,
    And why sae sad gang ye, O?'—
'O I hae kill'd my hawk sae gude,
    Mither, mither;
O I hae kill'd my hawk sae gude,
    And I had nae mair but he, O.'

'Your hawk's blude was never sae red,
    Edward, Edward;
Your hawk's blude was never sae red,
    My dear son, I tell thee, O.'—
'O I hae kill'd my red-roan steed,
    Mither, mither;
O I hae kill'd my red-roan steed,
    That erst was sae fair and free, O.'

'Your steed was auld, and ye hae got mair,
    Edward, Edward;
Your steed was auld, and ye hae got mair;
    Some other dule ye dree,[1] O.'—
'O I hae kill'd my father dear,
    Mither, mither;
O I hae kill'd my father dear,
    Alas, and wae is me, O!'

'And whatten penance will ye dree for that,
    Edward, Edward?
Whatten penance will ye dree for that?
    My dear son, now tell me, O.'—
'I'll set my feet in yonder boat,
    Mither, mither;
I'll set my feet in yonder boat,
    And I'll fare over the sea, O.'

'And what will ye do wi' your tow'rs and your ha',
    Edward, Edward?
And what will ye do wi' your tow'rs and your ha',
    That were sae fair to see, O?'—
'I'll let them stand till they doun fa',
    Mither, mither;
I'll let them stand till they doun fa',
    For here never mair maun I be, O.'

'And what will ye leave to your bairns and your
    wife,
    Edward, Edward?
And what will ye leave to your bairns and your
    wife,
    When ye gang owre the sea, O?'—

---

[1] grief you suffer.

'The warld's room: let them beg through life,
  Mither, mither;
The warld's room: let them beg through life;
  For them never mair will I see, O.'

'And what will ye leave to your ain mither dear,
  Edward, Edward?
And what will ye leave to your ain mither dear,
  My dear son, now tell me, O?'—
'The curse of hell frae me sall ye bear,
  Mither, mither;
The curse of hell frae me sall ye bear:
  Sic counsels ye gave to me, O!'

The Dowie Houms o' Yarrow

Late at een, drinkin' the wine,
  And ere they paid the lawin',[1]
They set a combat them between,
  To fight it in the dawin'.

'O stay at hame, my noble lord!
  O stay at hame, my marrow![2]
My cruel brother will you betray,
  On the dowie[3] houms o' Yarrow.'—

'O fare ye weel, my lady gay!
  O fare ye weel, my Sarah!
For I maun gae, tho' I ne'er return
  Frae the dowie banks o' Yarrow.'

She kiss'd his cheek, she kamed his hair,
  As she had done before, O;
She belted on his noble brand,
  An' he's awa to Yarrow.

---

[1] reckoning.   [2] married mate.   [3] doleful.

O he's gane up yon high, high hill—
  I wat he gaed wi' sorrow—
An' in a den spied nine arm'd men,
  I' the dowie houms[1] o' Yarrow.

'O are ye come to drink the wine,
  As ye hae doon before, O?
Or are ye come to wield the brand,
  On the dowie houms o' Yarrow?'—

'I am no come to drink the wine,
  As I hae done before, O,
But I am come to wield the brand,
  On the dowie houms o' Yarrow.'

Four he hurt an' five he slew,
  On the dowie houms o' Yarrow,
Till that stubborn knight came him behind,
  An' ran his body thorrow.

'Gae hame, gae hame, good brother John,
  An' tell your sister Sarah
To come an' lift her noble lord,
  Who's sleepin' sound on Yarrow.'

'Yestreen I dream'd a dolefu' dream;
  I ken'd there wad be sorrow;
I dream'd I pu'd the heather green,
  On the dowie banks o' Yarrow.'

She gaed up yon high, high hill—
  I wat she gaed wi' sorrow—
An' in a den spied nine dead men,
  On the dowie houms o' Yarrow.

[1] water-meads.

She kiss'd his cheek, she kamed his hair,
  As oft she did before, O;
She drank the red blood frae him ran,
  On the dowie houms o' Yarrow.

'O haud your tongue, my douchter dear,
  For what needs a' this sorrow?
I'll wed you on a better lord
  Than him you lost on Yarrow.'—

'O haud your tongue, my father dear,
  An' dinna grieve your Sarah;
A better lord was never born
  Than him I lost on Yarrow.

'Tak hame your ousen,[1] tak hame your kye,
  For they hae bred our sorrow;
I wiss that they had a' gane mad
  Whan they cam' first to Yarrow.'

Rare Willy drowned in Yarrow

'Willy's rare, and Willy's fair,
  And Willy's wondrous bonny;
And Willy heght[2] to marry me,
  Gin e'er he marryd ony.

'Yestreen I made my bed fu' braid,
  The night I'll make it narrow,
For a' the live-long winter's night
  I lie twin'd[3] of my marrow.[4]

'O came you by yon water-side?
  Pu'd you the rose or lily?
Or came you by yon meadow green?
  Or saw you my sweet Willy?'

[1] oxen.   [2] promised.   [3] deprived.   [4] mate.

She sought him east, she sought him west,
    She sought him braid and narrow;
Sine, in the clifting¹ of a craig,
    She found him drown'd in Yarrow.

Clyde's Water

'Ye gie corn to my horse,
    An' meat to my man;
For I will gae to my true love's gates
    This night, gin I can win.'

'O stay at hame, my son Willy,
    This ae bare night wi' me;
The best bed in a' my house
    Sall be well made to thee.'

'I carena for your beds, mither,
    I carena a pin;
For I'll gae to my love's gates
    This night, gin I can win.'

'Oh stay, my son Willy,
    This night wi' me;
The best hen in a' my roost
    Sall be well made ready for thee.'

'I carena for your hens, mither,
    I carena a pin;
For I'll gae to my love's gates
    This night, gin I can win.'

'Gin ye winna stay, my son Willy,
    This ae bare night wi' me,
Gin Clyde's waters be deep and fu' o' flood,
    My malison drown ye in.'

¹ cleft.

He rade up yon high hill,
  And down yon dowie den,
The roaring of Clyde's water
  Wad ha fleyed ten thousand men.

'O spare me, Clyde's water,
  O spare me as I gae!
Mak' me your wrack as I come back,
  But spare me as I gae!'

He rade in, and farther in,
  Till he came to the chin;
And he rade in, an' farther in,
  Till he came to dry land.
And when he came to his love's gates,
  He tirled at the pin.
'Open your gates, Meggie,
  Open your gates to me;
For my boots are fu' o' Clyde's water
  And the rain rins ower my chin.'

'I hae nae love thereout,' she[1] says,
  'I hae nae love within;
My true-love is in my arms twa,
  An' nane will I let in.'

'Open your gates, Meggie,
  This night to me;
For Clyde's water is fu' o' flood,
  And my mother's malison will drown me in.'

'Ane o' my chambers is fu' o' corn,' she says,
  'Anither is fu' o' hay;
The ither is fu' o' gentlemen;—
  An' they winna remove till day.'

---

[1] The mother impersonating her daughter.

Out waked her may Meggie,
    Out of her drussie dream.
'I dreamed a dream nou sin yestreen,
    God read a' dreams to guid,
That my true love Willy,
    Was staning at my bed-feet.'

'Nou lay still, my ae dochter,
    An' keep my back frae the call,[1]
For it's nae the space o' half an hour,
    Sen he gaed frae your hall.'

An' hey Willy, an' hou, Willy,
    An Willy, Winna ye turn agen?
But aye the louder that she cried,
    He rade against the wind.
He rade up yon high hill,
    And doun yon dowie den;
The roaring that was in Clyde's water
    Wad ha fleyed ten thousand men.
He rade in, an' farther in,
    Till he came to the chin;
An' he rade in, an' farther in,
    But never mair came out agen.

She has kissed his comely mou
    As she had done afore;
'Baith our mithers sall be alike sorry
    For we'll baith sleep soun in Clyde's water.'

There was na mair seen o' that guid lord,
    But his hat frae his head;
There was na mair seen o' that lady,
    But her kaim[2] and her sneed.[3]
Their mithers went up and doun the water
    Saying, 'Clyde's water din us wrong!'

---

[1] cold.   [2] comb.   [3] snood.

Helen of Kirkconnell

I wish I were where Helen lies,
Night and day on me she cries;
O that I were where Helen lies,
   On fair Kirkconnell lea!

Curst be the heart that thought the thought,
And curst the hand that fired the shot,
When in my arms burd Helen dropt,
   And died to succour me!

O think na ye my heart was sair,
When my Love dropp'd and spak nae mair!
There did she swoon wi' meikle care,
   On fair Kirkconnell lea.

As I went down the water side,
None but my foe to be my guide,
None but my foe to be my guide,
   On fair Kirkconnell lea;

I lighted down my sword to draw,
I hackèd him in pieces sma',
I hackèd him in pieces sma',
   For her sake that died for me.

O Helen fair, beyond compare!
I'll mak a garland o' thy hair,
Shall bind my heart for evermair,
   Until the day I dee!

O that I were where Helen lies!
Night and day on me she cries;
Out of my bed she bids me rise,
   Says, 'Haste, and come to me!'

O Helen fair! O Helen chaste!
If I were with thee, I'd be blest,
Where thou lies low an' taks thy rest,
   On fair Kirkconnell lea.

I wish my grave were growing green,
A winding-sheet drawn owre my een,
And I in Helen's arms lying,
   On fair Kirkconnell lea.

I wish I were where Helen lies!
Night and day on me she cries;
And I am weary of the skies,
   For her sake that died for me.

Bessie Bell and Mary Gray

O Bessie Bell and Mary Gray,
   They war twa bonnie lasses;
They biggit[1] a bower on yon burn-brae,
   And theekit[2] it o'er wi' rashes.

They theekit it o'er wi' rashes green,
   They theekit it o'er wi' heather;
But the pest cam frae the burrows-town,
   And slew them baith thegither.

They thought to lye in Methven kirkyard,
   Amang their noble kin;
But they maun lye in Stronach haugh,[3]
   To biek[4] forenent the sin.[5]

And Bessie Bell and Mary Gray,
   They war twa bonnie lasses;
They biggit a bower on yon burn-brae,
   And theekit it o'er wi' rashes.

---

[1] built.   [2] thatched.   [3] water-mead.   [4] bask.   [5] sun.

The Lowlands o' Holland

'My love has built a bonny ship, and set her on the sea,
With seven score good mariners to bear her com-
panie;
There's three score is sunk, and three score dead at sea,
And the Lowlands o' Holland has twin'd[1] my love
and me.

'My love he built another ship, and set her on the
main,
And nane but twenty mariners for to bring her hame;
But the weary wind began to rise, and the sea began
to rout,
My love then and his bonny ship turn'd wither-
shins[2] about.

'Then shall neither coif come on my head nor comb
come in my hair;
Then shall neither coal nor candle-light shine in my
bower mair;
Nor will I love another one until the day I die,
Sin' the Lowlands o' Holland has twin'd my love and
me.'—

'O haud your tongue, my daughter dear, be still and
be content;
There are mair lads in Galloway, ye need nae sair
lament.'—
'O there is none in Galloway, there's none at a' for
me,
For I never loved a love but one, and he's drown'd
in the sea.'

---

[1] parted.   [2] around against the sun.

Marie Hamilton

Marie Hamilton's to the kirk gane,
  Wi' ribbons in her hair;
The King thought mair o' Marie Hamilton
  Than ony that were there.

Marie Hamilton's to the kirk gane
  Wi' ribbons on her breast;
The King thought mair o' Marie Hamilton
  Than he listen'd to the priest.

Marie Hamilton's to the kirk gane,
  Wi' gloves upon her hands;
The King thought mair o' Marie Hamilton
  Than the Queen and a' her lands.

She hadna been about the King's court
  A month, but barely ane,
Till she was beloved by a' the King's court,
  And the King the only man.

She hadna been about the King's court
  A month, but barely three,
Till frae the King's court Marie Hamilton,
  Marie Hamilton durstna be.

The King is to the Abbey gane,
  To pu' the Abbey tree,
To scale[1] the babe frae Marie's heart;
  But the thing it wadna be.

O she has row'd[2] it in her apron,
  And set it on the sea—
'Gae sink ye or swim ye, bonny babe,
  Ye'se get nae mair o' me.'

    [1] drive away, get rid of.   [2] wrapped.

Word is to the kitchen gane,
   And word is to the ha',
And word is to the noble room
   Amang the ladies a',
That Marie Hamilton's brought to bed,
   And the bonny babe's miss'd and awa'.

Scarcely had she laid down again,
   And scarcely fa'en asleep,
When up and started our gude Queen
   Just at her bed-feet;
Saying—'Marie Hamilton, where's your babe?
   For I am sure I heard it greet.'[1]—

'O no, O no, my noble Queen!
   Think no sic thing to be;
'Twas but a stitch into my side,
   And sair it troubles me!'—

'Get up, get up, Marie Hamilton:
   Get up and follow me;
For I am going to Edinburgh town,
   A rich wedding for to see.'

O slowly, slowly rase she up,
   And slowly put she on;
And slowly rade she out the way
   Wi' mony a weary groan.

The Queen was clad in scarlet,
   Her merry maids all in green;
And every town that they cam to,
   They took Marie for the Queen.

[1] wail, cry.

'Ride hooly,[1] hooly, gentlemen,
    Ride hooly now wi' me!
For never, I am sure, a wearier burd
    Rade in your companie.'

But little wist Marie Hamilton,
    When she rade on the brown,
That she was gaen to Edinburgh town,
    And a' to be put down.

'Why weep ye sae, ye burgess wives,
    Why look ye sae on me?
O I am going to Edinburgh town,
    A rich wedding for to see.'

When she gaed up the Tolbooth stairs,
    The corks frae her heels did flee;
And lang or e'er she cam down again,
    She was condemn'd to die.

When she cam to the Netherbow port,
    She laugh'd loud laughters three;
But when she came to the gallows foot
    The tears blinded her e'e.

'Yestreen the Queen had four Maries,
    The night she'll hae but three;
There was Marie Seaton, and Marie Beaton,
    And Marie Carmichael, and me.

'O often have I dress'd my Queen,
    And put gowd upon her hair;
But now I've gotten for my reward
    The gallows to be my share.

[1] gently.

'Often have I dress'd my Queen
    And often made her bed;
But now I've gotten for my reward
    The gallows tree to tread.

'I charge ye all, ye mariners,
    When ye sail owre the faem,
Let neither my father nor mother get wit
    But that I'm coming hame.

'I charge ye all, ye mariners,
    That sail upon the sea,
That neither my father nor mother get wit
    The dog's death I'm to die.

'For if my father and mother got wit,
    And my bold brethren three,
O mickle wad be the gude red blude
    This day wad be spilt for me!

'O little did my mother ken,
    The day she cradled me,
The lands I was to travel in
    Or the death I was to die!'

The Gipsy Laddie

The gipsies came to our good lord's gate,
    And wow but they sang sweetly!
They sang sae sweet and sae very complete
    That down came the fair lady.

And she came tripping down the stair,
    And a' her maids before her;
As soon as they saw her weel-faured[1] face,
    They coost the glamour o'er her.

[1] well-favoured.

'Gae tak frae me this gay mantile,
   And bring to me a plaidie;
For if kith and kin and a' had sworn,
   I'll follow the gipsy laddie.

'Yestreen I lay in a well-made bed,
   And my good lord beside me;
This night I'll lie in a tenant's barn,
   Whatever shall betide me.'

'Come to your bed,' says Johnnie Faa,
   'Oh come to your bed, my dearie;
For I vow and I swear, by the hilt of my sword,
   That your lord shall nae mair come near ye.

'I'll go to bed to my Johnnie Faa,
   I'll go to bed to my dearie;
For I vow and I swear, by what passed yestreen,
   That my lord shall nae mair come near me.

'I'll mak a hap to my Johnnie Faa,
   And I'll mak a hap to my dearie;
And he's get a' the coat gaes round,
   And my lord shall nae mair come near me.'

And when our lord came hame at een,
   And speired for his fair lady,
The tane she cried, and the other replied,
   'She's away with the gipsy laddie.'

'Gae saddle to me the black, black steed,
   Gae saddle and make him ready;
Before that I either eat or sleep,
   I'll gae seek my fair lady.'

And we were fifteen well-made men,
   Although we were nae bonnie;
And we were a' put down for ane,
   A fair young wanton lady.

Barbara Allen

In Scarlet town, where I was born,
    There was a fair maid dwellin',
Made every youth cry *Well-a-way!*
    Her name was Barbara Allen.

All in the merry month of May,
    When green buds they were swellin',
Young Jemmy Grove on his death-bed lay,
    For love of Barbara Allen.

He sent his man in to her then,
    To the town where she was dwellin';
'O haste and come to my master dear,
    If your name be Barbara Allen.'

So slowly, slowly rase she up,
    And slowly she came nigh him,
And when she drew the curtain by—
    'Young man, I think you're dyin'.'

'O it's I am sick and very sick,
    And it's all for Barbara Allen.'—
'O the better for me ye'se never be,
    Tho' your heart's blood were a-spillin'!

'O dinna ye mind, young man,' says she,
    'When the red wine ye were fillin',
That ye made the healths go round and round,
    And slighted Barbara Allen?'

He turn'd his face unto the wall,
    And death was with him dealin':
'Adieu, adieu, my dear friends all,
    And be kind to Barbara Allen!'

As she was walking o'er the fields,
   She heard the dead-bell knellin';
And every jow[1] the dead-bell gave
   Cried 'Woe to Barbara Allen.'

'O mother, mother, make my bed,
   O make it saft and narrow:
My love has died for me to-day,
   I'll die for him to-morrow.

'Farewell,' she said, 'ye virgins all,
   And shun the fault I fell in:
Henceforth take warning by the fall
   Of cruel Barbara Allen.'

Thomas the Rhymer

True Thomas lay on Huntlie bank;
   A ferlie[2] he spied wi' his e'e;
And there he saw a ladye bright
   Come riding down by the Eildon Tree.

Her skirt was o' the grass-green silk,
   Her mantle o' the velvet fyne;
At ilka tett[3] o' horse's mane
   Hung fifty siller bells and nine.

True Thomas he pu'd aff his cap,
   And louted low down on his knee:
'Hail to thee, Mary, Queen of Heaven!
   For thy peer on earth could never be.'

'O no, O no, Thomas,' she said,
   'That name does not belang to me;
I'm but the Queen o' fair Elfland.
   That am hither come to visit thee.

[1] beat, toll.   [2] marvel.   [3] tuft.

'Harp and carp,[1] Thomas,' she said;
  'Harp and carp along wi' me;
And if ye dare to kiss my lips,
  Sure of your bodie I will be.'

'Betide me weal, betide me woe,
  That weird[2] shall never daunten me.'
Syne he has kiss'd her rosy lips,
  All underneath the Eildon Tree.

'Now ye maun go wi' me,' she said,
  'True Thomas, ye maun go wi' me;
And ye maun serve me seven years,
  Thro' weal or woe as may chance to be.'

She's mounted on her milk-white steed,
  She's ta'en true Thomas up behind;
And aye, whene'er her bridle rang,
  The steed gaed swifter than the wind.

O they rade on, and farther on,
  The steed gaed swifter than the wind;
Until they reach'd a desert wide,
  And living land was left behind.

'Light down, light down now, true Thomas,
  And lean your head upon my knee;
Abide ye there a little space,
  And I will show you ferlies three.

'O see ye not yon narrow road,
  So thick beset wi' thorns and briers?
That is the Path of Righteousness,
  Though after it but few inquires.

---

[1] play and recite (as a minstrel).   [2] doom.

'And see ye not yon braid, braid road,
   That lies across the lily leven?[1]
That is the Path of Wickedness,
   Though some call it the Road to Heaven.

'And see ye not yon bonny road
   That winds about the fernie brae?
That is the Road to fair Elfland,
   Where thou and I this night maun gae.

'But, Thomas, ye sall haud your tongue,
   Whatever ye may hear or see;
For speak ye word in Elfyn-land,
   Ye'll ne'er win back to your ain countrie.'

O they rade on, and farther on,
   And they waded rivers abune the knee;
And they saw neither sun nor moon,
   But they heard the roaring of the sea.

It was mirk, mirk night, there was nae starlight,
   They waded thro' red blude to the knee;
For a' the blude that's shed on the earth
   Rins through the springs o' that countrie.

Syne they came to a garden green,
   And she pu'd an apple frae a tree:
'Take this for thy wages, true Thomas;
   It will give thee the tongue that can never lee.'

'My tongue is my ain,' true Thomas he said;
   'A gudely gift ye wad gie to me!
I neither dought[2] to buy or sell
   At fair or tryst where I might be.

      [1] lawn.   [2] could.

'I dought neither speak to prince or peer,
   Nor ask of grace from fair ladye!'—
'Now haud thy peace, Thomas,' she said,
   'For as I say, so must it be.'

He has gotten a coat of the even cloth,[1]
   And a pair o' shoon of the velvet green;
And till seven years were gane and past,
   True Thomas on earth was never seen.

Binnorie

There were twa sisters sat in a bour;
   Binnorie, O Binnorie!
There cam a knight to be their wooer,
   By the bonnie milldams o' Binnorie.

He courted the eldest with glove and ring,
But he lo'ed the youngest abune a' thing.

The eldest she was vexèd sair,
And sair envìed her sister fair.

Upon a morning fair and clear,
She cried upon her sister dear:

'O sister, sister, tak my hand,
And we'll see our father's ships to land.'

She's ta'en her by the lily hand,
And led her down to the river-strand.

The youngest stood upon a stane,
The eldest cam and push'd her in.

'O sister, sister, reach your hand!
And ye sall be heir o' half my land:

[1] smooth cloth.

'O sister, reach me but your glove!
And sweet William sall be your love.'—

'Foul fa' the hand that I should take;
It twin'd[1] me o' my warldis make.[2]

'Your cherry cheeks and your yellow hair
Gar'd me gang maiden evermair.'

Sometimes she sank, sometimes she swam,
Until she cam to the miller's dam.

Out then cam the miller's son,
And saw the fair maid soummin'[3] in.

'O father, father, draw your dam!
There's either a mermaid or a milk-white swan.'

The miller hasted and drew his dam,
And there he found a drown'd womàn.

You couldna see her middle sma',
Her gowden girdle was sae braw.

You couldna see her lily feet,
Her gowden fringes were sae deep.

You couldna see her yellow hair
For the strings o' pearls was twisted there.

You couldna see her fingers sma',
Wi' diamond rings they were cover'd a'.

And by there cam a harper fine,
That harpit to the king at dine.

And when he look'd that lady on,
He sigh'd and made a heavy moan.

---

[1] robbed, deprived.   [2] my one mate in the world.   [3] swimming.

He's made a harp of her breast-bane,
Whose sound wad melt a heart of stane.

He's ta'en three locks o' her yellow hair,
And wi' them strung his harp sae rare.

He went into her father's hall,
And there was the court assembled all.

He laid his harp upon a stane,
And straight it began to play by lane.[1]

'O yonder sits my father, the King,
And yonder sits my mother, the Queen;

'And yonder stands my brother Hugh,
And by him my William, sweet and true.'

But the last tune that the harp play'd then—
    Binnorie, O Binnorie!
Was, 'Woe to my sister, false Helèn!'
    By the bonnie milldams o' Binnorie.

The Wife of Usher's Well

There lived a wife at Usher's well,
    And a wealthy wife was she;
She had three stout and stalwart sons,
    And sent them o'er the sea.

They hadna been a week from her,
    A week but barely ane,
When word came to the carline[2] wife
    That her three sons were gane.

---

[1] alone, of itself.   [2] old woman.

They hadna been a week from her,
    A week but barely three,
When word came to the carline wife
    That her sons she'd never see.

'I wish the wind may never cease,
    Nor fashes[1] in the flood,
Till my three sons come hame to me
    In earthly flesh and blood!'

It fell about the Martinmas,
    When nights are lang and mirk,
The carline wife's three sons came hame,
    And their hats were o' the birk.

It neither grew in syke[2] nor ditch,
    Nor yet in ony sheugh;[3]
But at the gates o' Paradise
    That birk grew fair eneugh.

'Blow up the fire, my maidens!
    Bring water from the well!
For a' my house shall feast this night,
    Since my three sons are well.'

And she has made to them a bed,
    She's made it large and wide;
And she's ta'en her mantle her about,
    Sat down at the bedside.

Up then crew the red, red cock,
    And up and crew the gray;
The eldest to the youngest said,
    ''Tis time we were away.'

---

[1] troubles.   [2] marsh.   [3] trench.

The cock he hadna craw'd but once,
    And clapp'd his wings at a',
When the youngest to the eldest said,
    'Brother, we must awa'.

'The cock doth craw, the day doth daw,
    The channerin'[1] worm doth chide;
Gin we be miss'd out o' our place,
    A sair pain we maun bide.'—

'Lie still, lie still but a little wee while,
    Lie still but if we may;
Gin my mother should miss us when she
      wakes,
    She'll go mad ere it be day.'—

'Fare ye weel, my mother dear!
    Fareweel to barn and byre!
And fare ye weel, the bonny lass
    That kindles my mother's fire!'

Tam Lin

'O I forbid you, maidens a',
    That wear gowd on your hair,
To come or gae by Carterhaugh,
    For young Tam Lin is there.

'For even about that knight's middle
    O' siller bells are nine;
And nae maid comes to Carterhaugh
    And a maid returns again.'

---

[1] fretting.

Fair Janet sat in her bonny bower,
 Sewing her silken seam,
And wish'd to be in Carterhaugh
 Amang the leaves sae green.

She's lat her seam fa' to her feet,
 The needle to her tae,[1]
And she's awa' to Carterhaugh
 As fast as she could gae.

And she has kilted her green kirtle
 A little abune her knee;
And she has braided her yellow hair
 A little abune her bree;[2]
And she has gaen for Carterhaugh
 As fast as she can hie.

She hadna pu'd a rose, a rose,
 A rose but barely ane,
When up and started young Tam Lin;
 Says, 'Ladye, let alane.

'What gars ye pu' the rose, Janet?
 What gars ye break the tree?
What gars ye come to Carterhaugh
 Without the leave o' me?'

'Weel may I pu' the rose,' she says,
 'And ask no leave at thee;
For Carterhaugh it is my ain,
 My daddy gave it me.'

He's ta'en her by the milk-white hand,
 And by the grass-green sleeve,
He's led her to the fairy ground
 At her he ask'd nae leave.

---

[1] toe. [2] eye-brow.

Janet has kilted her green kirtle
  A little abune her knee,
And she has snooded her yellow hair
  A little abune her bree,
And she is to her father's ha'
  As fast as she can hie.

But when she came to her father's ha',
  She look'd sae wan and pale,
They thought the lady had gotten a fright,
  Or with sickness she did ail.

Four and twenty ladies fair
  Were playing at the ba',
And out then came fair Janet
  Ance the flower amang them a'.

Four and twenty ladies fair
  Where playing at the chess,
And out then came fair Janet
  As green as onie glass.

Out then spak' an auld grey knight
  'Lay owre the Castle wa',
And says, 'Alas, fair Janet!
  For thee we'll be blamèd a'.'

'Hauld your tongue, ye auld-faced knight,
  Some ill death may ye die!
Father my bairn on whom I will,
  I'll father nane on thee.

'O if my love were an earthly knight,
  As he is an elfin gay,
I wadna gie my ain true-love
  For nae laird that ye hae.

'The steed that my true-love rides on
  Is fleeter nor the wind;
Wi' siller he is shod before,
  Wi' burning gold behind.'

Out then spak' her brither dear—
  He meant to do her harm:
'There grows an herb in Carterhaugh
  Will twine[1] you an' the bairn.'

Janet has kilted her green kirtle
  A little abune her knee,
And she has snooded her yellow hair
  A little abune her bree,
And she's awa' to Carterhaugh
  As fast as she can hie.

She hadna pu'd a leaf, a leaf,
  A leaf but only twae,
When up and started young Tam Lin,
  Says, 'Ladye, thou's pu' nae mae.

'How dar' ye pu' a leaf?' he says,
  'How dar' ye break the tree?
How dar' ye scathe[2] my babe,' he says,
  'That's between you and me?'

'O tell me, tell me, Tam,' she says,
  'For His sake that died on tree,
If ye were ever in holy chapel
  Or sain'd[3] in Christentie?'

'The truth I'll tell to thee, Janet,
  Ae word I winna lee;
A knight me got, and a lady me bore,
  As well as they did thee.

[1] part, sunder.   [2] harm.   [3] blessed, baptized.

'Roxburgh he was my grandfather,
   Took me with him to bide;
And ance it fell upon a day,
   As hunting I did ride,

'There came a wind out o' the north,
   A sharp wind an' a snell,[1]
A dead sleep it came over me
   And frae my horse I fell;
And the Queen o' Fairies she took me
   In yon green hill to dwell.

'And pleasant is the fairy land
   For those that in it dwell,
But ay at end of seven years
   They pay a teind[2] to hell;
I am sae fair and fu' o' flesh
   I'm fear'd 'twill be mysell.

'But the night is Hallowe'en, Janet,
   The morn is Hallowday;
Then win me, win me, an ye will,
   For weel I wat ye may.

'The night it is gude Hallowe'en,
   The fairy folk to ride,
And they that wad their true-love win,
   At Miles Cross they maun bide.'—

'But how should I you ken, Tam Lin,
   How should I borrow[3] you,
Amang a pack of uncouth[4] knights
   The like I never saw?'—

---

[1] keen, cold.   [2] tithe.   [3] ransom.   [4] unknown.

'You'll do you down to Miles Cross
    Between twel' hours and ane,
And fill your hands o' the holy water
    And cast your compass roun'.

'The first company that passes by,
    Say na, and let them gae;
The neist company that passes by,
    Say na, and do right sae;
The third company that passes by,
    Then I'll be ane o' thae.

'O first let pass the black, ladye,
    And syne let pass the brown;
But quickly run to the milk-white steed,
    Pu' ye his rider down.

'For some ride on the black, ladye,
    And some ride on the brown;
But I ride on a milk-white steed,
    A gowd star on my crown:
Because I was an earthly knight
    They gie me that renown.

'My right hand will be gloved, ladye,
    My left hand will be bare,
And thae's the tokens I gie thee:
    Nae doubt I will be there.

'Ye'll tak' my horse then by the head
    And let the bridle fa';
The Queen o' Elfin she'll cry out
    "True Tam Lin he's awa'!"

'They'll turn me in your arms, ladye,
    An aske[1] but and a snake;

---

[1] newt, lizard.

But hauld me fast, let me na gae,
 To be your warldis make.[1]

'They'll turn me in your arms, ladye,
 But and a deer so wild;
But hauld me fast, let me na gae,
 The father o' your child.

'They'll shape me in your arms, ladye,
 A hot iron at the fire;
But hauld me fast, let me na go,
 To be your heart's desire.

'They'll shape me last in your arms, Janet,
 A mother-naked man;
Cast your green mantle over me,
 And sae will I be won.'

Janet has kilted her green kirtle
 A little abune the knee;
And she has snooded her yellow hair
 A little abune her bree,
And she is on to Miles Cross
 As fast as she can hie.

About the dead hour o' the night
 She heard the bridles ring;
And Janet was as glad at that
 As any earthly thing.

And first gaed by the black, black steed,
 And syne gaed by the brown;
But fast she gript the milk-white steed
 And pu'd the rider down.

---

[1] mate, husband.

She's pu'd him frae the milk-white steed,
    An' loot[1] the bridle fa',
And up there rase an eldritch[2] cry,
    'True Tam Lin he's awa'!'

They shaped him in her arms twa
    An aske but and a snake;
But aye she grips and hau'ds him fast
    To be her warldis make.

They shaped him in her arms twa
    But and a deer sae wild;
But aye she grips and hau'ds him fast,
    The father o' her child.

They shaped him in her arms twa
    A hot iron at the fire;
But aye she grips and hau'ds him fast
    To be her heart's desire.

They shaped him in her arms at last
    A mother-naked man;
She cast her mantle over him,
    And sae her love she wan.

Up then spak' the Queen o' Fairies,
    Out o' a bush o' broom,
'She that has borrow'd young Tam Lin
    Has gotten a stately groom.'

Out then spak' the Queen o' Fairies,
    And an angry woman was she,
'She's ta'en awa' the bonniest knight
    In a' my companie!

[1] let.   [2] unearthly.

'But what I ken this night, Tam Lin,
　Gin I had kent yestreen,
I wad ta'en out thy heart o' flesh,
　And put in a heart o' stane.

'And adieu, Tam Lin! But gin I had kent
　A ladye wad borrow'd thee,
I wad ta'en out thy twa grey e'en,
　Put in twa e'en o' tree.¹

'And had I the wit yestreen, yestreen,
　That I have coft² this day,
I'd paid my teind seven times to hell
　Ere you had been won away!'

Fair Annie

It's narrow, narrow, mak your bed,
　And learn to lie your lane;
For I'm gaun owre the sea, Fair Annie,
　A braw bride to bring hame.
Wi' her I will get gowd and gear,
　Wi' you I ne'er gat nane.

'But wha will bake my bridal bread,
　Or brew my bridal ale?
And wha will welcome my bright bride,
　That I bring owre the dale?'—

'It's I will bake your bridal bread,
　And brew your bridal ale;
And I will welcome your bright bride,
　That you bring owre the dale.'—

¹ wood.　² bought.

'But she that welcomes my bright bride
　　Maun gang like maiden fair;
She maun lace on her robe sae jimp,[1]
　　And comely braid her hair.

'Bind up, bind up your yellow hair,
　　And tie it on your neck;
And see you look as maiden-like
　　As the day that first we met.'—

'O how can I gang maiden-like,
　　When maiden I am nane?
Have I not borne six sons to thee,
　　And am wi' child again?'—

'I'll put cooks into my kitchen,
　　And stewards in my hall,
And I'll have bakers for my bread,
　　And brewers for my ale;
But you're to welcome my bright bride,
　　That I bring owre the dale.'

Three months and a day were gane and past,
　　Fair Annie she gat word
That her love's ship was come at last,
　　Wi' his bright young bride aboard.

She's ta'en her young son in her arms,
　　Anither in her hand;
And she's gane up to the highest tower,
　　Looks over sea and land.

'Come doun, come doun, my mother dear,
　　Come aff the castle wa'!
I fear if langer ye stand there,
　　Ye'll let yoursell doun fa'.'

[1] slender, trim.

She's ta'en a cake o' the best bread,
    A stoup o' the best wine,
And a' the keys upon her arm,
    And to the yett[1] is gane.

'O ye're welcome hame, my ain gude lord,
    To your castles and your towers;
Ye're welcome hame, my ain gude lord,
    To your ha's, but and your bowers.
And welcome to your hame, fair lady!
    For a' that's here is yours.'

'O whatna lady's that, my lord,
    That welcomes you and me?
Gin I be lang about this place,
    Her friend I mean to be.'

Fair Annie served the lang tables
    Wi' the white bread and the wine;
But ay she drank the wan water
    To keep her colour fine.

And aye she served the lang tables
    Wi' the white bread and the brown,
And aye she turn'd her round about,
    Sae fast the tears fell doun.

She took a napkin lang and white,
    And hung it on a pin;
It was to wipe away the tears,
    As she gaed out and in.

When bells were rung and mass was sung,
    And a' men bound for bed,
The bridegroom and the bonny bride
    In ae chamber were laid.

[1] gate.

Fair Annie 's ta'en a harp in her hand,
  To harp thir twa asleep;
But ay, as she harpit and she sang,
  Fu' sairly did she weep.

'O gin my sons were seven rats,
  Rinnin' on the castle wa',
And I myself a great grey cat,
  I soon wad worry them a'!

'O gin my sons were seven hares,
  Rinnin' owre yon lily lea,
And I myself a good greyhound,
  Soon worried they a' should be!'

Then out and spak the bonny young bride,
  In bride-bed where she lay:
'That's like my sister Annie,' she says;
  'Wha is it doth sing and play?

'I'll put on my gown,' said the new-come bride
  'And my shoes upon my feet;
I will see wha doth sae sadly sing,
  And what is it gars her greet.

'What ails you, what ails you, my housekeeper,
  That ye mak sic a mane?
Has ony wine-barrel cast its girds,
  Or is a' your white bread gane?'—

'It isna because my wine is spilt,
  Or that my white bread's gane;
But because I've lost my true love's love,
  And he's wed to anither ane.'—

'Noo tell me wha was your father?' she says,
   'Noo tell me wha was your mither?
And had ye ony sister?' she says,
   'And had ye ever a brither?'—

'The Earl of Wemyss was my father,
   The Countess of Wemyss my mother,
Young Elinor she was my sister dear,
   And Lord John he was my brither.'—

'If the Earl of Wemyss was your father,
   I wot sae was he mine;
And it's O my sister Annie!
   Your love ye sallna tyne.[1]

'Tak your husband, my sister dear;
   You ne'er were wrang'd for me,
Beyond a kiss o' his merry mouth
   As we cam owre the sea.

'Seven ships, loaded weel,
   Cam owre the sea wi' me;
Ane o' them will take me hame,
   And six I'll gie to thee.'

Get up and Bar the Door

It fell about the Martinmas time,
   And a gay time it was then,
When our goodwife got puddings to make,
   And she's boil'd them in the pan.

The wind sae cauld blew south and north,
   And blew into the floor;
Quoth our goodman to our goodwife,
   'Gae out and bar the door.'—

[1] lose.

'My hand is in my hussyfskap,[1]
　Goodman, as ye may see;
An' it shou'dna be barr'd this hundred year,
　It's no be barr'd for me.'

They made a paction 'tween them twa,
　They made it firm and sure,
That the first word whae'er shou'd speak,
　Shou'd rise and bar the door.

Then by there came two gentlemen,
　At twelve o'clock at night,
And they could neither see house nor hall,
　Nor coal nor candle-light.

'Now whether is this a rich man's house,
　Or whether is it a poor?'
But ne'er a word wad ane o' them speak,
　For barring of the door.

And first they ate the white puddings,
　And then they ate the black.
Tho' muckle thought the goodwife to hersel'
　Yet ne'er a word she spake.

Then said the one unto the other,
　'Here, man, tak ye my knife;
Do ye tak aff the auld man's beard,
　And I'll kiss the goodwife.'—

'But there's nae water in the house,
　And what shall we do than?'—
'What ails ye at the pudding-broo,
　That boils into the pan?'

---

[1] I am busy with my housewifery.

O up then started our goodman,
    An angry man was he:
'Will ye kiss my wife before my een,
    And sca'd me wi' pudding-bree?'

Then up and started our goodwife,
    Gied three skips on the floor:
'Goodman, you've spoken the foremost word!
    Get up and bar the door.'

SIR ROBERT AYTON

1570–1638

Inconstancy Reproved

I do confess thou'rt smooth and fair,
    And I might have gone near to love thee,
Had I not found the slightest prayer
    That lips could speak, had power to move thee;
But I can let thee now alone
As worthy to be loved by none.

I do confess thou'rt sweet; yet find
    Thee such an unthrift of thy sweets,
Thy favours are but like the wind
    That kisseth everything it meets:
And since thou canst with more than one,
Thou'rt worthy to be kiss'd by none.

The morning rose that untouch'd stands
    Arm'd with her briers, how sweet she smells!
But pluck'd and strain'd through ruder hands,
    Her sweets no longer with her dwells:
But scent and beauty both are gone,
And leaves fall from her, one by one.

Such fate ere long will thee betide
  When thou hast handled been awhile,
Like fair flowers to be thrown aside;
  And thou shalt sigh, when I shall smile,
To see thy love to every one
Hath brought thee to be loved by none.

To an Inconstant Mistress

I loved thee once; I'll love no more—
  Thine be the grief as is the blame;
Thou art not what thou wast before,
  What reason I should be the same?
    He that can love unloved again,
    Hath better store of love than brain:
  God send me love my debts to pay,
  While unthrifts fool their love away!

Nothing could have my love o'erthrown
  If thou hadst still continued mine;
Yea, if thou hadst remain'd thine own,
  I might perchance have yet been thine.
    But thou thy freedom didst recall
    That it thou might elsewhere enthral:
  And then how could I but disdain
  A captive's captive to remain?

When new desires had conquer'd thee
  And changed the object of thy will,
It had been lethargy in me,
  Not constancy, to love thee still.
    Yea, it had been a sin to go
    And prostitute affection so:
  Since we are taught no prayers to say
  To such as must to others pray.

Yet do thou glory in thy choice—
   Thy choice of his good fortune boast;
I'll neither grieve nor yet rejoice
   To see him gain what I have lost:
     The height of my disdain shall be
     To laugh at him, to blush for thee;
   To love thee still, but go no more
   A-begging at a beggar's door.

The Exercise of Affection

There is no worldly pleasure here below
   Which by experience doth not folly prove,
But among all the follies that I know,
   The sweetest folly in the world is love.

But not that passion, which by fool's consent,
   Above the reason bears imperious sway,
Making their lifetime a perpetual Lent,
   As if a man were born to fast and pray.

No! that is not the humour I approve,
   As either yielding pleasure or promotion;
I like a mild and lukewarm zeal in love,
   Altho' I do not like it in devotion.

For it hath no coherence in my creed,
   To think that lovers die as they pretend:
If all that say they die, had died indeed,
   Sure long ere now the world had had an end.

Besides, we need not love but if we please,
   No destiny can force man's disposition,
And how can any die of that disease,
   Whereof himself may be his own physician?

But some seem so distracted of their wits,
　　That I would think it but a venial sin,
To take some of these innocents that sit
　　In Bedlam out, and put some lovers in.

Yet some men, rather than incur the slander
　　Of true apostates, will false martyrs prove;
But I am neither Iphis nor Leander,
　　I'll neither drown or hang myself for love.

Methinks a wise man's actions should be such
　　As always yield to reason's best advice,
Now for to love too little, or too much,
　　Are both extremes, and all extremes are vice.

Yet have I been a lover by report,
　　Yea, I have died for love as others do,
But praised be God, it was in such a sort,
　　That I revived within an hour or two.

Thus have I liv'd, thus have I loved till now,
　　And found no reason to repent me yet,
And whosoever otherwise will do,
　　His courage is as little as his wit.

WILLIAM DRUMMOND OF
HAWTHORNDEN

1585–1649

I know that all beneath the moon decays

I know that all beneath the moon decays,
And what by mortals in this world is brought,
In Time's great periods shall return to nought;
That fairest states have fatal nights and days;
I know how all the Muse's heavenly lays,

With toil of spright which are so dearly bought,
As idle sounds, of few or none are sought,
And that nought lighter is than airy praise;
I know frail beauty like the purple flower,
To which one morn oft birth and death affords;
That love a jarring is of minds' accords,
Where sense and will invassal reason's power:
Know what I list, this all can not me move,
But that, O me! I both must write and love.

Sleep, Silence' child, sweet father of soft rest

Sleep, Silence' child, sweet father of soft rest,
Prince, whose approach peace to all mortals brings,
Indifferent host to shepherds and to kings,
Sole comforter of minds with grief opprest;
Lo, by thy charming rod all breathing things
Lie slumb'ring, with forgetfulness possest,
And yet o'er me to spread thy drowsy wings
Thou spares, alas! who cannot be thy guest.
Since I am thine, O come, but with that face
To inward light which thou art wont to show,
With feigned solace ease a true-felt woe;
Or if, deaf god, thou do deny that grace,
Come as thou wilt, and what thou wilt bequeath,
I long to kiss the image of my death.

Like the Idalian queen

Like the Idalian queen,
Her hair about her eyne,
With neck and breast's ripe apples to be seen,
At first glance of the morn,
In Cyprus' gardens gathering those fair flow'rs
Which of her blood were born,

I saw, but fainting saw, my paramours.
The Graces naked danc'd about the place,
The winds and trees amaz'd
With silence on her gaz'd;
The flow'rs did smile, like those upon her face,
And as their aspen stalks those fingers band,
That she might read my case,
A hyacinth I wish'd me in her hand.

Phoebus, arise

Phoebus, arise,
And paint the sable skies
With azure, white, and red;
Rouse Memnon's mother from her Tithon's bed,
That she thy career may with roses spread;
The nightingales thy coming each where sing;
Make an eternal spring,
Give life to this dark world which lieth dead;
Spread forth thy golden hair
In larger locks than thou wast wont before,
And, emperor-like, decore
With diadem of pearl thy temples fair:
Chase hence the ugly night,
Which serves but to make dear thy glorious light.
This is that happy morn,
That day, long-wished day,
Of all my life so dark
(If cruel stars have not my ruin sworn,
And fates not hope betray),
Which, only white, deserves
A diamond for ever should it mark:
This is the morn should bring unto this grove
My love, to hear and recompense my love.
Fair king, who all preserves,

But show thy blushing beams,
And thou two sweeter eyes
Shalt see, than those which by Peneus' streams
Did once thy heart surprise;
Nay, suns, which shine as clear
As thou when two thou did to Rome appear.
Now, Flora, deck thyself in fairest guise;
If that ye, winds, would hear
A voice surpassing far Amphion's lyre,
Your stormy chiding stay;
Let zephyr only breathe,
And with her tresses play,
Kissing sometimes those purple ports of death.
The winds all silent are,
And Phoebus in his chair,
Ensaffroning sea and air,
Makes vanish every star:
Night like a drunkard reels
Beyond the hills to shun his flaming wheels;
The fields with flow'rs are deck'd in every hue,
The clouds bespangle with bright gold their blue:
Here is the pleasant place,
And ev'ry thing, save her, who all should grace.

For the Baptist

The last and greatest herald of heaven's King,
Girt with rough skins, hies to the deserts wild,
Among that savage brood the woods forth bring,
Which he than man more harmless found and mild:
His food was locusts, and what young doth spring,
With honey that from virgin hives distill'd;
Parch'd body, hollow eyes, some uncouth thing
Made him appear, long since from earth exil'd.
There burst he forth: 'All ye, whose hopes rely

On God, with me amidst these deserts mourn;
Repent, repent, and from old errors turn.'
Who listen'd to his voice, obey'd his cry?
   Only the echoes, which he made relent,
   Rung from their marble caves, 'Repent, repent!'

Doth then the world go thus, doth all thus move?

Doth then the world go thus, doth all thus move?
Is this the justice which on earth we find?
Is this that firm decree which all doth bind?
Are these your influences, Powers above?
Those souls which vice's moody mists most blind,
Blind Fortune blindly most their friend doth prove;
And they who thee, poor idol, Virtue, love,
Ply like a feather toss'd by storm and wind.
Ah! if a Providence doth sway this all,
Why should best minds groan under most distress,
Or why should pride humility make thrall,
And injuries the innocent oppress?
   Heavens, hinder, stop this fate, or grant a time
   When good may have, as well as bad, their prime.

JAMES GRAHAM, MARQUIS OF MONTROSE

1612–1650

My dear and only Love

My dear and only Love, I pray
   That little world of thee
Be govern'd by no other sway
   Than purest monarchy;

For if confusion have a part
   (Which virtuous souls abhor),
And hold a synod in thine heart,
   I'll never love thee more.

Like Alexander I will reign,
   And I will reign alone;
My thoughts did evermore disdain
   A rival on my throne.
He either fears his fate too much,
   Or his deserts are small,
That dares not put it to the touch,
   To gain or lose it all.

And in the empire of thine heart,
   Where I should solely be,
If others do pretend a part
   Or dare to vie with me,
Or if *Committees* thou erect,
   And go on such a score,
I'll laugh and sing at thy neglect,
   And never love thee more.

But if thou wilt prove faithful then,
   And constant of thy word,
I'll make thee glorious by my pen
   And famous by my sword;
I'll serve thee in such noble ways
   Was never heard before;
I'll crown and deck thee all with bays,
   And love thee more and more.

Lines on the Execution of King Charles the First

Great, good, and just, could I but rate
My grief, and thy too rigid fate,

I'd weep the world in such a strain
As it should deluge once again.
But since thy loud-tongued blood demands supplies
More from Briareus' hands than Argus' eyes,
I'll sing thine obsequies with trumpet sounds,
And write thine epitaph in blood and wounds.

ANON.

(From *The Tea-Table Miscellany*, 1724–1737.)

The Gaberlunzie[1] *Man*

The pawky auld carle cam ower the lea
Wi' mony good-e'ens and days to me,
Saying, 'Gudewife, for your courtesie,
    Will you lodge a silly poor man?'
The night was cauld, the carle was wat,
And down ayont the ingle he sat;
My dochter's shoulders he 'gan to clap,
    And cadgily[2] ranted and sang.

'O wow!' quo' he, 'were I as free
As first when I saw this countrie,
How blyth and merry wad I be!
    And I wad nevir think lang.'
He grew canty,[3] and she grew fain,
But little did her auld minny ken
What thir twa togither were say'n
    When wooing they were sa thrang.

[1] strolling beggar.   [2] merrily.   [3] cheerful.

'An' O!' quo' he, 'an' ye were as black
As e'er the crown of your daddy's hat,
'Tis I wad lay thee by my back,
 And awa' wi' me thou sould gang.'
'An' O!' quo' she, 'an' I were as white
As e'er the snaw lay on the dike,
I'd clead me braw and lady-like,
 And awa' wi' thee I would gang.'

Between the twa was made a plot;
They raise a wee before the cock,
And wilily they shot the lock,
 And fast to the bent are gane.
Up in the morn the auld wife raise,
And at her leisure put on her claiths,
Syne to the servant's bed she gaes,
 To speir for the silly poor man.

She gaed to the bed where the beggar lay,
The strae was cauld, he was away;
She clapt her hand, cried 'Waladay!
 For some of our gear will be gane.'
Some ran to coffers and some to kist,
But nought was stown, that could be mist;
She danced her lane, cried 'Praise be blest,
 I have lodg'd a leal poor man.

'Since naething's awa' as we can learn,
The kirn's to kirn and milk to earn;
Gae but the house, lass, and waken my bairn
 And bid her come quickly ben.'
The servant gaed where the dochter lay,
The sheets were cauld, she was away,
And fast to her goodwife did say,
 'She's aff with the gaberlunzie man.'

'O fy gar ride and fy gar rin,
And haste ye find these traitors again;
For she's be burnt, and he's be slain,
 The wearifu' gaberlunzie man.'
Some rade upo' horse, some ran afit,
The wife was wud, and out of her wit:
She could na gang, nor yet could she sit,
 But ay she curs'd and she bann'd.

Meantime far 'hind out o'er the lea,
Fu' snug in a glen, where nane could see,
The twa, with kindly sport and glee,
 Cut frae a new cheese a whang:[1]
The priving[2] was gude, it pleas'd them baith.
To lo'e her for ay, he ga'e her his aith.
Quo' she, 'To leave thee I will be laith,
 My winsome gaberlunzie man.

'O kend my minny[3] I were wi' you,
Ill-fardly wad she crook her mou';
Sic a poor man she'd never trow,
 After the gaberlunzie man.'
'My dear,' quo' he, 'ye're yet ower young,
And hae na learn'd the beggar's tongue,
To follow me frae toun to toun,
 And carry the gaberlunzie on.

'Wi' cauk and keel[4] I'll win your bread,
And spindles and whorles for them wha need,
Whilk is a gentle trade indeed,
 The gaberlunzie to carry, O.
I'll bow my leg, and crook my knee,
And draw a black clout ower my e'e;
A cripple or blind they will ca' me,
 While we sall sing and be merry, O.'

---

[1] thick slice. [2] tasting. [3] mother. [4] chalk and ruddle.

Waly, Waly

O waly, waly, up the bank,
    And waly, waly, doun the brae,
And waly, waly, yon burn-side,
    Where I and my Love wont to gae!
I lean'd my back unto an aik,
    I thocht it was a trustie tree;
But first it bow'd and syne it brak—
    Sae my true love did lichtlie me.

O waly, waly, gin love be bonnie
    A little time while it is new!
But when 'tis auld it waxeth cauld,
    And fades awa' like morning dew.
O wherefore should I busk my heid,
    Or wherefore should I kame my hair?
For my true Love has me forsook,
    And says he'll never lo'e me mair.

Now Arthur's Seat sall be my bed,
    The sheets sall ne'er be 'filed by me;
Saint Anton's well sall be my drink;
    Since my true Love has forsaken me.
Marti'mas wind, when wilt thou blaw,
    And shake the green leaves aff the tree?
O gentle Death, when wilt thou come?
    For of my life I am wearìe.

'Tis not the frost, that freezes fell,
    Nor blawing snaw's inclemencie,
'Tis not sic cauld that makes me cry;
    But my Love's heart grown cauld to me.
When we cam in by Glasgow toun,
    We were a comely sicht to see;

My Love was clad in the black velvèt,
    And I mysel in cramasie.[1]

But had I wist, before I kist,
    That love had been sae ill to win,
I had lock'd my heart in a case o' gowd,
    And pinn'd it wi' a siller pin.
And O! if my young babe were born,
    And set upon the nurse's knee;
And I mysel were dead and gane,
    And the green grass growing over me!

Jocky said to Jeany

Jocky said to Jeany, Jeany, wilt thou do't?
Ne'er a fit, quo' Jeany, for my tocher-good,[2]
For my tocher-good, I winna marry thee.
E'ens ye like, quo' Jocky, ye may let it be.

I hae gowd and gear, I hae land eneugh,
I hae seven good owsen ganging in a pleugh,
Ganging in a pleugh, and linking o'er the lee,
And gin ye winna take me, I can let ye be.

I hae a good ha' house, a barn and a byre,
A stack afore the door, I'll make a rantin fire,
I'll make a rantin fire, and merry shall we be:
And gin ye winna take me, I can let ye be.

Jeany said to Jocky, Gin ye winna tell,
Ye shall be the lad, I'll be the lass mysell.
Ye're a bonny lad, and I'm a lassie free,
Ye're welcomer to take me than to let me be.

<hr />

[1] crimson.   [2] dowry.

LADY GRISELL BAILLIE
1665–1746

There ance was a may

There ance was a may, and she loo'd na men;
She biggit her bonnie bower doun in yon glen;
But now she cries, Dool! and well-a-day!
Come doun the green gait[1] and come here away!

When bonnie young Johnnie cam' ower the sea,
He said he saw naething sae lovely as me;
He hecht[2] me baith rings and mony braw things,—
And werena my heart licht I wad dee.

He had a wee titty[3] that loo'd na me,
Because I was twice as bonnie as she;
She raised such a pother 'twixt him and his mother
That werena my heart licht I wad dee.

The day it was set, and the bridal to be:
The wife took a dwam,[4] and lay doun to dee;
She maned and she graned out o' dolour and pain,
Till he vow'd he never wad see me again.

His kin was for ane of a higher degree,
Said, What had he to do wi' the like of me?
Albeit I was bonnie, I wasna for Johnnie,—
And werena my heart licht I wad dee.

They said I had neither cow nor calf,
Nor dribbles o' drink rins through the draff,
Nor pickles o' meal rins through the mill-e'e;
And werena my heart licht I wad dee.

[1] way.　　[2] promised.　　[3] sister.　　[4] swoon.

His titty she was baith wylie and slee:
She spied me as I cam' ower the lea;
And then she ran in and made a loud din,—
Believe your ain een an' ye trow na me.

His bonnet stood aye fu' round on his brow,—
His auld ane look'd aye as weel as some's new;
But now he lets 't wear ony gait it will hing,
And casts himself dowie upon the corn-bing.[1]

And now he gaes daund'ring about the dykes,
And a' he dow do is to hund the tykes:
The live-lang nicht he ne'er steeks his e'e;
And werena my heart licht I wad dee.

Were I but young for thee, as I hae been,
We should hae been gallopin' doun on yon green,
And linkin' it on the lily-white lea,—
And wow! gin I were but young for thee!

ALLAN RAMSAY

1686–1758

The Lass o' Patie's Mill

The lass o' Patie's mill,
  So bonny, blythe, and gay,
In spite of all my skill,
  Hath stole my heart away.
When tedding[2] of the hay,
  Bare-headed on the green,
Love 'midst her locks did play,
  And wanton'd in her een.

---

[1] heap of corn.   [2] spreading.

Her arms, white, round, and smooth,
  Breasts rising in their dawn,
To age it would give youth,
  To press them with his hand.
Thro' all my spirits ran
  An extasy of bliss,
When I such sweetness fan'd
  Wrapt in a balmy kiss.

Without the help of art,
  Like flowers which grace the wild,
She did her sweets impart,
  Whene'er she spoke or smil'd.
Her looks they were so mild,
  Free from affected pride,
She me to love beguil'd;
  I wish'd her for my bride.

O had I all the wealth
  Hopetoun's high mountains fill,
Insur'd lang life and health,
  And pleasure at my will;
I'd promise and fulfil,
  That none but bonny she,
The lass o' Patie's mill,
  Shou'd share the same with me.

My Peggy

My Peggy is a young thing
  Just enter'd in her teens,
Fair as the day, and sweet as May,
Fair as the day, and always gay.
  My Peggy is a young thing.
  And I'm na very auld,

Yet weel I like to meet her at
The wauking[1] o' the fauld.

My Peggy speaks sae sweetly,
Whene'er we meet alane,
I wish nae mair to lay my care,
I wish nae mair o' a' that's rare.
My Peggy speaks sae sweetly,
To a' the lave I'm cauld,
But she gars a' my spirits glow
At wauking o' the fauld.

My Peggy smiles sae kindly
Whene'er I whisper love,
That I look doun on a' the toun,
That I look doun upon a croun.
My Peggy smiles sae kindly,
It maks me blythe and bauld,
An' naething gies me sic delight
As wauking o' the fauld.

My Peggy sings sae saftly
When on my pipe I play,
By a' the rest it is confest,
By a' the rest that she sings best.
My Peggy sings sae saftly,
And in her sangs are tauld
Wi' innocence, the wale[2] o' sense,
At wauking o' the fauld.

Look up to Pentland's tow'ring tap

Look up to Pentland's tow'ring tap,
Buried beneath big wreaths o' snaw,
O'er ilka cleugh,[3] ilk scar[4] an' slap,[5]
As high as ony Roman wa'.

---

[1] watching.   [2] choice.   [3] hollow.   [4] cliff.   [5] pass.

Driving their ba's frae whins or tee,
    There's no ae gowfer to be seen;
Nor douser[1] fouk, wysing a-jee[2]
    The byas bouls[3] on Tamson's green.

Then fling on coals, an' ripe[4] the ribs,
    An' beek[5] the house baith butt an' ben;[6]
That mutchkin[7]-stoup it hauds but dribs,[8]
    Then let's get in the tappit hen.[9]

Guid claret best keeps out the cauld,
    An' drives awa the winter soon;
It maks a man baith gash[10] an' bauld,
    An' heaves his saul ayont the moon.

Leave to the gods your ilka[11] care;
    If that they think us worth their while,
They can a rowth[12] o' blessings spare,
    Which will our fashious[13] fears beguile.

For what they hae a mind to do,
    That will they do, shou'd we gang wud;
If they command the storms to blaw,
    Then upo' sight the hailstanes thud.

But soon as e'er they cry, Be quiet,
    The blatt'ring winds daur nae mair move,
But cour into their caves, an' wait
    The high command o' supreme Jove.

Let neist day come as it thinks fit,
    The present minute's only ours;
On pleasure let's employ our wit,
    An' laugh at fortune's feckless[14] pow'rs.

---

[1] quieter.   [2] gently pushing off the straight.   [3] biased bowls.
[4] poke.   [5] heat.   [6] in both its rooms.   [7] pint.   [8] drops.
[9] Scots quart measure.   [10] talkative.   [11] every.   [12] abundance.
[13] vexing.   [14] weak and foolish.

Be sure ye dinna quat the grip
    O' ilka joy whan ye are young,
Before auld age your vitals nip,
    An' lay ye twafald o'er a rung.[1]

Sweet youth's a blythe an' heartsome time;
    Then, lads an' lasses, while it's May,
Gae pu' the gowan[2] in its prime,
    Before it wither an' decay.

Watch the saft minutes o' delight,
    Whan Jenny speaks beneath her breath,
An' kisses, laying a' the wyte[3]
    On you, if she kepp ony skaith.[4]

Haith[5] ye're ill-bred, she'll smiling say,
    Ye'll worry me, ye greedy rook;
Syne frae your arms she'll rin away,
    An' hide hersell in some dark nook;

Her laugh will lead you to the place
    Whare lies the happiness you want,
An' plainly tells you to your face,
    Nineteen nay-says[6] are hauf a grant.

Now to her heaving bosom cling,
    An' sweetly toolie[7] for a kiss,
Frae her fair finger whup a ring,
    As taiken o' a future bliss.

These bennisons, I'm very sure,
    Are o' the gods' indulgent grant;
Then, surly carles, whisht, forbear
    To plague us wi' your whining cant.

(*Imitations of Horace: Carm. I, 9.*)

---

[1] doubled over a staff.   [2] daisy.   [3] blame.   [4] catch any harm.
[5] faith.   [6] denials.   [7] struggle.

Up in the Air

Now the sun's gane out o' sight,
Beet the ingle,[1] an' snuff the light;
In glens the fairies skip an' dance,
An' witches wallop o'er to France.
    Up in the air
    On my bonny grey mare;
An' I see her yet, an' I see her yet.
    Up in, etc.

The wind's drifting hail an' snaw
O'er frozen hags[2] like a foot ba';
Nae starns keek[3] thro' the azure slit,
It's cauld an' mirk as ony pit.
    The man i' the moon
    Is carousing aboon,
D'ye see, d'ye see, d'ye see him yet.
    The man, etc.

Tak your glass to clear your een,
It's the elixir hales[4] the spleen,
Baith wit and mirth it will inspire,
An' gently puffs the lover's fire.
    Up i' the air,
    It drives away care;
Hae wi' ye, hae wi' ye, an' hae wi' ye, lads, yet.
    Up in, etc.

Steek the doors, keep out the frost;
Come, Willy, gie's about your toast;
Till't lads, an' lilt it out,
An' let us hae a blythesome bout.

---

[1] stir up the fire.   [2] marshes.   [3] stars peep.   [4] heals.

Up wi't there, there,
Dinna cheat, but drink fair,
Huzza, huzza, an' huzza, lads, yet.
Up wi't, etc.

JAMES THOMSON

1700–1748

Winter

Now, when the cheerless empire of the sky
To Capricorn the Centaur-Archer yields,
And fierce Aquarius stains the inverted year—
Hung o'er the farthest verge of heaven, the sun
Scarce spreads o'er ether the dejected day.
Faint are his gleams, and ineffectual shoot
His struggling rays in horizontal lines
Through the thick air; as clothed in cloudy storm,
Weak, wan, and broad, he skirts the southern sky;
And, soon descending, to the long dark night,
Wide-shading all, the prostrate world resigns.
Nor is the night unwished; while vital heat,
Light, life, and joy the dubious day forsake.
Meantime, in sable cincture, shadows vast,
Deep-tinged and damp, and congregated clouds,
And all the vapoury turbulence of heaven
Involve the face of things. Thus Winter falls,
A heavy gloom oppressive o'er the world,
Through Nature shedding influence malign,
And rouses up the seeds of dark disease.
The soul of man dies in him, loathing life,
And black with more than melancholy views.
The cattle droop; and o'er the furrowed land,
Fresh from the plough, the dun discoloured flocks,

Untended spreading, crop the wholesome root.
Along the woods, along the moorish fens,
Sighs the sad genius of the coming storm;
And up among the loose disjointed cliffs
And fractured mountains wild, the brawling brook
And cave, presageful, send a hollow moan,
Resounding long in listening fancy's ear.

Then comes the father of the tempest forth,
Wrapt in black glooms. First, joyless rains obscure
Drive through the mingling skies with vapour foul,
Dash on the mountain's brow, and shake the woods
That grumbling wave below. The unsightly plain
Lies a brown deluge; as the low-bent clouds
Pour flood on flood, yet unexhausted still
Combine, and, deepening into night, shut up
The day's fair face. The wanderers of heaven,
Each to his home, retire; save those that love
To take their pastime in the troubled air,
Or skimming flutter round the dimply pool.
The cattle from the untasted fields return
And ask, with meaning low, their wonted stalls,
Or ruminate in the contiguous shade.
Thither the household feathery people crowd,
The crested cock, with all his female train,
Pensive and dripping; while the cottage-hind
Hangs o'er the enlivening blaze, and taleful there
Recounts his simple frolic: much he talks,
And much he laughs, nor recks the storm that blows
Without, and rattles on his humble roof.

Wide o'er the brim, with many a torrent swelled,
And the mixed ruin of its banks o'erspread,
At last the roused-up river pours along:
Resistless, roaring, dreadful, down it comes,
From the rude mountain and the mossy wild,

Tumbling through rocks abrupt, and sounding far;
Then o'er the sanded valley floating spreads,
Calm, sluggish, silent; till again, constrained
Between two meeting hills, it bursts a way
Where rocks and woods o'erhang the turbid stream;
There, gathering triple force, rapid and deep,
It boils, and wheels, and foams, and thunders through.

Nature! great parent! whose unceasing hand
Rolls round the Seasons of the changeful year,
How mighty, how majestic are thy works!
With what a pleasing dread they swell the soul,
That sees astonished, and astonished sings!
Ye too, ye winds! that now begin to blow
With boisterous sweep, I raise my voice to you.
Where are your stores, ye powerful beings! say,
Where your aerial magazines reserved
To swell the brooding terrors of the storm?
In what far-distant region of the sky,
Hushed in deep silence, sleep you when 'tis calm?

When from the pallid sky the Sun descends,
With many a spot, that o'er his glaring orb
Uncertain wanders, stained; red fiery streaks
Begin to flush around. The reeling clouds
Stagger with dizzy poise, as doubting yet
Which master to obey; while, rising slow,
Blank in the leaden-coloured east, the moon
Wears a wan circle round her blunted horns.
Seen through the turbid, fluctuating air,
The stars obtuse emit a shivering ray;
Or frequent seem to shoot athwart the gloom,
And long behind them trail the whitening blaze.
Snatched in short eddies, plays the withered leaf;
And on the flood the dancing feather floats.
With broadened nostrils to the sky upturned,

The conscious heifer snuffs the stormy gale.
Even, as the matron, at her nightly task,
With pensive labour draws the flaxen thread,
The wasted taper and the crackling flame
Foretell the blast. But chief the plumy race,
The tenants of the sky, its changes speak.
Retiring from the downs, where all day long
They picked their scanty fare, a blackening train
Of clamorous rooks thick-urge their weary flight,
And seek the closing shelter of the grove.
Assiduous, in his bower, the wailing owl
Plies his sad song. The cormorant on high
Wheels from the deep, and screams along the land.
Loud shrieks the soaring hern; and with wild wing
The circling sea-fowl cleave the flaky clouds.
Ocean, unequal pressed, with broken tide
And blind commotion heaves; while from the shore,
Eat into caverns by the restless wave,
And forest-rustling mountain comes a voice
That, solemn-sounding, bids the world prepare.
Then issues forth the storm with sudden burst,
And hurls the whole precipitated air
Down in a torrent. On the passive main
Descends the ethereal force, and with strong gust
Turns from its bottom the discoloured deep.
Through the black night that sits immense around,
Lashed into foam, the fierce-conflicting brine
Seems o'er a thousand raging waves to burn.
Meantime the mountain-billows, to the clouds
In dreadful tumult swelled, surge above surge,
Burst into chaos with tremendous roar,
And anchored navies from their stations drive
Wild as the winds, across the howling waste
Of mighty waters: now the inflated wave
Straining they scale, and now impetuous shoot

Into the secret chambers of the deep,
The wintry Baltic thundering o'er their head.
Emerging thence again, before the breath
Of full-exerted heaven they wing their course,
And dart on distant coasts—if some sharp rock
Or shoal insidious break not their career,
And in loose fragments fling them floating round.

Nor less at land the loosened tempest reigns.
The mountain thunders, and its sturdy sons
Stoop to the bottom of the rocks they shade.
Lone on the midnight steep, and all aghast,
The dark wayfaring stranger breathless toils,
And, often falling, climbs against the blast.
Low waves the rooted forest, vexed, and sheds
What of its tarnished honours yet remain—
Dashed down and scattered, by the tearing wind's
Assiduous fury, its gigantic limbs.
Thus struggling through the dissipated grove,
The whirling tempest raves along the plain;
And, on the cottage thatched or lordly roof
Keen-fastening, shakes them to the solid base.
Sleep frighted flies; and round the rocking dome,
For entrance eager, howls the savage blast.
Then too, they say, through all the burdened air
Long groans are heard, shrill sounds, and distant
    sighs,
That, uttered by the demon of the night,
Warn the devoted wretch of woe and death.

Huge uproar lords it wide. The clouds, com-
    mixed
With stars swift-gliding, sweep along the sky.
All Nature reels: till Nature's King, who oft
Amid tempestuous darkness dwells alone,
And on the wings of the careering wind

Walks dreadfully serene, commands a calm;
Then straight air, sea, and earth are hushed at once.

As yet 'tis midnight deep. The weary clouds,
Slow-meeting, mingle into solid gloom.
Now, while the drowsy world lies lost in sleep,
Let me associate with the serious Night,
And Contemplation, her sedate compeer;
Let me shake off the intrusive cares of day,
And lay the meddling senses all aside.

Where now, ye lying vanities of life!
Ye ever-tempting, ever-cheating train!
Where are you now? and what is your amount?
Vexation, disappointment, and remorse.
Sad, sickening thought! and yet deluded man,
A scene of crude disjointed visions past,
And broken slumbers, rises still resolved,
With new-flushed hopes, to run the giddy round.

Father of light and life! thou Good Supreme!
O teach me what is good! teach me Thyself!
Save me from folly, vanity, and vice,
From every low pursuit; and feed my soul
With knowledge, conscious peace, and virtue pure—
Sacred, substantial, never-fading bliss!

The keener tempests come: and, fuming dun
From all the livid east or piercing north,
Thick clouds ascend, in whose capacious womb
A vapoury deluge lies, to snow congealed.
Heavy they roll their fleecy world along,
And the sky saddens with the gathered storm.
Through the hushed air the whitening shower des-
    cends,
At first thin-wavering; till at last the flakes
Fall broad and wide and fast, dimming the day

With a continual flow. The cherished fields
Put on their winter-robe of purest white.
'Tis brightness all; save where the new snow melts
Along the mazy current. Low the woods
Bow their hoar head; and, ere the languid sun
Faint from the west emits his evening ray,
Earth's universal face, deep-hid and chill,
Is one wild dazzling waste, that buries wide
The works of man. Drooping, the labourer-ox
Stands covered o'er with snow, and then demands
The fruit of all his toil. The fowls of heaven,
Tamed by the cruel season, crowd around
The winnowing tree, and claim the little boon
Which Providence assigns them. One alone,
The redbreast, sacred to the household gods,
Wisely regardful of the embroiling sky,
In joyless fields and thorny thickets leaves
His shivering mates, and pays to trusted man
His annual visit. Half afraid, he first
Against the window beats; then brisk alights
On the warm hearth; then, hopping o'er the floor,
Eyes all the smiling family askance,
And pecks, and starts, and wonders where he is—
Till, more familiar grown, the table-crumbs
Attract his slender feet. The foodless wilds
Pour forth their brown inhabitants. The hare,
Though timorous of heart, and hard beset
By death in various forms, dark snares, and dogs,
And more unpitying men, the garden seeks,
Urged on by fearless want. The bleating kind
Eye the bleak heaven, and next the glistening earth,
With looks of dumb despair; then, sad-dispersed,
Dig for the withered herb through heaps of snow.

Now, shepherds, to your helpless charge be kind:

Baffle the raging year, and fill their pens
With food at will; lodge them below the storm,
And watch them strict: for, from the bellowing east,
In this dire season, oft the whirlwind's wing
Sweeps up the burden of whole wintry plains
In one wide waft, and o'er the hapless flocks,
Hid in the hollow of two neighbouring hills,
The billowy tempest whelms; till, upward urged,
The valley to a shining mountain swells,
Tipt with a wreath high-curling in the sky.

As thus the snows arise, and, foul and fierce,
All Winter drives along the darkened air,
In his own loose-revolving fields the swain
Disastered stands; sees other hills ascend,
Of unknown joyless brow; and other scenes,
Of horrid prospect, shag the trackless plain;
Nor finds the river nor the forest, hid
Beneath the formless wild; but wanders on
From hill to dale, still more and more astray—
Impatient flouncing through the drifted heaps,
Stung with the thoughts of home: the thoughts of
      home
Rush on his nerves and call their vigour forth
In many a vain attempt. How sinks his soul!
What black despair, what horror fills his heart,
When, for the dusky spot which fancy feigned
His tufted cottage rising through the snow,
He meets the roughness of the middle waste,
Far from the track and blest abode of man;
While round him night resistless closes fast,
And every tempest, howling o'er his head,
Renders the savage wilderness more wild.
Then throng the busy shapes into his mind
Of covered pits, unfathomably deep,

A dire descent! beyond the power of frost;
Of faithless bogs; of precipices huge,
Smoothed up with snow; and (what is land unknown,
What water) of the still unfrozen spring,
In the loose marsh or solitary lake,
Where the fresh fountain from the bottom boils.
These check his fearful steps; and down he sinks
Beneath the shelter of the shapeless drift,
Thinking o'er all the bitterness of death,
Mixed with the tender anguish nature shoots
Through the wrung bosom of the dying man—
His wife, his children, and his friends unseen.
In vain for him the officious wife prepares
The fire fair-blazing and the vestment warm;
In vain his little children, peeping out
Into the mingling storm, demand their sire
With tears of artless innocence. Alas!
Nor wife nor children more shall he behold,
Nor friends, nor sacred home. On every nerve
The deadly Winter seizes, shuts up sense,
And, o'er his inmost vitals creeping cold,
Lays him along the snows a stiffened corse,
Stretched out, and bleaching in the northern blast.

(*The Seasons, Winter*, ll. 41–321.)

To Amanda

Come, dear Amanda, quit the town,
    And to the rural hamlets fly;
Behold! the wintry storms are gone,
    A gentle radiance glads the sky;

The birds awake, the flowers appear,
    Earth spreads a verdant couch for thee;
'Tis joy and music all we hear,
    'Tis love and beauty all we see.

Come, let us mark the gradual spring,
  How peeps the bud, the blossom blows;
Till Philomel begins to sing,
  And perfect May to swell the rose.

Even so thy rising charms improve,
  As life's warm season grows more bright;
And, opening to the sighs of love,
  Thy beauties glow with full delight.

To Fortune

For ever, Fortune, wilt thou prove
An unrelenting foe to love,
And, when we meet a mutual heart,
Come in between and bid us part;

Bid us sigh on from day to day,
And wish, and wish the soul away;
Till youth and genial years are flown,
And all the life of life is gone?

But busy, busy still art thou,
To bind the loveless joyless vow,
The heart from pleasure to delude,
And join the gentle to the rude.

For once, O Fortune! hear my prayer,
And I absolve thy future care—
All other blessings I resign;
Make but the dear Amanda mine!

Enchanted Ground

In lowly dale, fast by a river's side,
With woody hill o'er hill encompassed round,
A most enchanting wizard did abide,
Than whom a fiend more fell is nowhere found.

It was, I ween, a lovely spot of ground;
And there a season atween June and May,
Half prankt with spring, with summer half im-
    browned,
A listless climate made, where, sooth to say,
No living wight could work, ne carèd even for play.

Was nought around but images of rest:
Sleep-soothing groves, and quiet lawns between;
And flowery beds that slumbrous influence kest,
From poppies breathed; and beds of pleasant green,
Where never yet was creeping creature seen.
Meantime unnumbered glittering streamlets
    played,
And hurlèd everywhere their waters sheen;
That, as they bickered through the sunny glade,
Though restless still themselves, a lulling murmur
    made.

Joined to the prattle of the purling rills,
Were heard the lowing herds along the vale,
And flocks loud-bleating from the distant hills,
And vacant shepherds piping in the dale:
And now and then sweet Philomel would wail,
Or stock-doves plain amid the forest deep,
That drowsy rustled to the sighing gale;
And still a coil the grasshopper did keep:
Yet all these sounds yblent inclinèd all to sleep.

Full in the passage of the vale, above,
A sable, silent, solemn forest stood;
Where nought but shadowy forms were seen to move,
As Idless fancied in her dreaming mood.
And up the hills, on either side, a wood
Of blackening pines, ay waving to and fro,
Sent forth a sleepy horror through the blood;

And where this valley winded out, below,
The murmuring main was heard, and scarcely heard,
   to flow.

A pleasing land of drowsyhed it was:
Of dreams that wave before the half-shut eye;
And of gay castles in the clouds that pass,
For ever flushing round a summer sky:
There eke the soft delights, that witchingly
Instil a wanton sweetness through the breast,
And the calm pleasures always hovered nigh;
But whate'er smacked of noyance, or unrest,
Was far far off expelled from this delicious nest.

        (*The Castle of Indolence*, stanzas II–VI.)

Finis

As those we love decay, we die in part,
String after string is severed from the heart;
Till loosened life, at last but breathing clay,
Without one pang is glad to fall away.
Unhappy he who latest feels the blow,
Whose eyes have wept o'er every friend laid low,
Dragged lingering on from partial death to death,
Till, dying, all he can resign is breath.

      (*On the death of Mr. William Aikman the Painter*, ll. 35-42.)

ANON.

Low doun in the Broom

My daddie is a cankert carle,[1]
   He'll no twine[2] wi' his gear;
My minnie she's a scauldin' wife,[3]
   Hauds a' the house asteer.[4]

---

[1] crusty old man. [2] part. [3] My mother she's a scolding woman.
[4] keeps all the house in a turmoil.

But let them say, or let them do,
    It's a' ane to me,
For he's low doun, he's in the broom,
    That's waitin' on me:
Waitin' on me, my love,
    He's waitin' on me:
For he's low doun, he's in the broom,
    That's waitin' on me.

My auntie Kate sits at her wheel,
    And sair she lightlies me;
But weel I ken it's a' envy,
    For ne'er a joe[1] has she.

My cousin Kate was sair beguiled
    Wi' Johnnie o' the Glen;
And aye sinsyne she cries, Beware
    O' fause deluding men.

Gleed[2] Sandy he cam west yestreen,
    And speired[3] when I saw Pate;
And aye sinsyne the neebors round
    They jeer me air and late.
    But let them say, or let them do,
        It's a' ane to me,
    For he's low doun, he's in the broom,
        That's waitin' on me:
    Waitin' on me, my love,
        He's waitin' on me:
    For he's low doun, he's in the broom,
        That's waitin' on me.

---

[1] sweetheart.   [2] squinting.   [3] asked.

Aye Waukin' O!

O spring's a pleasant time,
 Flowers o' every colour—
The sweet bird builds her nest,
 And I long for my lover.
  Aye waukin' O,
   Waukin' aye, and weary,
  Sleep can I get nane,
   For thinkin' o' my dearie.

O I'm wat, wat,
 O I'm wat and weary;
Yet fain I'd rise and run
 If I thought to meet my dearie.

When I sleep I dream,
 When I wauk I'm eerie;
Sleep can I get nane,
 For thinkin' o' my dearie.

Lanely night comes on;
 A' the lave are sleeping;
I think on my love,
 And blear my een wi' greeting.

Feather-beds are soft,
 Painted rooms are bonnie;
But a kiss o' my dear love
 Is better far than ony.

O for Friday's night,
 Friday at the gloaming!
O for Friday's night!
 Friday's lang o' coming.
  Aye waukin' O,
   Waukin' aye, and weary,
  Sleep can I get nane,
   For thinkin' o' my dearie.

ALISON RUTHERFORD
(MRS. COCKBURN)
1712–1794

The Flowers of the Forest

I've seen the smiling of Fortune beguiling,
   I've tasted her favours, and felt her decay:
Sweet is her blessing, and kind her caressing;
   But soon it is fled—it is fled far away.

I've seen the Forest adornèd the foremost
   With flowers of the fairest—most pleasant and gay:
Full sweet was their blooming—their scent the air
     perfuming;
   But now they are wither'd and a' wede away.

I've seen the morning with gold the hills adorning,
   And the red tempest storming before parting day:
I've seen Tweed's silver streams, glittering in the
     sunny beams,
   Grow drumly[1] and dark as they roll'd on their way.

O fickle Fortune! why this cruel sporting?
   Why thus perplex us poor sons of a day?
Thy frowns cannot fear me, thy smiles cannot cheer
     me—
   Since the Flowers of the Forest are a' wede away.

TOBIAS SMOLLETT
1721–1771

Ode to Leven Water

On Leven's banks, while free to rove,
And tune the rural pipe to love,

[1] muddy.

I envied not the happiest swain
That ever trod the Arcadian plain.
  Pure stream, in whose transparent wave
My youthful limbs I wont to lave;
No torrents stain thy limpid source,
No rocks impede thy dimpling course,
That sweetly warbles o'er its bed,
With white round polished pebbles spread;
While, lightly poised, the scaly brood
In myriads cleave thy crystal flood;
The springing trout in speckled pride,
The salmon, monarch of the tide;
The ruthless pike, intent on war,
The silver eel, and mottled par.
Devolving from thy parent lake,
A charming maze thy waters make,
By bowers of birch and groves of pine,
And edges flowered with eglantine.
  Still on thy banks so gaily green
May numerous herds and flocks be seen:
And lasses chanting o'er the pail,
And shepherds piping in the dale;
And ancient faith that knows no guile,
And industry embrowned with toil;
And hearts resolved and hands prepared
The blessings they enjoy to guard!

JOHN SKINNER
1721–1807

Tullochgorum

Come, gie's a sang, Montgomery cry'd,
And lay your disputes a' aside;
What signifies't for folks to chide
  For what was done before them?

Let Whig and Tory a' agree,
  Whig and Tory, Whig and Tory,
  Whig and Tory a' agree
    To drop their whigmigmorum;
Let Whig and Tory a' agree
To spend this night wi' mirth and glee,
And cheerfu' sing, alang wi' me,
    The Reel o' Tullochgorum.

O Tullochgorum's my delight,
It gars us a' in ane unite,
And ony sumph[1] that keeps up spite,
  In conscience I abhor him.
Blithe and merry we'll be a',
  Blithe and merry, blithe and merry,
  Blithe and merry we'll be a'
    And mak a cheerfu' quorum.
For blithe and merry we'll be a'
As lang as we hae breath to draw,
And dance, till we be like to fa',
    The Reel o' Tullochgorum.

What needs there be sae great a fraise[2]
Wi' dringing[3] dull Italian lays,
I wadna gie our ain strathspeys
  For half a hunder score o' them:
They're dowf and dowie[4] at the best,
  Dowf and dowie, dowf and dowie,
  Dowf and dowie at the best,
    Wi' a' their variorum;
They're dowf and dowie at the best,
Their allegros and a' the rest;
They canna please a Scottish taste
    Compared wi' Tullochgorum.

[1] blockhead.   [2] fuss.   [3] droning.   [4] dull and heavy.

Let warldly worms their minds oppress
Wi' fears o' want and double cess,[1]
And sullen sots themselves distress
   Wi' keeping up decorum.
Shall we sae sour and sulky sit,
  Sour and sulky, sour and sulky,
  Sour and sulky shall we sit
    Like auld philosophorum?
Shall we sae sour and sulky sit,
Wi' neither sense, nor mirth, nor wit,
Nor ever rise to shake a fit
    To the Reel o' Tullochgorum?

May choicest blessings aye attend
Each honest, open-hearted friend,
And calm and quiet be his end,
   And a' that's good watch o'er him;
May peace and plenty be his lot,
  Peace and plenty, peace and plenty,
  Peace and plenty be his lot,
    And dainties a great store o' them;
May peace and plenty be his lot,
Unstained by any vicious spot,
And may he never want a groat,
    That's fond o' Tullochgorum!

But for the sullen, frumpish fool,
Who wants to be oppression's tool,
May envy gnaw his rotten soul,
   And discontent devour him;
May dule and sorrow be his chance,
  Dule and sorrow, dule and sorrow,
  Dule and sorrow be his chance,
    And nane say, Wae's me for him!

[1] tax.

May dule and sorrow be his chance,
And a' the ills that come frae France,
Whae'er he be that winna dance
The Reel o' Tullochgorum.

JEAN ELLIOT

1727–1805

The Flowers of the Forest

I've heard them lilting at our yowe-milking—
Lasses a-lilting before dawn of day;
But now they are moaning on ilka green loaning—
The Flowers of the Forest are a' wede away.

At buchts,[1] in the morning, nae blythe lads are
scorning;
Lasses are lonely and dowie and wae;—
Nae daffin', nae gabbin'—but sighing and sabbing
Ilk ane lifts her leglin[2] and hies her away.

In hairst, at the shearing, nae youths now are jeer-
ing—
Bandsters[3] are runkled[4] and lyart[5] or grey:
At fair or at preaching, nae wooing, nae fleeching[6]—
The Flowers of the Forest are a' wede away.

At e'en, in the gloaming, nae swankies[7] are roaming,
'Bout stacks with the lasses at bogle to play;
But ilk maid sits drearie, lamenting her dearie—
The Flowers of the Forest are a' wede away.

---

[1] sheep-folds. [2] milk-pail. [3] binders. [4] wrinkled.
[5] grizzled. [6] flattering. [7] smart young fellows.

Dool and wae for the order sent our lads to the
    Border!
    The English, for ance, by guile wan the day;—
The Flowers of the Forest, that foucht aye the fore-
    most—
    The prime of our land—are cauld in the clay.

We'll hear nae mair lilting at the yowe-milking;
    Women and bairns are heartless and wae,
Sighing and moaning on ilka green loaning—
    The Flowers of the Forest are a' wede away.

WILLIAM JULIUS MICKLE

1734–1788

The Sailor's Wife

And are ye sure the news is true?
    And are ye sure he's weel?
Is this a time to think o' wark?
    Ye jauds, fling bye your wheel!
Is this the time to spin a thread,
    When Colin's at the door?
Rax[1] down my cloak—I'll to the quay,
    And see him come ashore.
      For there's nae luck aboot the house,
        There's nae luck ava;
      There's little pleasure in the house
        When our gudeman's awa'.

And gie to me my bigonet,[2]
    My bishop's satin gown;
For I maun tell the bailie's wife
    That Colin's in the town.

      [1] reach.   [2] linen cap.

My Turkey slippers maun gae on,
    My hose o' pearly blue,—
It's a' to pleasure our gudeman,
    For he's baith leal and true.

Rise up and mak' a clean fireside,
    Put on the muckle pot;
Gie little Kate her button gown,
    And Jock his Sunday coat;
And mak' their shoon as black as slaes,
    Their stockin's white as snaw,—
It's a' to please my ain gudeman—
    He likes to see them braw.

There's twa fat hens upon the bauk,[1]
    Hae fed this month and mair;
Mak' haste and thraw[2] their necks about,
    That Colin weel may fare;
And spread the table neat and clean—
    Gar ilka thing look braw;
For wha can tell how Colin fared
    When he was far awa'?

Sae true his heart, sae smooth his speech,
    His breath like caller air;
His very foot has music in't
    As he comes up the stair.
And will I see his face again?
    And will I hear him speak?
I'm downright dizzy wi' the thought,—
    In troth I'm like to greet!

If Colin's weel, and weel content,
    I hae nae mair to crave;
And gin I live to keep him sae,
    I'm blest aboon the lave.

[1] cross-beam.   [2] wring.

And will I see his face again,
  And will I hear him speak?—
I'm downright dizzy wi' the thought,—
  In troth I'm like to greet!
    For there's nae luck aboot the house,
      There's nae luck ava;
    There's little pleasure in the house
      When our gudeman's awa'.

ROBERT CUNNINGHAME-GRAHAM OF GARTMORE

1735–1797

If doughty deeds

If doughty deeds my lady please,
  Right soon I'll mount my steed;
And strong his arm and fast his seat,
  That bears frae me the meed.
I'll wear thy colours in my cap,
  Thy picture in my heart;
And he that bends not to thine eye
  Shall rue it to his smart!
    Then tell me how to woo thee, Love;
      O tell me how to woo thee!
    For thy dear sake nae care I'll take,
      Tho' ne'er another trow me.

If gay attire delight thine eye
  I'll dight me in array;
I'll tend thy chamber door all night,
  And squire thee all the day,
If sweetest sounds can win thine ear,
  These sounds I'll strive to catch;

Thy voice I'll steal to woo thysel',
   That voice that nane can match.
      Then tell me how to woo thee, Love . . .

But if fond love thy heart can gain,
   I never broke a vow;
Nae maiden lays her skaith to me,
   I never loved but you.
For you alone I ride the ring,
   For you I wear the blue;
For you alone I strive to sing,
   O tell me how to woo!
      Then tell me how to woo thee, Love;
        O tell me how to woo thee!
      For thy dear sake nae care I'll take
      Tho' ne'er another trow me.

JAMES BEATTIE

1735–1803

An Epitaph

Escaped the gloom of mortal life, a soul
   Here leaves its mouldering tenement of clay,
Safe—where no cares their whelming billows roll!
   No doubts bewilder, and no hopes betray.

Like thee, I once have stemm'd the sea of life;
   Like thee, have languish'd after empty joys;
Like thee, have labour'd in the stormy strife,
   Been grieved with trifles, and amused with toys.

Yet for a while, 'gainst passion's threatful blast,
   Let steady reason urge the struggling oar;
Shot through the dreary gloom, the morn, at last,
   Gives to thy longing eye the blissful shore.

Forget my frailties—thou art also frail;
Forgive my lapses, for thyself may'st fall;
Nor read unmoved my artless, tender tale—
I was a friend, oh man, to thee, to all!

MICHAEL BRUCE

1746–1767

To the Cuckoo

Hail, beauteous stranger of the grove!
   Thou messenger of Spring!
Now Heaven repairs thy rural seat,
   And woods thy welcome sing.

What time the daisy decks the green,
   Thy certain voice we hear:
Hast thou a star to guide thy path,
   Or mark the rolling year?

Delightful visitant, with thee
   I hail the time of flowers;
And hear the sound of music sweet
   From birds among the bowers.

The schoolboy, wandering through the wood,
   To pull the primrose gay,
Starts the new voice of Spring to hear,
   And imitates thy lay.

What time the pea puts on the bloom,
   Thou fliest thy vocal vale—
An annual guest, in other lands,
   Another Spring to hail.

Sweet bird! thy bower is ever green,
    Thy sky is ever clear;
Thou hast no sorrow in thy song.
    No winter in thy year!

Alas! sweet bird! not so my fate;
    Dark scowling skys I see
Fast gathering round, and fraught with woe
    And ninety years to me.

O could I fly, I'd fly with thee!
    We'd make, with joyful wing,
Our annual visit o'er the globe—
    Companions of the Spring.

From *Elegy: In Spring*

Now Spring returns: but not to me returns—
    The vernal joy my better years have known;
Dim in my breast life's dying taper burns,
    And all the joys of life with health are flown.

Starting and shivering in th' inconstant wind,
    Meagre and pale—the ghost of what I was,
Beneath some blasted tree I lie reclined,
    And count the silent moments as they pass—

The wingèd moments, whose unstaying speed
    No art can stop, or in their course arrest;—
Whose flight shall shortly count me with the dead,
    And lay me down in peace with them that rest.

Oft morning dreams presage approaching fate;—
    And morning dreams, as poets tell, are true:
Led by pale ghosts, I enter Death's dark gate,
    And bid the realms of light and life adieu.

I hear the helpless wail, the shriek of woe;
  I see the muddy wave, the dreary shore,
The sluggish streams that slowly creep below,
  Which mortals visit—and return no more.

Farewell, ye blooming fields! ye cheerful plains!
  Enough for me the churchyard's lonely mound,
Where Melancholy with still Silence reigns,
  And the rank grass waves o'er the cheerless ground.

There let me wander at the shut of eve,
  When Sleep sits dewy on the labourer's eyes,—
The world and all its busy follies leave,
  And talk with Wisdom where my Daphnis lies.

There let me sleep forgotten in the clay,
  When Death shall shut these weary aching eyes,—
Rest in the hopes of an eternal day,
  Till the long night is gone, and the last morn arise.

JOHN LOGAN

1748–1788

The Braes of Yarrow

Thy braes were bonny, Yarrow stream,
When first on them I met my lover;
Thy braes how dreary, Yarrow stream,
When now thy waves his body cover!
For ever now, O Yarrow stream!
Thou aar to me a stream of sorrow;
For never on thy banks shall I
Behold my love, the flower of Yarrow.

He promised me a milk-white steed,
To bear me to his father's bowers;
He promised me a little page,
To squire me to his father's towers;
He promised me a wedding-ring,—
The wedding-day was fix'd to-morrow:
Now he is wedded to his grave,
Alas! his watery grave in Yarrow.

Sweet were his words when last we met;
My passion I as freely told him:
Clasp'd in his arms, I little thought
That I should never more behold him!
Scarce was he gone, I saw his ghost;
It vanish'd with a shriek of sorrow:
Thrice did the water-wraith ascend,
And gave a doleful groan thro' Yarrow.

His mother from the window look'd,
With all the longing of a mother;
His little sister weeping walk'd
The greenwood path to meet her brother:
They sought him east, they sought him west,
They sought him all the Forest thorough;
They only saw the cloud of night,
They only heard the roar of Yarrow.

No longer from thy window look—
Thou hast no son, thou tender mother!
No longer walk, thou little maid;
Alas! thou hast no more a brother.
No longer seek him east or west,
And search no more the Forest thorough;
For, wandering in the night so dark,
He fell a lifeless corpse in Yarrow.

The tear shall never leave my cheek,
No other youth shall be my marrow—
I'll seek thy body in the stream,
And then with thee I'll sleep in Yarrow.
—The tear did never leave her cheek,
No other youth became her marrow;
She found his body in the stream,
And now with him she sleeps in Yarrow.

ROBERT FERGUSSON

1750–1774

The Daft Days

Now mirk December's dowie face
Glow'rs owre the rigs[1] wi' sour grimace,
While, thro' his *minimum* o' space
        The bleer-e'ed sun,
Wi' blinkin' light and stealin' pace,
        His race doth run.

Frae naked groves nae birdie sings;
To shepherd's pipe nae hillock rings;
The breeze nae od'rous flavour brings
        Frae Borean cave;
And dwynin' Nature droops her wings,
        Wi' visage grave.

Mankind but scanty pleasure glean
Frae snawy hill or barren plain,
Whan Winter, 'midst his nippin' train,
        Wi' frozen spear,
Sends drift owre a' his bleak domain,
        And guides the weir.[2]

[1] ridges in a ploughed field.   [2] war.

Auld Reikie! thou'rt the canty[1] hole;
A bield[2] for mony a cauldrife[3] soul,
Wha snugly at thine ingle loll,
> Baith warm and couth;[4]
While round they gar the bicker[5] roll,
> To weet their mouth.

Whan merry Yule-day comes, I trow,
You'll scantlins find a hungry mou;
Sma' are our cares, our stamacks fou
> O' gusty[6] gear,
And kickshaws, strangers to our view
> Sin' fairn-year.[7]

Ye browster wives! now busk ye braw,
And fling your sorrows far awa;
Then, come and gie's the tither blaw
> O' reaming[8] ale,
Mair precious than the Well o' Spa,
> Our hearts to heal.

Then, tho' at odds wi' a' the warl',
Amang oursels we'll never quarrel;
Tho' Discord gie a canker'd snarl,
> To spoil our glee,
As lang's there's pith into the barrel,
> We'll drink and gree.

Fiddlers! your pins in temper fix,
And roset[9] weel your fiddlesticks;
But banish vile Italian tricks
> Frae our your quorum;
Nor fortes wi' pianos mix;—
> Gie's Tullochgorum.

---

[1] cosy. [2] shelter. [3] chilly. [4] comfortable.
[5] wooden drinking vessel. [6] tasty. [7] yester-year.
[8] foaming. [9] resin.

For nought can cheer the heart sae weel,
As can a canty Highland reel;
It even vivifies the heel
    To skip and dance:
Lifeless is he wha canna feel
    Its influence.

Let mirth abound; let social cheer
Invest the dawnin' o' the year;
Let blithesome Innocence appear,
    To crown our joy:
Nor Envy, wi' sarcastic sneer,
    Our bliss destroy.

And thou, great god of *Aquavitæ!*
Wha sways the empire o' this city;—
Whan fou, we're sometimes capernoity;—[1]
    Be thou prepar'd
To hedge us frae that black banditti,
    The City Guard.

Braid Claith

Ye wha are fain to hae your name
Wrote i' the bonny book o' Fame,
Let merit nae pretension claim
    To laurell'd wreath,
But hap[2] ye weel, baith back and wame,[3]
    In gude Braid Claith.

He that some ells o' this may fa',[4]
And slae-black hat on pow like snaw,
Bids bauld to bear the gree[5] awa,
    Wi' a' this graith,[6]
Whan bienly[7] clad wi' shell fu' braw
    O' gude Braid Claith.

[1] muddled.   [2] cover.   [3] belly.   [4] obtain.   [5] prize.
[6] equipment.   [7] comfortably.

Waesuck[1] for him wha has nae feck[2] o't!
For he's a gowk[3] they're sure to geck[4] at,
A chiel that ne'er will be respeckit
    While he draws breath,
Till his four quarters are bedeckit
    Wi' gude Braid Claith.

On Sabbath-days the barber spark,
Whan he has done wi' scrapin' wark,
Wi' siller broachie[5] in his sark,[6]
    Gangs trigly,[7] faith!
Or to the Meadow, or the Park,
    In gude Braid Claith.

Weel might ye trow, to see them there,
That they to shave your haffits[8] bare,
Or curl and sleek a pickle[9] hair,
    Wad be right laith,
Whan pacing wi' a gawsy[10] air
    In gude Braid Claith.

If ony mettl'd stirrah[11] green[12]
For favour frae a lady's een,
He maunna care for being seen
    Before he sheath
His body in a scabbard clean
    O' gude Braid Claith.

For, gin he come wi' coat thread-bare,
A feg for him she winna care,
But crook her bonny mou' fu' sair,
    And scald[13] him baith.
Wooers should ay their travel spare
    Without Braid Claith.

[1] alas. [2] abundance. [3] fool. [4] mock. [5] brooch. [6] shirt.
[7] smartly. [8] sides of the head. [9] little. [10] consequential.
  [11] young fellow. [12] long. [13] scold.

Braid Claith lends fouk an unco heese,[1]
Maks mony kail-worms[2] butterflies,
Gives mony a doctor his degrees
    For little skaith:[3]
In short, you may be what you please
    Wi' gude Braid Claith.

For thof ye had as wise a snout on
As Shakespeare or Sir Isaac Newton,
Your judgment fouk wad hae a doubt on,
    I'll tak my aith,
Till they cou'd see ye wi' a suit on
    O' gude Braid Claith.

The Farmer's Ingle

Whan gloamin' grey out-owre the welkin keeks;
 Whan Batie ca's his owsen to the byre;
When Thrasher John, sair dung,[4] his barn-door
  steeks,[5]
 And lusty lasses at the dightin'[6] tire;
What bangs fu' leal the e'enings coming cauld,
 And gars snaw-tappit Winter freeze in vain;
Gars dowie mortals look baith blithe and bauld,
 Nor fley'd[7] wi' a' the poortith o' the plain;
 Begin, my Muse! and chant in hamely strain.

Frae the big stack, weel winnow't on the hill,
 Wi' divots theekit frae[8] the weet and drift;
Sods, peats, and heathery trufs the chimley fill,
 And gar their thickening smeek salute the lift.
The gudeman, new come hame, is blithe to find,
 Whan he out-owre the hallan[9] flings his een,

---

[1] folk a wonderful hoist.   [2] caterpillars.   [3] trouble.
[4] overcome (by fatigue).   [5] shuts.   [6] cleaning corn.   [7] affrighted.
[8] covered with sods as a protection against.   [9] partition.

That ilka turn is handled to his mind;
　　That a' his housie looks sae cosh and clean;
　　For cleanly house loes he, tho' e'er sae mean.

Weel kens the gudewife, that the pleughs require
　　A heartsome meltith,[1] and refreshin' synd[2]
O' nappy liquor,[3] owre a bleezin' fire:
　　Sair wark and poortith downa weel be join'd.
Wi' butter'd bannocks now the girdle reeks;
　　I' the far nook the bowie[4] briskly reams;
The readied kail stands by the chimley cheeks,
　　And haud the riggin's[5] het wi' welcome streams,
　　Whilk than the daintiest kitchen[6] nicer seems.

Frae this, lat gentler gabs a lesson lear:
　　Wad they to labouring lend an eident[7] hand,
They'd rax[8] fell strang upo' the simplest fare,
　　Nor find their stamacks ever at a stand.
Fu' hale and healthy wad they pass the day;
　　At night, in calmest slumbers dose fu' sound;
Nor doctor need their weary life to spae,
　　Nor drogs their noddle and their sense confound,
　　Till death slip sleely on, and gie the hindmost
　　wound.

On sicken[9] food has mony a doughty deed
　　By Caledonia's ancestors been done;
By this did mony a wight fu' weirlike bleed
　　In brulzies[10] frae the dawn to set o' sun.
'Twas this that braced their gardies[11] stiff and strang;
　　That bent the deadly yew in ancient days;
Laid Denmark's daring sons on yird[12] alang;
　　Gar'd Scottish thristles bang the Roman bays;
　　For near our crest their heads they doughtna raise.

---

[1] meal.　[2] draught.　[3] ale.　[4] ale cask.　[5] rafters.　[6] relish.
[7] earnest.　[8] grew.　[9] such.　[10] broil, brattle.　[11] arms.　[12] earth.

The couthy cracks[1] begin whan supper's owre;
   The cheering bicker gars them glibly gash[2]
O' Simmer's showery blinks, and Winter sour,
   Whase floods did erst their mailin's[3] produce hash.
'Bout kirk and market eke their tales gae on;
   How Jock woo'd Jenny here to be his bride;
And there, how Marion, for a bastard son,
   Upo' the cutty-stool[4] was force to ride;
   The waefu' scauld[5] o' our Mess John[6] to bide.

The fient[7] a cheep's amang the bairnies now;
   For a' their anger 's wi' their hunger gane:
Ay maun the childer, wi' a fastin mou',
   Grumble and greet, and mak an unco mane.
In rangles[8] round, before the ingle's lowe,[9]
   Frae Gudame's mouth auld-warld tales they hear,
O' warlocks loupin round the wirrikow:[10]
   O' ghaists that win[11] in glen and kirkyard drear,
   Whilk touzles a' their tap,[12] and gars them shake
     wi' fear!

For weel she trows that fiends and fairies be
   Sent frae the deil to fleetch[13] us to our ill;
That kye hae tint their milk wi' evil ee;
   And corn been scowder'd[14] on the glowin kill.
O mock na this, my friends! but rather mourn,
   Ye in life's brawest spring wi' reason clear;
Wi' eild our idle fancies a' return,
   And dim our dolefu' days wi' bairnly fear;
   The mind 's ay cradled whan the grave is near.

[1] chats. [2] talk. [3] farm. [4] stool of repentance. [5] scolding.
[6] parson. [7] devil. [8] crowds. [9] glow. [10] hobgoblin. [11] dwell.
[12] makes their hair stand on end. [13] deceive. [14] burned.

Yet thrift, industrious, bides her latest days,
    Tho' age her sair-dow'd[1] front wi' runcles wave;
Yet frae the russet lap the spindle plays;
    Her e'enin stent[2] reels she as weel's the lave.
On some feast-day, the wee things, buskit braw,
    Shall heeze[3] her heart up wi' a silent joy,
Fu' cadgie[4] that her head was up, and saw
    Her ain spun cleedin on a darlin oy;[5]
    Careless tho' death shou'd mak the feast her foy.[6]

In its auld lerroch[7] yet the deas[8] remains,
    Whare the gudeman aft streeks[9] him at his ease;
A warm and canny lean for weary banes
    O' lab'rers doil'd[10] upon the wintry leas.
Round him will baudrins[11] and the collie come,
    To wag their tail, and cast a thankfu' ee
To him wha kindly flings them mony a crum
    O' kebbuck whang'd,[12] and dainty fadge[13] to prie;
    This a' the boon they crave, and a' the fee.

Frae him the lads their mornin' counsel tak;
    What stacks he wants to thrash; what rigs to till;
How big a birn[14] maun lie on Bassie's back,
    For meal and mu'ter[15] to the thirlin mill.[16]
Neist, the gudewife her hirelin damsels bids
    Glow'r thro' the byre, and see the hawkies[17] bound;
Tak tent, 'case Crummy tak her wonted tids,[18]
    And ca' the laiglen's[19] treasure on the ground,
    Whilk spills a kebbuck nice, or yellow pound.

---

[1] faded.   [2] quantity of work.   [3] lift.   [4] proud.   [5] grandchild.
[6] farewell to life.   [7] place.   [8] couch.   [9] stretches.
[10] tired.   [11] cat.   [12] cheese cut.   [13] bread.   [14] burden.
        [15] portion of meal retained by miller as his fee.
[16] mill to which farmer is thirled or bound.   [17] cows.
            [18] whims.   [19] milk-pail.

Then a' the house for sleep begin to grien,[1]
   Their joints to slack frae industry a-while;
The leaden god fa's heavy on their een,
   And hafflins steeks them frae their daily toil;
The cruizie[2] too can only blink and bleer;
   The restit ingle's[3] done the maist it dow;
Tacksman and cotter eke to bed maun steer,
   Upo' the cod[4] to clear their drumly[5] pow,
   Till wauken'd by the dawnin's ruddy glow.

Peace to the husbandman and a' his tribe,
   Whase care fells a' our wants frae year to year!
Lang may his sock[6] and cou'ter[7] turn the glybe,[8]
   And bauks o' corn bend down wi' laded ear!
May Scotia's simmers ay look gay and green;
   Her yellow har'sts frae scowry blasts decreed!
May a' her tenants sit fu' snug and bien,
   Frae the hard grip o' ails, and poortith freed;
   And a lang lasting train o' peacefu' hours succeed!

The Lee Rigg

Will ye gang o'er the lee-rigg,[9]
   My ain kind deary O!
And cuddle there sae kindly
   Wi' me, my kind deary O?

At thornie-dike[10] and birken tree[11]
   We'll daff,[12] and ne'er be weary O:
They'll scug ill een[13] frae you and me,
   Mine ain kind deary O.

---

[1] long.   [2] primitive oil lamp.   [3] stirred up fire.   [4] pillow.
[5] dull.   [6] ploughshare.   [7] coulter.   [8] glebe.   [9] grass field.
[10] hawthorn hedge.   [11] birch tree.   [12] dally.   [13] screen hostile eyes.

Nae herds wi' kent or colly[1] there,
  Shall ever come to fear ye O;
But lav'rocks, whistling in the air,
  Shall woo, like me, their deary O!

While others herd their lambs and ewes,
  And toil for warld's gear, my jo,
Upon the lee my pleasure grows,
  Wi' you, my kind deary O!

LADY ANNE LINDSAY

1750–1825

Auld Robin Gray

When the sheep are in the fauld, and the kye at
  hame,
And a' the warld to rest are gane,
The waes o' my heart fa' in showers frae my e'e,
While my gudeman lies sound by me.

Young Jamie lo'ed me weel, and sought me for his
  bride;
But saving a croun he had naething else beside:
To make the croun a pund, young Jamie gaed to sea;
And the croun and the pund were baith for me.

He hadna been awa' a week but only twa,
When my father brak his arm, and the cow was
  stown awa';
My mother she fell sick,—and my Jamie at the sea—
And auld Robin Gray came-a-courtin' me.

---

[1] shepherd's stick or dog.

My father couldna work, and my mother couldna
    spin;
I toil'd day and night, but their bread I couldna
    win;
Auld Rob maintain'd them baith, and wi' tears in
    his e'e
Said, 'Jennie, for their sakes, O, marry me!'

My heart it said nay; I look'd for Jamie back;
But the wind it blew high, and the ship it was a
    wrack;
His ship it was a wrack—Why didna Jamie dee?
Or why do I live to cry, Wae's me!

My father urged me sair: my mother didna speak;
But she look'd in my face till my heart was like to
    break:
They gi'ed him my hand, tho' my heart was in the
    sea;
Sae auld Robin Gray he was gudeman to me.

I hadna been a wife a week but only four,
When mournfu' as I sat on the stane at the door,
I saw my Jamie's wraith,—for I couldna think it he,
Till he said, 'I'm come hame to marry thee.'

O sair, sair did we greet, and muckle did we say;
We took but ae kiss, and we tore ourselves away:
I wish that I were dead, but I'm no like to dee;
And why was I born to say, Wae's me!

I gang like a ghaist, and I carena to spin;
I daurna think on Jamie, for that wad be a sin;
But I'll do my best a gude wife aye to be,
For auld Robin Gray he is kind unto me.

ROBERT BURNS

1759–1796

Robin

There was a lad was born in Kyle,
But whatna day o' whatna style,
I doubt it's hardly worth the while
   To be sae nice wi' Robin.

   Robin was a rovin' boy,
      Rantin rovin', rantin rovin';
   Robin was a rovin' boy,
      Rantin rovin' Robin!

Our monarch's hindmost year but ane
Was five and twenty days begun,
'Twas then a blast o' Janwar win'
   Blew hansel in on Robin.

The gossip keekit in his loof,[1]
Quo' she, wha lives will see the proof,
This waly[2] boy will be nae coof—[3]
   I think we'll ca' him Robin.

He'll hae misfortunes great and sma',
But aye a heart aboon them a';
He'll be a credit till us a',
   We'll a' be proud o' Robin.

But sure as three times three mak nine,
I see, by ilka score and line,
This chap will dearly like our kin',
   So leeze me on[4] thee, Robin.

---

[1] peeped in his palm.   [2] big, fine.   [3] ninny.   [4] commend me to.

Guid faith, quo' she, I doubt ye gar
The bonnie lasses lie aspar,
But twenty fauts ye may hae waur,
    So blessin's on thee, Robin.

    Robin was a rovin' boy,
        Rantin rovin', rantin rovin';
    Robin was a rovin' boy,
        Rantin rovin' Robin!

Epistle to William Simpson, Ochiltree

May 1785.

I gat your letter, winsome Willie;
Wi' gratefu' heart I thank you brawlie;
Tho' I maun say't, I wad be silly,
        And unco vain,
Should I believe, my coaxin' billie,[1]
        Your flatterin' strain.

But I'se believe ye kindly meant it,
I sud be laith to think ye hinted
Ironic satire, sidelins sklented[2]
        On my poor Musie;
Tho' in sic phraisin'[3] terms ye've penn'd it,
        I scarce excuse ye.

My senses wad be in a creel,
Should I but dare a hope to speel,
Wi' Allan,[4] or wi' Gilbertfield,[5]
        The braes o' fame;
Or Fergusson, the writer chiel,[6]
        A deathless name.

[1] fellow.   [2] turned sidelong.   [3] flattering.   [4] Ramsay.
    [5] Hamilton of Gilbertfield.   [6] lawyer-fellow.

(O Fergusson! thy glorious parts
Ill suited law's dry, musty arts!
My curse upon your whunstane hearts,
    Ye E'nbrugh gentry!
The tythe o' what ye waste at cartes[1]
    Wad stow'd[2] his pantry!)

Yet when a tale comes i' my head,
Or lasses gie my heart a screed,[3]
As whiles they're like to be my dead[4]
    (O sad disease!)
I kittle[5] up my rustic reed;
    It gies me ease.

Auld Coila,[6] now, may fidge fu' fain,[7]
She's gotten poets o' her ain,
Chiels wha their chanters winna hain,[8]
    But tune their lays,
Till echoes a' resound again
    Her weel-sung praise.

Nae poet thought her worth his while,
To set her name in measur'd style;
She lay like some unkenned-of isle
    Beside New Holland,
Or whare wild-meeting oceans boil
    Besouth Magellan.

Ramsay an' famous Fergusson
Gied Forth an' Tay a lift aboon;
Yarrow an' Tweed, to mony a tune,
    Owre Scotland rings,
While Irwin, Lugar, Ayr, an' Doon,
    Naebody sings.

---

[1] cards. [2] would have stored. [3] tear, rent. [4] death.
[5] tickle. [6] Kyle, district in Ayrshire. [7] tingle with delight.
[8] will not spare their pipes.

Th' Illissus, Tiber, Thames, an' Seine,
Glide sweet in mony a tunefu' line!
But, Willie, set your fit to mine,
    An' cock your crest!
We'll gar our streams and burnies shine
    Up wi' the best.

We'll sing Auld Coila's plains an' fells,
Her moors red-brown wi' heather bells,
Her banks an' braes, her dens an' dells,
    Where glorious Wallace
Aft bare the gree,[1] as story tells,
    Frae Southron billies.

At Wallace' name, what Scottish blood
But boils up in a spring-tide flood!
Oft have our fearless fathers strode
    By Wallace' side,
Still pressing onward, red-wat shod,
    Or glorious died.

O, sweet are Coila's haughs[2] an' woods,
When lintwhites[3] chant amang the buds,
And jinkin[4] hares, in amorous whids,[5]
    Their loves enjoy,
While thro' the braes the cushat croods
    With wailfu' cry!

Ev'n winter bleak has charms to me
When winds rave thro' the naked tree;
Or frosts on hills of Ochiltree
    Are hoary gray:
Or blinding drifts wild-furious flee,
    Dark'ning the day!

[1] prize. [2] hollows. [3] linnets. [4] dodging. [5] gambols.

O Nature! a' thy shews an' forms,
To feeling, pensive hearts hae charms!
Whether the summer kindly warms,
                    Wi' life an' light,
Or winter howls, in gusty storms,
                    The lang, dark night!

The Muse, nae poet ever fand her,
Till by himsel he learn'd to wander
Adown some trotting burn's meander,
                    An' no think lang;
O sweet to stray an' pensive ponder
                    A heart-felt sang!

The war'ly race may drudge an' drive
Hog-shouther,[1] jundie,[2] stretch, an' strive—
Let me fair Nature's face descrive,
                    And I, wi' pleasure,
Shall let the busy, grumbling hive
                    Bum owre their treasure.

Fareweel, my rhyme-composing brither!
We've been owre lang unkenn'd to ither:
Now let us lay our heads thegither,
                    In love fraternal;
May Envy wallop in a tether,[3]
                    Black fiend, infernal!

While Highlandmen hate tolls an' taxes;
While moorlan' herds like guid fat braxies,[4]
While terra firma on her axis
                    Diurnal turns,
Count on a friend, in faith an' practice,
                    In ROBERT BURNS.

[1] push.   [2] elbow.   [3] dangle in a rope.
[4] sheep that have died of disease.

Holy Willie's Prayer

'And send the godly in a pet to pray'

POPE

O Thou, that in the heavens does dwell,
Wha, as it pleases best Thysel',
Sends ane to heaven an' ten to hell,
      A' for thy glory,
And no for onie guid or ill
      They've done afore Thee!

I bless and praise Thy matchless might,
When thousands Thou hast left in night
That I am here afore Thy sight,
      For gifts an' grace
A burning and a shining light
      To a' this place.

What was I, or my generation,
That I should get sic exaltation,
I wha deserv'd most just damnation
      For broken laws,
Sax thousand years ere my creation,
      Thro' Adam's cause.

When from my mither's womb I fell,
Thou might hae plung'd me deep in hell,
To gnash my gooms, and weep and wail,
      In burnin' lakes,
Where damnèd devils roar and yell
      Chain'd to their stakes.

Yet I am here a chosen sample,
To show thy grace is great and ample;
I'm here a pillar o' Thy temple,
      Strong as a rock,
A guide, a buckler, and example,
      To a' Thy flock.

O Lord, Thou kens what zeal I bear,
When drinkers drink, an' swearers swear,
An' singing here, an' dancin' there,
   Wi' great and sma';
For I am keepit by Thy fear
   Free frae them a'.

But yet, O Lord! confess I must
At time I'm fash'd wi' fleshly lust:
An' sometimes, too, in warldly trust,
   Vile self gets in;
But Thou remembers we are dust,
   Defil'd wi' sin.

O Lord! yestreen, Thou kens, wi' Meg—
Thy pardon I sincerely beg;
O! may't ne'er be a livin plague
   To my dishonour,
An' I'll ne'er lift a lawless leg
   Again upon her.

Besides, I farther maun allow,
Wi' Leezie's lass, three times I trow—
But Lord, that Friday I was fou,
   When I cam near her;
Or else, Thou kens, Thy servant true
   Wad never steer her.

Maybe Thou lets this fleshly thorn
Buffet Thy servant e'en and morn,
Lest he owre proud and high shou'd turn,
   That he's sae gifted:
If sae, Thy han' maun e'en be borne,
   Until Thou lift it.

Lord, bless Thy chosen in this place,
For here Thou has a chosen race:
But God confound their stubborn face,
  An' blast their name,
Wha bring Thy elders to disgrace
  An' public shame.

Lord, mind Gaw'n Hamilton's deserts;
He drinks, an' swears, an' plays at cartes,
Yet has sae mony takin arts,
  Wi' great and sma',
Frae God's ain priest the people's hearts
  He steals awa.

An' when we chasten'd him therefor,
Thou kens how he bred sic a splore,
An' set the warld in a roar
  O' laughing at us;—
Curse Thou his basket and his store,
  Kail an' potatoes.

Lord, hear my earnest cry and pray'r,
Against that Presbyt'ry o' Ayr;
Thy strong right hand, Lord, make it bare
  Upo' their heads;
Lord, visit them, an' dinna spare,
  For their misdeeds.

O Lord, my God! that glib-tongu'd Aiken,
My vera heart and flesh are quakin',
To think how we stood sweatin, shakin,
  An' p—'d wi' dread,
While he, wi' hingin lip an' snakin,
  Held up his head.

Lord, in Thy day o' vengeance try him,
Lord, visit them wha did employ him,
And pass not in Thy mercy by them,
            Nor hear their pray'r,
But for thy people's sake destroy them,
            An' dinna spare.

But Lord, remember me an' mine
Wi' mercies temporal and divine,
That I for grace an' gear may shine,
            Excell'd by nane,
And a' the glory shall be thine,
            Amen, Amen!

Whistle o'er the lave o't

First when Maggy was my care,
Heaven, I thought, was in her air;
Now we're married—spier[1] nae mair—
            Whistle o'er the lave o't.—[2]
Meg was meek, and Meg was mild,
Bonnie Meg was Nature's child;
Wiser men than me's beguil'd—
            Whistle o'er the lave o't.

How we live, my Meg and me,
How we love, and how we 'gree,
I care na by how few may see;
            Whistle o'er the lave o't.—
Wha I wish were maggots' meat,
Dish'd up in her winding sheet,
I could write—but Meg wad see't—
            Whistle o'er the lave o't.

[1] ask.   [2] rest of it.

Macpherson's Farewell

Farewell, ye dungeons dark and strong,
   The wretch's destinie!
Macpherson's time will not be long
   On yonder gallows-tree.

     Sae rantingly, sae wantonly,
      Sae dauntingly gaed he;
     He play'd a spring,[1] and danc'd it round,
      Below the gallows-tree.

Oh! what is death but parting breath?—
   On mony a bloody plain
I've dar'd his face, and in this place
   I scorn him yet again!

Untie these bands from off my hands,
   And bring to me my sword!
And there's no a man in all Scotland
   But I'll brave him at a word.

I've liv'd a life of sturt[2] and strife;
   I die by treacherie:
It burns my heart I must depart,
   And not avengèd be.

Now farewell light—thou sunshine bright,
   And all beneath the sky!
May coward shame distain his name,
   The wretch that dares not die!

---

[1] dance-tune.   [2] trouble.

From *The Jolly Beggars*

See the smoking bowl before us!
　Mark our jovial ragged ring!
Round and round take up the chorus,
　And in raptures let us sing.

Chorus

　A fig those by law protected!
　　Liberty's a glorious feast!
　Courts for cowards were erected,
　　Churches built to please the priest.

What is title? what is treasure?
　What is reputation's care?
If we lead a life of pleasure,
　'Tis no matter how or where!
　　A fig, etc.

With the ready trick and fable,
　Round we wander all the day;
And at night, in barn or stable,
　Hug our doxies on the hay.
　　A fig, etc.

Does the train-attended carriage
　Thro' the country lighter rove?
Does the sober bed of marriage
　Witness brighter scenes of love?
　　A fig, etc.

Life is all a variorum,
　We regard not how it goes;
Let them cant about decorum
　Who have characters to lose.
　　A fig, etc.

Here's to budgets, bags, and wallets!
Here's to all the wandering train!
Here's our ragged brats and callets![1]
One and all cry out—Amen!

Chorus

A fig for those by law protected!
Liberty's a glorious feast!
Courts for cowards were erected,
    Churches built to please the priest.

From *The Vision*

The sun had clos'd the winter day,
The curlers quat their roaring play,
An' hunger'd maukin[2] ta'en her way
    To kail-yards green,
While faithless snaws ilk step betray
    Whare she has been.

The thresher's weary flingin'-tree[3]
The lee-lang day had tirèd me;
And when the day had clos'd his e'e,
    Far i' the west,
Ben i' the spence,[4] right pensivelie,
    I gaed to rest.

There, lanely, by the ingle-cheek,[5]
I sat and e'ed the spewing reek,[6]
That fill'd, wi' hoast-provoking[7] smeek,[8]
    The auld clay biggin;[9]
And heard the restless rattons[10] squeak
    About the riggin.[11]

---

[1] wenches. [2] hare. [3] flail. [4] within, in the parlour. [5] fireside.
[6] volleying smoke. [7] cough-provoking. [8] drift. [9] building.
[10] rats. [11] roof-tree.

All in this mottie,[1] misty clime,
I backward mus'd on wasted time,
How I had spent my youthfu' prime,
    And done naething,
But stringin' blethers up in rhyme,
    For fools to sing.

Had I to guid advice but harkit,
I might, by this, hae led a market,
Or strutted in a bank an' clerkit
    My cash account:
While here, half-mad, half-fed, half-sarkit,
    Is a' th' amount.

         (Stanzas 1–5.)

From *A Winter Night*

When biting Boreas, fell and doure,[2]
Sharp shivers thro' the leafless bow'r;
When Phœbus gies a short-liv'd glow'r[3]
    Far south the lift,[4]
Dim-dark'ning through the flaky show'r,
    Or whirling drift:

Ae night the storm the steeples rocked,
Poor labour sweet in sleep was locked,
While burns, wi' snawy wreaths up-choked,
    Wild-eddying swirl,
Or thro' the mining outlet bocked,[5]
    Down headlong hurl.

List'ning the doors an' winnocks rattle,
I thought me on the ourie[6] cattle,

---

[1] dusty.   [2] hard.   [3] stare.   [4] sky.   [5] vomited.   [6] shivering.

Or silly sheep, wha bide this brattle[1]
    O' winter war,
And thro' the drift, deep-lairing sprattle,[2]
    Beneath a scaur.[3]

Ilk happing bird, wee, helpless thing!
That, in the merry months o' spring,
Delighted me to hear thee sing,
    What comes o' thee?
Whare wilt thou cow'r thy chittering wing,
    An' close thy e'e?

Ev'n you, on murd'ring errands toil'd,
Lone from your savage homes exil'd,
The blood-stain'd roost, and sheep-cote spoil'd
    My heart forgets,
While pitiless the tempest wild
    Sore on you beats.

       (Stanzas 1–5.)

To a Mouse

On turning her up in her nest with the plough,
November 1785

Wee, sleekit, cow'rin', tim'rous beastie,
Oh, what a panic's in thy breastie!
Thou need na start awa sae hasty,
    Wi' bickering brattle![4]
I wad be laith[5] to rin an' chase thee,
    Wi' murd'ring pattle![6]

---

[1] noisy onset. [2] scramble. [3] cliff. [4] hurrying scamper.
    [5] loth.   [6] plough-staff.

I'm truly sorry man's dominion
Has broken nature's social union,
An' justifies that ill opinion
    Which makes thee startle
At me, thy poor earth-born companion,
    An' fellow-mortal!

I doubt na, whyles, but thou may thieve;
What then? poor beastie, thou maun live!
A daimen icker[1] in a thrave[2]
    'S a sma' request:
I'll get a blessin' wi' the lave,[3]
    And never miss't!

Thy wee bit housie, too, in ruin!
Its silly wa's the win's are strewin'!
An' naething, now, to big[4] a new ane,
    O' foggage[5] green!
An' bleak December's winds ensuin',
    Baith snell[6] and keen!

Thou saw the fields laid bare an' waste,
An' weary winter comin' fast,
An' cozie here, beneath the blast,
    Thou thought to dwell,
'Till crash! the cruel coulter past
    Out thro' thy cell.

That wee bit heap o' leaves an' stibble
Has cost thee mony a weary nibble!
Now thou's turn'd out, for a' thy trouble,
    But[7] house or hald,
To thole the winter's sleety dribble,
    An' cranreuch[8] cauld!

---

[1] odd ear. [2] twenty-four sheaves. [3] remainder. [4] build.
[5] coarse grass. [6] bitter. [7] without. [8] hoar-frost.

But, Mousie, thou art no thy lane,
In proving foresight may be vain:
The best-laid schemes o' mice an' men,
        Gang aft agley,[1]
An' lea'e us nought but grief and pain
        For promis'd joy!

Still thou art blest, compar'd wi' me!
The present only toucheth thee:
But, och! I backward cast my ee,
        On prospects drear!
An' forward, tho' I canna see,
        I guess an' fear!

Epistle to James Smith

Dear Smith, the slee'st, paukie thief,
That e'er attempted stealth or rief,[2]
Ye surely hae some warlock-breef[3]
        Owre human hearts;
For ne'er a bosom yet was prief
        Against your arts.

For me, I swear by sun an' moon,
And ev'ry star that blinks aboon,
Ye've cost me twenty pair of shoon
        Just gaun to see you;
And ev'ry ither pair that's done,
        Mair ta'en I'm wi' you.

That auld capricious carlin, Nature,
To mak amends for scrimpit[4] stature,
She's turn'd you aff, a human creature
        On her first plan;
And in her freaks, on every feature
        She's wrote, 'The Man'.

[1] askew.   [2] robbery or plunder.   [3] wizard-spell.   [4] stunted.

Just now I've ta'en the fit o' rhyme,
My barmie noddle 's¹ working prime,
My fancy yerkit up sublime
    Wi' hasty summon:
Hae ye a leisure moment's time
    To hear what's comin'?

Some rhyme a neibor's name to lash;
Some rhyme (vain thought!) for needfu' cash;
Some rhyme to court the countra clash,²
    An' raise a din;
For me, an aim I never fash;³
    I rhyme for fun.

The star that rules my luckless lot,
Has fated me the russet coat,
An' damn'd my fortune to the groat;
    But in requit,
Has blest me wi' a random shot
    O' countra wit.

This while my notion's ta'en a sklent,⁴
To try my fate in guid, black prent;
But still, the mair I'm that way bent,
    Something cries 'Hoolie!⁵
I rede you, honest man, tak tent!⁶
    Ye'll shaw your folly.

'There's ither poets much your betters,
Far seen in Greek, deep men o' letters,
Hae thought they had ensur'd their debtors,
    A' future ages;
Now months deform in shapeless tatters
    Their unknown pages.'

---

¹ seething brain. ² gossip. ³ bother. ⁴ turn. ⁵ softly. ⁶ heed.

Then fareweel hopes o' laurel-boughs,
To garland my poetic brows!
Henceforth I'll rove where busy ploughs
   Are whistling thrang,[1]
An' teach the lanely heights an' howes[2]
   My rustic sang.

I'll wander on, wi' tentless[3] heed
How never-halting moments speed,
Till fate shall snap the brittle thread;
   Then, all unknown,
I'll lay me with th' inglorious dead,
   Forgot and gone!

But why o' death begin a tale?
Just now we're living sound and hale,
Then top and maintop crowd the sail,
   Heave Care o'er side!
And large, before Enjoyment's gale,
   Let's tak the tide.

This life, sae far's I understand,
Is a' enchanted fairy-land,
Where Pleasure is the magic wand,
   That, wielded right,
Maks hours like minutes, hand in hand,
   Dance by fu' light.

The magic wand then let us wield;
For, ance that five-and-forty's speel'd,[4]
See crazy, weary, joyless Eild,[5]
   Wi' wrinkled face,
Comes hoastin',[6] hirplin',[7] owre the field,
   Wi' creepin' pace.

---

[1] crowded on all sides.   [2] hollows.   [3] careless.   [4] climbed.
   [5] Age.   [6] coughing.   [7] limping.

When ance life's day draws near the gloamin',
Then fareweel vacant careless roamin';
An' fareweel cheerfu' tankards foamin',
        An' social noise;
An' fareweel, dear deluding Woman!
        The joy of joys!

O Life! how pleasant is thy morning,
Young Fancy's rays the hills adorning!
Cold-pausing Caution's lesson scorning,
        We frisk away,
Like school-boys, at th' expected warning,
        To joy an' play.

We wander there, we wander here,
We eye the rose upon the brier,
Unmindful that the thorn is near,
        Among the leaves;
And tho' the puny wound appear,
        Short while it grieves.

Some, lucky, find a flow'ry spot,
For which they never toil'd nor swat;
They drink the sweet and eat the fat,
        But[1] care or pain;
And, haply, eye the barren hut
        With high disdain.

With steady aim some Fortune chase;
Keen Hope does ev'ry sinew brace;
Thro' fair, thro' foul, they urge the race,
        And seize the prey:
Then cannie,[2] in some cozie place,
        They close the day.

---

[1] without.   [2] quietly.

And others, like your humble servan',
Poor wights! nae rules nor roads observin';
To right or left, eternal swervin',
         They zigzag on;
Till curst with age, obscure an' starvin',
         They aften groan.

Alas! what bitter toil an' straining—
But truce with peevish, poor complaining!
Is fortune's fickle Luna waning?
         E'en let her gang!
Beneath what light she has remaining,
         Let 's sing our sang.

My pen I here fling to the door,
And kneel, ye Pow'rs! and warm implore,
'Tho' I should wander terra o'er,
         In all her climes,
Grant me but this, I ask no more,
         Ay rowth[1] o' rhymes.

'Gie dreeping[2] roasts to countra lairds.
Till icicles hing frae their beards;
Gie fine braw claes to fine life-guards,
         And maids of honour!
And yill[3] an' whiskey gie to cairds,[4]
         Until they sconner.[5]

'A title, Dempster merits it;
A garter gie to Willie Pitt;
Gie wealth to some be-ledger'd cit,
         In cent. per cent.,
But gie me real, sterling wit,
         And I'm content.

[1] abundance.   [2] dripping.   [3] ale.   [4] tinkers.   [5] grow squeamish.

'While ye are pleas'd to keep me hale,
I'll sit down o'er my scanty meal,
Be't water-brose, or muslin-kail,[1]
        Wi' cheerfu' face,
As lang's the Muses dinna fail
        To say the grace.'

An anxious e'e I never throws
Behint my lug,[2] or by my nose;
I jouk[3] beneath Misfortune's blows
        As weel's I may;
Sworn foe to sorrow, care, and prose,
        I rhyme away.

O ye douce folk, that live by rule,
Grave, tideless-blooded, calm an' cool,
Compar'd wi' you—O fool! fool! fool!
        How much unlike!
Your hearts are just a standing pool,
        Your lives a dyke!

Nae hair-brain'd, sentimental traces,
In your unletter'd, nameless faces!
In arioso trills and graces
        Ye never stray,
But, gravissimo, solemn basses
        Ye hum away.

Ye are sae grave, nae doubt ye're wise;
Nae ferly[4] tho' ye do despise
The hairum-scairum, ram-stam boys,
        The rattling squad:
I see you upward cast your eyes—
        Ye ken the road.

---

[1] broth made without meat.   [2] ear.   [3] duck.   [4] wonder.

Whilst I—but I shall haud me there—
Wi' you I'll scarce gang onywhere:
Then, Jamie, I shall say nae mair,
                    But quit my sang,
Content wi' you to mak a pair,
                    Whare'er I gang.

Tam o' Shanter

When chapman billies[1] leave the street,
And drouthy[2] neebors neebors meet;
As market-days are wearin late,
An' folk begin to tak the gate;[3]
While we sit sousing at the nappy,[4]
An' gettin' fou[5] and unco[6] happy,
We think na on the lang Scots miles,
The mosses,[7] waters, slaps,[8] and styles,
That lie between us and our hame,
Whare sits our sulky, sullen dame,
Gathering her brows like gathering storm,
Nursing her wrath to keep it warm.

This truth fand honest Tam o' Shanter,
As he frae Ayr ae night did canter
(Auld Ayr, wham ne'er a town surpasses,
For honest men an' bonny lasses).

O Tam! hadst thou but been sae wise,
As ta'en thy ain wife Kate's advice!
She tauld thee weel thou wast a skellum,[9]
A bletherin',[10] blusterin', drunken blellum;[11]
That frae November till October,
Ae market-day thou was na sober;
That ilka melder,[12] wi' the miller,

---

[1] pedlar fellows.   [2] thirsty.   [3] road.   [4] ale.   [5] drunk.
[6] wonderfully.   [7] bogs.   [8] breaches.   [9] worthless fellow.
[10] chattering.   [11] idle fellow.   [12] meal-grinding.

Thou sat as lang as thou had siller;[1]
That ev'ry naig was ca'd[2] a shoe on,
The smith and thee gat roarin' fou on;
That at the Lord's house, ev'n on Sunday,
Thou drank wi' Kirkton Jean till Monday.
She prophesy'd that, late or soon,
Thou wad be found, deep drown'd in Doon!
Or catch'd wi' warlocks in the mirk,
By Alloway's auld, haunted kirk.
Ah, gentle dames! it gars me greet
To think how mony counsels sweet,
How mony lengthen'd, sage advices,
The husband frae the wife despises!

But to our tale:—Ae market night,
Tam had got planted unco right;
Fast by an ingle, bleezing finely,
Wi' reaming swats,[3] that drank divinely;
An' at his elbow, Souter Johnie,
His ancient, trusty, drouthy crony;
Tam lo'ed him like a vera brither;
They had been fou for weeks thegither!
The night drave on wi' sangs an' clatter;
An' aye the ale was growing better:
The landlady and Tam grew gracious,
Wi' favours secret, sweet, and precious;
The Souter tauld his queerest stories;
The landlord's laugh was ready chorus:
The storm without might rair and rustle—
Tam didna mind the storm a whistle.

Care, mad to see a man sae happy,
E'en drown'd himsel amang the nappy!
As bees flee hame wi' lades o' treasure,
The minutes wing'd their way wi' pleasure:

---

[1] money.   [2] put.   [3] foaming new ale.

Kings may be blest, but Tam was glorious,
O'er a' the ills o' life victorious!

But pleasures are like poppies spread,
You seize the flow'r, its bloom is shed!
Or like the snowfall in the river,
A moment white—then melts for ever;
Or like the borealis race,
That flit ere you can point their place;
Or like the rainbow's lovely form,
Evanishing amid the storm.—
Nae man can tether time or tide;
The hour approaches Tam maun ride;
That hour, o' night's black arch the keystane,
That dreary hour he mounts his beast in;
An' sic a night he taks the road in,
As ne'er poor sinner was abroad in.

The wind blew as 'twad blawn its last;
The rattling show'rs rose on the blast;
The speedy gleams the darkness swallow'd;
Loud, deep, and lang, the thunder bellow'd:
That night, a child might understand,
The Deil had business on his hand.

Weel mounted on his grey mare, Meg—
A better never lifted leg—
Tam skelpit on thro' dub[1] an' mire,
Despising wind, an' rain, an' fire;
Whiles holding fast his guid blue bonnet;
Whiles crooning o'er some auld Scots sonnet;
Whiles glow'ring round wi' prudent cares,
Lest bogles catch him unawares;
Kirk-Alloway was drawing nigh,
Where ghaists an' houlets nightly cry.

[1] puddle.

By this time he was cross the foord,
Whare in the snaw the chapman smoor'd;[1]
An' past the birks and meikle stane,
Whare drunken Charlie brak's neck-bane;
An' thro' the whins, an' by the cairn,
Whare hunters fand the murder'd bairn;
An' near the thorn, aboon the well,
Whare Mungo's mither hang'd hersel.
Before him Doon pours a' his floods;
The doublin' storm roars thro' the woods;
The lightnings flash frae pole to pole;
Near and more near the thunders roll;
When, glimmerin' thro' the groanin trees,
Kirk-Alloway seem'd in a bleeze;
Thro' ilka bore[2] the beams were glancin';
An' loud resounded mirth and dancin'.

Inspirin' bold John Barleycorn!
What dangers thou canst mak us scorn!
Wi' tippenny,[3] we fear nae evil;
Wi' usquabae[4] we'll face the Devil!
That swats sae ream'd in Tammie's noddle,
Fair play, he car'd na deils a boddle.
But Maggie stood, right sair astonish'd,
'Till, by the heel an' hand admonish'd,
She ventur'd forward on the light;
An', wow! Tam saw an unco sight!
Warlocks an' witches in a dance;
Nae cotillion brent new frae France,
But hornpipes, jigs, strathspeys, an' reels
Put life an' mettle in their heels:
At winnock-bunker[5] in the east,
There sat auld Nick, in shape o' beast;
A towzie[6] tyke, black, grim, an' large,

---

[1] smothered.　[2] chink.　[3] ale.　[4] whisky.　[5] window-seat.　[6] **shaggy.**

To gie them music was his charge;
He screw'd the pipes and gart them skirl,[1]
Till roof and rafters a' did dirl.[2]
Coffins stood round, like open presses;[3]
That shaw'd the dead in their last dresses;
And (by some dev'lish cantraip sleight[4])
Each in its cauld hand held a light:
By which heroic Tam was able
To note upon the haly table,
A murderer's banes in gibbet airns;
Twa span-lang, wee, unchristen'd bairns;
A thief, new-cutted frae a rape—
Wi' his last gasp his gab[5] did gape;
Five tomahawks, wi' bluid red-rusted,
Five scimitars, wi' murder crusted;
A garter, which a babe had strangled;
A knife, a father's throat had mangled,
Whom his ain son o' life bereft,
The grey hairs yet stack to the heft;
Wi' mair o' horrible an' awfu',
Which ev'n to name wad be unlawfu'.

As Tammie glowr'd, amaz'd, an' curious,
The mirth an' fun grew fast an' furious:
The piper loud an' louder blew,
The dancers quick an' quicker flew;
They reel'd, they set, they cross'd, they cleekit,[6]
'Till ilka carlin swat and reekit,[7]
An' coost her duddies[8] to the wark,
An' linket[9] at it in her sark!

Now Tam! O Tam! had thae been queans
A' plump an' strappin' in their teens;

---

[1] squeal. [2] ring. [3] cupboards. [4] magic trick. [5] mouth.
[6] took hands. [7] beldam sweated and steamed. [8] clothes.
[9] tripped.

Their sarks, instead o' creeshie[1] flannen,
Been snaw-white seventeen hunder linen!
Thir breeks o' mine, my only pair,
That ance were plush, o' guid blue hair,
I wad hae gi'en them aff my hurdies,
For ae blink o' the bonnie burdies![2]

But withered beldams, auld an' droll,
Rigwoodie[3] hags, wad spean[4] a foal,
Lowping an' flinging on a crummock,[5]
I wonder didna turn thy stomach.

But Tam kenn'd what was what fu' brawlie,
There was ae winsome wench an' walie,[6]
That night enlisted in the core[7]
(Lang after kenn'd on Carrick shore;
For mony a beast to dead she shot,
An' perish'd mony a bonnie boat,
An' shook baith meikle corn an' bear,
An' kept the country-side in fear),
Her cutty sark,[8] o' Paisley harn,[9]
That, while a lassie, she had worn,
In longitude tho' sorely scanty,
It was her best, an' she was vauntie.[10]

Ah! little kenn'd thy reverend Grannie,
That sark she coft[11] for her wee Nannie,
Wi' twa pund Scots ('twas a' her riches),
Wad ever grac'd a dance of witches!

But here my Muse her wing maun cour;[12]
Sic flights are far beyond her pow'r;
To sing how Nannie lap an' flang
(A souple jade she was, an' strang),

[1] greasy.   [2] girls.   [3] lean, ancient.   [4] wean.   [5] staff.
[6] jolly.   [7] corps.   [8] short shift.   [9] coarse cloth.
            [10] proud.   [11] bought.   [12] stoop.

An' how Tam stood, like ane bewitch'd,
An' thought his very een enrich'd;
Ev'n Satan glowr'd, an' fidg'd fu' fain,
An' hotched an' blew wi' might an' main:
'Till first ae caper, syne anither,
Tam tint[1] his reason a' thegither,
An' roars out, 'Weel done, Cutty-sark!'
An' in an instant a' was dark:
An' scarcely had he Maggie rallied,
When out the hellish legion sallied.

As bees bizz out wi' angry fyke,[2]
When plunderin' herds assail their byke;[3]
As open pussie's[4] mortal foes,
When, pop! she starts before their nose;
As eager runs the market-crowd,
When 'Catch the thief!' resounds aloud;
So Maggie runs, the witches follow,
Wi' mony an eldritch[5] screech an' hollow.

Ah, Tam! ah, Tam! thou'lt get thy fairin',
In hell they'll roast thee like a herrin'!
In vain thy Kate awaits thy comin'!
Kate soon will be a woefu' woman!
Now, do thy speedy utmost, Meg,
An' win the key-stane o' the brig;
There, at them thou thy tail may toss,
A running stream they darena cross;
But ere the key-stane she could make,
The fient[6] a tail she had to shake!
For Nannie, far before the rest,
Hard upon noble Maggie prest,
An' flew at Tam wi' furious ettle;[7]

[1] lost. [2] fuss. [3] hive. [4] the hare's. [5] unearthly.
[6] devil. [7] aim.

But little wist she Maggie's mettle—
Ae spring brought off her master hale,
But left behind her ain grey tail:
The carlin claught[1] her by the rump,
An' left poor Maggie scarce a stump.

Now, wha this tale o' truth shall read,
Ilk man and mother's son take heed:
Whane'er to drink you are inclin'd,
Or cutty-sarks run in your mind,
Think! ye may buy the joys o'er dear—
Remember Tam o' Shanter's meare.

Contented wi' little

Contented wi' little, and cantie[2] wi' mair,
Whene'er I forgather wi' sorrow and care,
I gie them a skelp,[3] as they're creeping alang,
Wi, a cog[4] o' sweet swats,[5] and an auld Scottish sang.

I whyles[6] claw the elbow o' troublesome thought;
But man is a sodger, and life is a faught;[7]
My mirth and guid humour are coin in my pouch,
And my freedom's my lairdship nae monarch dare
    touch.

A towmond[8] o' trouble, should that be my fa',[9]
A night o' guid fellowship sowthers[10] it a':
When at the blithe end o' our journey at last,
Wha the deil ever thinks o' the road he has past?

Blind chance, let her snapper and stoyte[11] on her way;
Be't to me, be't frae me, e'en let the jade gae:
Come ease, or come travail; come pleasure or pain;
My warst word is,—'Welcome, and welcome again!'

---

[1] seized.   [2] happy.   [3] smack.   [4] wooden vessel.   [5] new ale.
[6] sometimes.   [7] fight.   [8] twelvemonth.   [9] lot.   [10] solders.
[11] stumble and stagger.

O merry hae I been teethin' a heckle

O merry hae I been teethin' a heckle,[1]
   And merry hae I been shapin' a spoon;
And merry hae I been cloutin[2] a kettle,
   And kissin' my Katie when a' was done
O a' the lang day I ca'[3] at my hammer,
   An' a' the lang day I whistle and sing,
A' the lang night I cuddle my kimmer,[4]
   An' a' the lang night as happy's a king.

Bitter in dool[5] I lickit my winnins[6]
   O' marrying Bess, to gie her a slave:
Blest be the hour she cool'd in her linnens,
   And blithe be the bird that sings on her grave!
Come to my arms, my Katie, my Katie,
   An' come to my arms and kiss me again!
Drunken or sober, here 's to thee, Katie!
   And blest be the day I did it again.

The Rigs o' Barley

It was upon a Lammas night,
   When corn rigs[7] are bonnie,
Beneath the moon's unclouded light,
   I held awa to Annie:
The time flew by wi' tentless[8] heed,
   Till 'tween the late and early,
Wi' sma' persuasion she agreed
   To see me thro' the barley.

The sky was blue, the wind was still,
   The moon was shining clearly;

[1] hackling-comb.   [2] patching.   [3] work with.   [4] sweetheart.
[5] sorrow.   [6] earnings.   [7] ridges.   [8] careless.

I set her down, wi' right good will,
  Amang the rigs o' barley:
I kent her heart was a' my ain;
  I lov'd her most sincerely:
I kiss'd her owre and owre again,
  Amang the rigs o' barley.

I lock'd her in my fond embrace!
  Her heart was beating rarely:
My blessings on that happy place,
  Amang the rigs o' barley!
But by the moon and stars so bright,
  That shone that hour so clearly!
She aye shall bless that happy night,
  Amang the rigs o' barley.

I hae been blithe wi' comrades dear;
  I hae been merry drinking,
I hae been joyfu' gath'rin' gear;
  I hae been happy thinking:
But a' the pleasures e'er I saw,
  Tho' three times doubl'd fairly,
That happy night was worth them a',
  Amang the rigs o' barley.

Chorus

Corn rigs an' barley rigs,
  An' corn rigs are bonnie:
I'll ne'er forget that happy night,
  Amang the rigs wi' Annie.

I'll aye ca' in by yon town

I'll aye ca'[1] in by yon town,[2]
  And by yon garden green, again;

---

[1] call.   [2] group of cottages.

I'll aye ca' in by yon town,
   And see my bonnie Jean again.
There's nane sall ken, there's nane sall guess,
   What brings me back the gate¹ again;
But she my fairest faithfu' lass,
   And stownlins² we sall meet again.

She'll wander by the aiken³ tree,
   When trystin'-time draws near again;
And when her lovely form I see,
   O haith,⁴ she's doubly dear again!
I'll aye ca' in by yon town,
   And by yon garden green again;
I'll aye ca' in by yon town,
   And see my bonnie Jean again.

A red, red rose

O, my luve's like a red, red rose,
   That's newly sprung in June:
O, my luve's like the melodie
   That's sweetly played in tune.

As fair art thou, my bonnie lass,
   So deep in luve am I;
And I will luve thee still, my dear,
   Till a' the seas gang dry.

Till a' the seas gang dry, my dear,
   And the rocks melt wi' the sun:
And I will luve thee still, my dear,
   While the sands o' life shall run.

And fare thee well, my only luve!
   And fare thee well a while!
And I will come again, my luve,
   Though it were ten thousand mile.

¹ this way.   ² by stealth.   ³ oak.   ⁴ faith.

My Tocher's the Jewel

O meikle thinks my luve o' my beauty,
    And meikle thinks my luve o' my kin;
But little thinks my luve I ken brawlie
    My tocher's[1] the jewel has charms for him.
    It's a' for the apple he'll nourish the tree,
    It's a' for the hiney[2] he'll cherish the bee.
My laddie's sae meikle in luve wi' the siller,
    He canna hae luve to spare for me.

Your proffer o' luve's an airle-penny,[3]
    My tocher's the bargain ye wad buy;
But an ye be crafty, I am cunnin',
    Sae ye wi' anither your fortune may try.
Ye're like to the timmer[4] o' yon rotten wood,
    Ye're like to the bark o' yon rotten tree,
Ye'll slip frae me like a knotless thread,
    And ye'll crack[5] your credit wi' mair nor me.

[1]dowry   [2]honey   [3]small hansel   [4]timber   [5]flaw

The Lea Rig

When o'er the hill the eastern star
    Tells bughtin-time[2] is near, my jo;[3]
And owsen frae the furrow'd field
    Return sae dowf[4] and weary, O;
Down by the burn, where scented birks
    Wi' dew are hanging clear, my jo;
I'll meet thee on the lea-rig,[5]
    My ain kind dearie, O!

[1]scared.   [2]folding-time.   [3]sweetheart.   [4]dull.   [5]grassy ridge.

In mirkest glen, at midnight hour,
   I'd rove, and ne'er be eerie, O!
If thro' that glen I gaed to thee,
   My ain kind dearie, O!
Altho' the night were ne'er sae wild,
   And I were ne'er sae wearie, O,
I'd meet thee on the lea-rig,
   My ain kind dearie, O!

The hunter lo'es the morning sun,
   To rouse the mountain deer, my jo;
At noon the fisher seeks the glen,
   Along the burn to steer, my jo;
Gie me the hour o' gloamin' grey,
   It makes my heart sae cheery, O,
To meet thee on the lea-rig,
   My ain kind dearie, O!

Ae fond kiss

Ae fond kiss, and then we sever;
Ae farewell, and then, for ever!
Deep in heart-wrung tears I'll pledge thee,
Warring sighs and groans I'll wage thee.
Who shall say that fortune grieves him,
While the star of hope she leaves him?
Me, nae cheerfu' twinkle lights me:
Dark despair around benights me.

I'll ne'er blame my partial fancy,
Naething could resist my Nancy!
But to see her was to love her;
Love but her, and love for ever.
Had we never lov'd sae kindly,
Had we never lov'd sae blindly,

Never met—or never parted—
We had ne'er been broken-hearted.

Fare thee weel, thou first and fairest!
Fare thee weel, thou best and dearest!
Thine be ilka[1] joy and treasure,
Peace, Enjoyment, Love, and Pleasure!
Ae fond kiss, and then we sever;
Ae farewell, alas! for ever!
Deep in heart-wrung tears I'll pledge thee,
Warring sighs and groans I'll wage thee!

My Bonnie Mary

Go fetch to me a pint o' wine,
   An' fill it in a silver tassie;[2]
That I may drink, before I go,
   A service to my bonnie lassie;
The boat rocks at the pier o' Leith;
   Fu' loud the wind blaws frae the ferry;
The ship rides by the Berwick-Law,
   And I maun leave my bonnie Mary.

The trumpets sound, the banners fly,
   The glittering spears are rankèd ready;
The shouts o' war are heard afar,
   The battle closes thick and bloody!
It's not the roar o' sea or shore
   Wad make me langer wish to tarry;
Nor shout o' war that's heard afar—
   It's leaving thee, my bonnie Mary.

[1] every.   [2] goblet.

The banks of Doon

Ye flowery banks o' bonnie Doon,
   How can ye bloom sae fair;
How can ye chant, ye little birds,
   And I sae fu' o' care?

Thou'll break my heart, thou bonnie bird,
   That sings upon the bough;
Thou minds me o' the happy days
   When my fause luve was true.

Thou'll break my heart, thou bonnie bird,
   That sings beside thy mate;
For sae I sat, and sae I sang,
   And wist na o' my fate.

Aft hae I rov'd by bonnie Doon,
   To see the woodbine twine,
And ilka[1] bird sang o' its luve,
   And sae did I o' mine.

Wi' lightsome heart I pu'd a rose,
   Frae off its thorny tree;
And my fause luver staw the rose,
   But left the thorn wi' me.

Bess and her Spinning-wheel

O leeze[2] me on my spinning-wheel,
And leeze me on my rock[3] and reel;
Frae tap to tae that cleeds[4] me bien,[5]
And haps me fiel[6] and warm at e'en!

[1] each.   [2] commend me to.   [3] distaff.   [4] clothes.
             [5] comfortably.   [6] well.

I'll set me down and sing and spin,
While laigh descends the simmer sun,
Blest wi' content, and milk and meal—
O leeze me on my spinning-wheel!

On ilka[1] hand the burnies trot,
And meet below my theekit[2] cot;
The scented birk and hawthorn white,
Across the pool their arms unite,
Alike to screen the birdie's nest,
And little fishes' caller[3] rest:
The sun blinks kindly in the biel',[4]
Where blithe I turn my spinning-wheel.

On lofty aiks[5] the cushats wail,
And echo cons the doolfu' tale;
The lintwhites[6] in the hazel braes,
Delighted, rival ither's lays:
The craik[7] amang the clover hay,
The paitrick[8] whirrin' o'er the ley,[9]
The swallow jinkin'[10] round my shiel,[11]
Amuse me at my spinning-wheel.

Wi' sma' to sell, and less to buy,
Aboon distress, below envy,
O wha would leave this humble state,
For a' the pride of a' the great?
Amid their flaring, idle toys,
Amid their cumbrous, dinsome[12] joys,
Can they the peace and pleasure feel
Of Bessie at her spinning-wheel?

---

[1] either. [2] thatched. [3] cool. [4] shelter. [5] oaks.
[6] linnets. [7] corn-crake. [8] partridge. [9] meadow.
[10] darting. [11] cot. [12] noisy.

Tam Glen

My heart is a-breaking, dear Tittie![1]
   Some counsel unto me come len',
To anger them a' is a pity,
   But what will I do wi' Tam Glen?

I'm thinking, wi' sic a braw fallow,
   In poortith[2] I might mak a fen'![3]
What care I in riches to wallow,
   If I mauna marry Tam Glen?

There's Lowrie the laird o' Drumeller,
   'Guid day to you, brute!' he comes ben:
He brags and he blaws o' his siller,
   But when will he dance like Tam Glen?

My minnie[4] does constantly deave[5] me,
   And bids me beware o' young men;
They flatter, she says, to deceive me,
   But wha can think sae o' Tam Glen?

My daddie says, gin I'll forsake him,
   He'll gie me guid hunder marks ten:
But, if it's ordain'd I maun take him,
   O wha will I get but Tam Glen?

Yestreen at the Valentines' dealing,
   My heart to my mou' gied a sten;[6]
For thrice I drew ane without failing,
   And thrice it was written—Tam Glen.

The last Halloween I lay waukin—
   My droukit[7] sark-sleeve, as ye ken;
His likeness cam up the house staukin
   And the very grey breeks o' Tam Glen!

[1] sister.   [2] poverty.   [3] shift.   [4] mother.   [5] deafen.
[6] leap.   [7] dripping.

Come counsel, dear Tittie! don't tarry—
I'll gie you my bonnie black hen,
Gif ye will advise me to marry
The lad I loe dearly, Tam Glen.

Somebody

My heart is sair—I darena tell—
    My heart is sair for Somebody;
I could wake a winter night
    For the sake o' Somebody.
        Ohon! for Somebody!
        O-hey! for Somebody!
I could range the world around,
    For the sake o' Somebody!

Ye Powers that smile on virtuous love,
    O, sweetly smile on Somebody!
Frae ilka[1] danger keep him free,
    And send me safe my Somebody.
        Ohon! for Somebody!
        O-hey! for Somebody!
I wad do—what wad I not?
    For the sake o' Somebody!

Duncan Gray

Duncan Gray cam here to woo,
    Ha, ha, the wooing o't,
On blythe Yule night when we were fou,
    Ha, ha, the wooing o't.
Maggie coost her head fu' high,
Look'd asklent[2] and unco skeigh,[3]
Gart[4] poor Duncan stand abeigh;[5]
    Ha, ha, the wooing o't.

[1] every.   [2] askance.   [3] very skittish.   [4] made.   [5] off.

Duncan fleech'd,[1] and Duncan pray'd,
   Ha, ha, the wooing o't;
Meg was deaf as Ailsa Craig,
   Ha, ha, the wooing o't.
Duncan sigh'd baith out and in,
Grat[2] his een baith bleer't and blin',
Spak o' lowpin[3] o'er a linn;[4]
   Ha, ha, the wooing o't.

Time and chance are but a tide:
   Ha, ha, the wooing o't;
Slighted love is sair to bide;[5]
   Ha, ha, the wooing o't.
Shall I, like a fool, quoth he,
For a haughty hizzie die?
She may gae to—France for me!
   Ha, ha, the wooing o't.

How it comes let doctors tell;
   Ha, ha, the wooing o't;
Meg grew sick—as he grew hale;
   Ha, ha, the wooing o't.
Something in her bosom wrings,
For relief a sigh she brings;
And O, her een, they spak sic things!
   Ha, ha, the wooing o't.

Duncan was a lad o' grace;
   Ha, ha, the wooing o't;
Maggie's was a piteous case;
   Ha, ha, the wooing o't.
Duncan could na be her death,
Swelling pity smoor'd[6] his wrath;
Now they're crouse[7] and canty[8] baith;
   Ha, ha, the wooing o't.

---

[1] wheedled.   [2] wept.   [3] jumping.   [4] waterfall.
[5] sore to endure.   [6] smothered.   [7] cheerful.   [8] merry.

O, for ane-and-twenty

Chorus

An' O, for ane-and-twenty, Tam!
    And hey, sweet ane-and-twenty, Tam!
I'll learn my kin a rattlin' sang,
    An I saw ane-and-twenty, Tam.

They snool[1] me sair, and haud me down,
    And gar[2] me look like bluntie,[3] Tam;
But three short years will soon wheel roun'—
    And then comes ane-and-twenty, Tam.

A gleib[4] o' lan', a claut o' gear,[5]
    Was left me by my auntie, Tam;
At kith or kin I need na spier,[6]
    An I saw ane-and-twenty, Tam.

They'll hae me wed a wealthy coof,[7]
    Tho' I mysel hae plenty, Tam:
But hear'st thou, laddie—there's my loof—[8]
    I'm thine at ane-and-twenty, Tam.

O whistle, and I'll come to ye, my lad

O whistle, and I'll come to ye, my lad!
O whistle, and I'll come to ye, my lad!
Tho' father and mither and a' should gae mad,
O whistle, and I'll come to ye, my lad!

But warily tent,[9] when ye come to court me,
And come na unless the back-yett[10] be a-jee;[11]
Syne[12] up the back-stile, and let naebody see,
And come as ye were na comin' to me,
And come as ye were na comin' to me!

---

[1] snub. [2] make. [3] stupid. [4] glebe. [5] handful of money. [6] ask.
[7] ninny. [8] palm. [9] take heed. [10] gate. [11] ajar. [12] then.

At kirk, or at market, whene'er ye meet me,
Gang by me as tho' that ye car'd na a flie;
But steal me a blink o' your bonnie black e'e,
Yet look as ye were na lookin' at me,
Yet look as ye were na lookin' at me!

Aye vow and protest that ye care na for me,
And whyles ye may lightly[1] my beauty a wee;
But court na anither, tho' jokin' ye be,
For fear that she wyle[2] your fancy frae me,
For fear that she wyle your fancy frae me!

O whistle, and I'll come to ye, my lad!
O whistle, and I'll come to ye, my lad!
Tho' father and mither and a' should gae mad,
O whistle, and I'll come to ye, my lad!

The Farewell

It was a' for our rightfu' king,
  We left fair Scotland's strand;
It was a' for our rightfu' king,
  We e'er saw Irish land, my dear,
  We e'er saw Irish land.

Now a' is done that men can do,
  And a' is done in vain;
My love and native land farewell,
  For I maun cross the main, my dear,
  For I maun cross the main.

He turned him right, and round about,
  Upon the Irish shore;
And gae his bridle-reins a shake,
  With adieu for evermore, my dear,
  With adieu for evermore.

[1] slight.   [2] entice.

The sodger from the wars returns,
　The sailor frae the main;
But I hae parted frae my love,
　Never to meet again, my dear,
　Never to meet again.

When day is gane, and night is come,
　And a' folk bound to sleep;
I think on him that's far awa,
　The lee-lang night, and weep, my dear,
　The lee-lang night, and weep.

Auld Lang Syne

Should auld acquaintance be forgot,
　And never brought to mind?
Should auld acquaintance be forgot,
　And auld lang syne?

　　For auld lang syne, my dear,
　　　For auld lang syne,
　　We'll tak a cup o' kindness yet
　　　For auld lang syne!

And surely you'll be[1] your pint-stoup,
　And surely I'll be mine;
And we'll tak a cup o' kindness yet
　For auld lang syne!

We twa hae run about the braes,
　And pu'd the gowans[2] fine;
But we've wandered mony a weary fit[3]
　Sin auld lang syne.

　　　[1] pay for.　　　[2] daisies.　　　[3] foot.

We twa hae paidl'd in the burn,
   Frae morning sun till dine;[1]
But seas between us braid hae roar'd
   Sin auld lang syne!

And there's a hand, my trusty fiere,[2]
   And gie's a hand o' thine;
And we'll tak a right guid-willie waught[3]
   For auld lang syne.

     For auld lang syne, my dear,
      For auld lang syne,
     We'll tak a cup o' kindness yet
      For auld lang syne!

JOHN MAYNE

1759–1836

From *Glasgow*

Hail, Glasgow! famed for ilka thing
That heart can wish or siller bring!
May Peace, wi' healing on her wing,
   Aye nestle here;
And Plenty gar thy childer sing
   The lee-lang year!

Within the tinkling o' thy bells
How mony a happy body dwells!
Where they get bread they ken themsels;
   But I'll declare
They're aye bien-like, and, what precels,
   Hae fouth to spare.

---

[1] noon.   [2] comrade.   [3] draught.

If ye've a knacky son or twa,
To Glasgow College send them a',
Wi' whilk, for gospel, or for law,
  Or classic lair,
Ye'll find few places hereawa'
  That can compare.

There ane may be, for sma' propyne,
Physician, lawyer, or divine.
The gem, lang buried i' the mine,
  Is polished here,
Till a' its hidden beauties shine,
  And sparkle clear.

Nor is it students, and nae mair,
That climb in crowds our College stair.
Thither the learned, far-famed, repair
  To clear their notions,
And pay to Alma Mater there
  Their warm devotions.

'Mang ither names that consecrate,
And stamp a country gude or great,
We boast o' some that might compete,
  Or claim alliance
Wi' a' that's grand in Kirk or State,
  In art or science.

Here great Buchanan[1] learnt to scan
The verse that mak's him mair than man.
Cullen[2] and Hunter[3] here began
  Their first probations,

---

[1] George Buchanan (1506–82), tragedian and poet in Latin.
[2] William Cullen (1710–90), chemist and professor at Edinburgh University.
[3] William Hunter (1718–1783), surgeon and obstetrician.

And Smith,[1] frae Glasgow, formed his plan—
'The Wealth o' Nations'.

In ilka house, frae man to boy,
A' hands in Glasgow find employ;
Even little maids, wi' meikle joy,
    Flower lawn and gauze,
Or clip wi' care the silken soy
    For ladies' braws.

Their fathers weave, their mothers spin
The muslin robe, so fine and thin
That, frae the ankle to the chin,
    It aft discloses
The beauteous symmetry within—
    Limbs, neck, and bosies.

Look through the town! The houses here
Like noble palaces appear;
A' things the face o' gladness wear—
    The market's thrang,
Business is brisk, and a's asteer
    The streets alang.

Clean-keepit streets! so lang and braid,
The distant objects seem to fade;
And then, for shelter or for shade
    Frae sun or shower,
Piazzas lend their friendly aid
    At ony hour.

Wond'ring, we see new streets extending,
New squares wi' public buildings blending,

[1] Adam Smith (1723–90), Professor of Moral Philosophy at
Glasgow University (1751–64).

Brigs, stately brigs, in arches bending
  Across the Clyde,
And turrets, kirks, and spires ascending
  In lofty pride.

High owre the lave St. Mungo rears
His sacred fane, the pride of years,
And stretching upward to the spheres,
  His spire afar
To weary travellers appears
  A leading star.

'Tween twa and three wi' daily care,
The gentry to the Cross repair—
The politician, wi' grave air,
  Deliberating;
Merchants and manufacturers there
  Negociating.

It's not by slothfulness and ease
That Glasgow's canty ingles bleeze;
To gi'e her inland trade a heeze
  As weel's her foreign,
She's joined the east and western seas
  Together, roaring.

Frae Forth, athort the land, to Clyde,
Her barks a' winds and weathers glide,
And on the bosom o' the tide,
  Wi' gentle motion,
Her vessels like a forest ride
  And kiss auld Ocean.

Nor only hers what trade imparts.
She's great in arms as weel as arts;

Her gallant sons, wi' loyal hearts,
  A' tak' the field,
Resolved, when knaves would scatter darts,
  Their king to shield.

And yet, though armed they thus appear,
They only arm while danger's near.
When peace, blest peace! to them maist dear,
  Dispels the gloom,
They for the shuttle change the spear,
  And ply the loom.

Hail, Industry! thou richest gem
That shines in Virtue's diadem!
While Indolence, wi' tattered hem
  Around her knee,
Sits chittering like the withered stem
  O' some boss tree;

To thee we owe the flocks o' sheep
That glad Ben Lomond's cloud-capped steep;
The pregnant mines that yield yon heap
  O' massy coals;
And a' the tenants o' the deep,
  Caught here in shoals;

And a' the villas round that gleam;
Like spangles i' the sunny beam;
The bonnie haughs that laughing seem
  Wi' plenty growing;
And a' the bleachfields on ilk stream
  Through Clydesdale flowing.

Hence Commerce spreads her sails to a'
The Indies and America:

Whatever mak's ae penny twa,
   By wind or tide
Is wafted to the Broomielaw
   On bonnie Clyde.

O Glasgow! famed for ilka thing
That heart can wish or siller bring!
May nowther care nor sorrow ding
   Thy childer dear,
But peace and plenty gar them sing
   Frae year to year!

LADY NAIRNE

1766–1845

The Laird o' Cockpen

The Laird o' Cockpen, he 's proud an' he's great,
His mind is ta'en up wi' things o' the State:
He wanted a wife, his braw house to keep;
But favour wi' wooin' was fashous[1] to seek.

Down by the dyke-side a lady did dwell;
At his table-head he thought she'd look well—
McClish's ae daughter o' Claverse-ha' Lee,
A penniless lass wi' a lang pedigree.

His wig was weel pouther'd and as gude as new;
His waistcoat was white, his coat it was blue:
He put on a ring, a sword, and cock'd hat,—
And wha could refuse the Laird wi' a' that?

He took the grey mare, and rade cannily,
An' rapp'd at the yett[2] o' Claverse-ha' Lee:
'Gae tell Mistress Jean to come speedily ben,—
She's wanted to speak to the Laird o' Cockpen.'

---

       [1] troublesome.   [2] gate.

Mistress Jean was makin' the elder-flower wine:
'And what brings the Laird at sic a like time?'
She put aff her apron and on her silk goun,
Her mutch[1] wi' red ribbons, and gaed awa doun.

An' when she cam' ben he bow'd fu' low;
An' what was his errand he soon let her know.
Amazed was the Laird when the lady said 'Na';—
And wi' a laigh curtsey she turn'd awa.

Dumfounder'd was he; nae sigh did he gie,
He mounted his mare, he rade cannily;
And aften he thought as he gaed thro' the glen,
,She's daft to refuse the Laird o' Cockpen!'

And, now that the Laird his exit had made,
Mistress Jean she reflected on what she had said:
'Oh, for ane I'll get better, it's waur I'll get ten!
I was daft to refuse the Laird o' Cockpen.'

Next time that the Laird and the lady were seen
They were gaun arm-in-arm to the kirk on the green:
Now she sits in the ha', like a weel-tappit[2] hen;
But as yet there's nae chickens appear'd at Cockpen.

(The last two stanzas were written by Miss Susan Ferrier.)

Will ye no come back again?

Bonnie Charlie's now awa,
  Safely owre the friendly main;
Mony a heart will break in twa,
  Should he ne'er come back again.

> Will ye no come back again?
>   Will ye no come back again?
> Better lo'ed ye canna be,
>   Will ye no come back again?

[1] cap.   [2] crested.

Ye trusted in your Hieland men,
    They trusted you, dear Charlie;
They kent you hiding in the glen,
    Your cleadin was but barely.

English bribes were a' in vain,
    An' e'en though puirer we may be;
Siller canna buy the heart
    That beats aye for thine and thee.

We watched thee in the gloaming[1] hour,
    We watched thee in the morning grey;
Tho' thirty thousand pounds they'd gi'e,
    Oh there is nane that wad betray!

Sweet's the laverock's note and lang,
    Lilting wildly up the glen;
But aye to me he sings ae sang,
    Will ye no come back again?

JAMES HOGG

1770–1835

Lock the door, Lariston

'Lock the door, Lariston, lion of Liddesdale;
Lock the door, Lariston, Lowther comes on;
        The Armstrongs are flying,
        The widows are crying,
The Castletown's burning, and Oliver's gone!

'Lock the door, Lariston—high on the weather-gleam
See how the Saxon plumes bob on the sky—
        Yeomen and carbineer,
        Billman and halberdier,
Fierce is the foray, and far is the cry!

---

[1] twilight.

'Bewcastle brandishes high his broad scimitar;
Ridley is riding his fleet-footed grey;
　　　Hidley and Howard there,
　　　Wandale and Windermere;
Lock the door, Lariston; hold them at bay.

'Why dost thou smile, noble Elliot of Lariston?
Why does the joy-candle gleam in thine eye?
　　　Thou bold Border ranger,
　　　Beware of thy danger;
Thy foes are relentless, determined, and nigh.'

Jack Elliot raised up his steel bonnet and lookit,
His hand grasp'd the sword with a nervous embrace
　　　'Ah, welcome, brave foemen,
　　　On earth there are no men
More gallant to meet in the foray or chase!

'Little know you of the hearts I have hidden here;
Little know you of our moss-troopers' might—
　　　Linhope and Sorbie true,
　　　Sundhope and Milburn too,
Gentle in manner, but lions in fight!

'I have Mangerton, Ogilvie, Raeburn, and Netherbie,
Old Sim of Whitram, and all his array;
　　　Come all Northumberland,
　　　Teesdale and Cumberland,
Here at the Breaken tower end shall the fray!'

Scowled the broad sun o'er the links of green Liddes-
　　dale,
Red as the beacon-light tipped he the wold;
　　　Many a bold martial eye
　　　Mirror'd that morning sky,
Never more oped on his orbit of gold.

Shrill was the bugle's note, dreadful the warrior's
    shout,
Lances and halberds in splinters were borne;
       Helmet and hauberk then
       Braved the claymore in vain,
Buckler and armlet in shivers were shorn.

See how they wane—the proud files of the Winder-
    mere!
Howard! ah, woe to thy hopes of the day!
       Hear the wide welkin rend,
       While the Scots' shouts ascend—
'Elliot of Lariston, Elliot for aye!'

The Witch o' Fife

Hurray, hurray, the jade's away,
    Like a rocket of air with her bandalet!
I'm up in the air on my bonnie grey mare,
    But I see her yet, I see her yet.
I'll ring the skirts o' the gowden wain
    Wi' curb an' bit, wi' curb an' bit:
An' catch the Bear by the frozen mane—
    An' I see her yet, I see her yet.

Away, away, o'er mountain an' main,
    To sing at the morning's rosy yett;
An' water my mare at its fountain clear—
    But I see her yet, I see her yet.
Away, thou bonnie witch o' Fife,
    On foam of the air to heave an' flit,
An' little reck thou of a poet's life,
    For he sees thee yet, he sees thee yet!

A Witch's Chant

Thou art weary, weary, weary,
Thou art weary and far away!
Hear me, gentle spirit, hear me;
Come before the dawn of day.

I hear a small voice from the hill,
The vapour is deadly, pale, and still—
A murmuring sough is on the wood,
And the witching star is red as blood.

And in the cleft of heaven I scan
The giant form of a naked man;
His eye is like the burning brand,
And he holds a sword in his right hand.

All is not well: by dint of spell,
Somewhere between the heaven and hell
There is this night a wild deray;
The spirits have wander'd from their way.

The purple drops shall tinge the moon,
As she wanders through the midnight noon;
And the dawning heaven shall all be red
With blood by guilty angels shed.

Be as it will, I have the skill
To work by good or work by ill;
Then here's for pain, and here's for thrall,
And here's for conscience, worst of all!

Another chant, and then, and then,
Spirits shall come or Christian men—
Come from the earth, the air, or the sea:
Great Gil-Moules, I cry to thee!

Sleep'st thou, wakest thou, lord of the wind!
Mount thy steeds and gallop them blind;
And the long-tailed fiery dragon outfly,
The rocket of heaven, the bomb of the sky.

Over the dog-star, over the wain,
Over the cloud, and the rainbow's mane,
Over the mountain, and over the sea,
Haste—haste—haste to me!

Then here's for trouble and here's for smart,
And here's for the pang that seeks the heart;
Here's for madness, and here's for thrall,
And here's for conscience, the worst of all!

Bonny Kilmeny gaed up the glen

Bonny Kilmeny gaed up the glen,
But it wasna to meet Duneira's men,
Nor the rosy monk of the isle to see,
For Kilmeny was pure as pure could be.
It was only to hear the yorlin[1] sing,
And pu' the cress-flower round the spring;
The scarlet hypp and the hindberrye,[2]
And the nut that hung frae the hazel tree;
For Kilmeny was pure as pure could be.
But lang may her minny look o'er the wa',
And lang may she seek i' the green-wood shaw;
Lang the laird of Duneira blame,
And lang, lang greet or Kilmeny come hame!
　　When many a day had come and fled,
When grief grew calm, and hope was dead,
When mass for Kilmeny's soul had been sung,
When the bedes-man had prayed, and the dead bell
　　rung,

[1] yellow-hammer.   [2] raspberry.

Late, late in a gloamin' when all was still,
When the fringe was red on the westlin hill,
The wood was sere, the moon i' the wane,
The reek o' the cot hung over the plain,
Like a little wee cloud in the world its lane;
When the ingle lowed with an eiry leme,[1]
Late, late in the gloamin' Kilmeny came hame!
'Kilmeny, Kilmeny, where have you been?
Lang hae we sought baith holt and dean;
By linn, by ford, and green-wood tree,
Yet you are halesome and fair to see.
Where gat you that joup[2] o' the lily schene?
That bonny snood[3] of the birk sae green?
And these roses, the fairest that ever were seen?
Kilmeny, Kilmeny, where have you been?'
   Kilmeny looked up with a lovely grace,
But nae smile was seen on Kilmeny's face;
As still was her look, and as still was her ee,
As the stillness that lay on the emerant lea,
Or the mist that sleeps on a waveless sea.
For Kilmeny had been she knew not where,
And Kilmeny had seen what she could not declare;
Kilmeny had been where the cock never crew,
Where the rain never fell, and the wind never blew;
But it seemed as the harp of the sky had rung,
And the airs of heaven played round her tongue,
When she spake of the lovely forms she had seen,
And a land where sin had never been;
A land of love, and a land of light,
Withouten sun, or moon, or night;
Where the river swa'd a living stream,
And the light a pure celestial beam:

---

[1] fire glowed with an uncanny light.   [2] bodice, loose jacket.
[3] ribbon, fillet.

The land of vision it would seem,
A still, an everlasting dream. . . .
When seven lang years had come and fled;
When grief was calm, and hope was dead;
When scarce was remembered Kilmeny's name,
Late, late in a gloamin' Kilmeny came hame!

(*Kilmeny*, ll. 1–51 and 276–9.)

The Village of Balmaquhapple

D'ye ken the big village of Balmaquhapple,
The great muckle village of Balmaquhapple?
'Tis steep'd in iniquity up to the thrapple,[1]
An' what's to become o' poor Balmaquhapple?
Fling a' aff your bannets,[2] an' kneel for your life, fo'ks,
And pray to St Andrew, the god o' the Fife fo'ks;
Gar a' the hills yout[3] wi' sheer vociferation,
And thus you may cry on sic needfu' occasion:

'O, blessed St Andrew, if e'er ye could pity fo'k,
Men fo'k or women fo'k, country or city fo'k.
Come for this aince[4] wi' the auld thief to grapple,
An' save the great village of Balmaquhapple
Frae drinking an' leeing, an' flyting[5] an' swearing.

An' sins that ye wad be affrontit at hearing,
An' cheating an' stealing; O, grant them redemption,
All save an' except the few after to mention:

'There's Johnny the elder, wha hopes ne'er to need
      ye,
Sae pawkie,[6] sae holy, sae gruff, an' sae greedy;

---

            [1]throat   [2]bonnets   [3]make . . . roar
            [4]once   [5]calling names   [6]sly

Wha prays every hour as the wayfarer passes,
But aye at a hole where he watches the lasses;
He's cheated a thousand, an' e'en to this day yet,
Can cheat a young lass, or they're leears[1] that say it;
Then gie him his gate; he's sae slee an' sae civil,
Perhaps in the end he may wheedle the devil.

'There's Cappie the cobbler, an' Tammie the tinman,
An Dickie the brewer, an' Peter the skinman,
An' Geordie our deacon, for want of a better,
An Bess, wha delights in the sins that beset her.
O, worthy St Andrew, we canna compel ye,
But ye ken as weel as a body can tell ye,
If these gang to heaven, we'll a' be sae shockit,
Your garret o' blue will but thinly be stockit.

'But for a' the rest, for the women's sake, save them,
Their bodies at least, an' their sauls, if they have
    them;
But it puzzles Jock Lesley, an' sma' it avails,
If they dwell in their stamocks, their heads, or their
    tails.
An' save, without word of confession auricular,
The clerk's bonny daughters, an' Bell in particular;
For ye ken that their beauty's the pride an' the staple
Of the great wicked village of Balmaquhapple!'

SIR WALTER SCOTT

1771–1832

My own, my native land!

Breathes there the man with soul so dead,
Who never to himself hath said,

[1] liars

This is my own, my native land!
Whose heart hath ne'er within him burn'd
As home his footsteps he hath turn'd,
From wandering on a foreign strand!
If such there breathe, go, mark him well;
For him no minstrel raptures swell;
High though his titles, proud his name,
Boundless his wealth as wish can claim;
Despite these titles, power, and pelf,
The wretch, concentred all in self,
Living, shall forfeit fair renown,
And, doubly dying, shall go down
To the vile dust, from whence he sprung,
Unwept, unhonour'd, and unsung.

O Caledonia! stern and wild,
Meet nurse for a poetic child!
Land of brown heath and shaggy wood,
Land of the mountain and the flood,
Land of my sires! what mortal hand
Can e'er untie the filial band
That knits me to thy rugged strand?
Still, as I view each well-known scene,
Think what is now and what hath been,
Seems as, to me, of all bereft,
Sole friends thy woods and streams were left;
And thus I love them better still,
Even in extremity of ill.

(*Lay of the Last Minstrel*, Canto VI, stanzas 1–2.)

November in Ettrick Forest

November's sky is chill and drear,
November's leaf is red and sear:
Late, gazing down the steepy linn,
That hems our little garden in,

Low in its dark and narrow glen
You scarce the rivulet might ken,
So thick the tangled greenwood grew,
So feeble trill'd the streamlet through:
Now, murmuring hoarse, and frequent seen
Through bush and brier, no longer green,
An angry brook, it sweeps the glade,
Brawls over rock and wild cascade,
And, foaming brown with doubled speed,
Hurries its waters to the Tweed.

No longer Autumn's glowing red
Upon our Forest hills is shed;
No more beneath the evening beam
Fair Tweed reflects their purple gleam;
Away hath pass'd the heather-bell
That bloom'd so rich on Needpathfell;
Sallow his brow; and russet bare
Are now the sister-heights of Yair.
The sheep, before the pinching heaven,
To shelter'd dale and down are driven,
Where yet some faded herbage pines,
And yet a watery sunbeam shines:
In meek despondency they eye
The wither'd sward and wintry sky,
And far beneath their summer hill,
Stray sadly by Glenkinnon's rill:
The shepherd shifts his mantle's fold,
And wraps him closer from the cold;
His dogs no merry circles wheel,
But shivering follow at his heel;
A cowering glance they often cast,
As deeper moans the gathering blast.

(*Marmion*, Introduction to Canto I.)

March, march, Ettrick and Teviotdale

March, march, Ettrick and Teviotdale,
 Why the deil dinna ye march forward in order?
March, march, Eskdale and Liddesdale,
 All the Blue Bonnets are bound for the Border.
   Many a banner spread,
   Flutters above your head,
  Many a crest that is famous in story.
   Mount and make ready then,
   Sons of the mountain glen,
  Fight for the Queen and the old Scottish glory.

Come from the hills where your hirsels are grazing,
 Come from the glen of the buck and the roe;
Come to the crag where the beacon is blazing,
 Come with the buckler, the lance, and the bow.
   Trumpets are sounding,
   War-steeds are bounding,
  Stand to your arms then, and march in good
   order;
   England shall many a day
   Tell of the bloody fray,
  When the Blue Bonnets came over the Border.

      (*The Monastery*, Chapter xxv.)

Harlaw

'The herring loves the merry moonlight,
 The mackerel loves the wind,
But the oyster loves the dredging sang,
 For they come of a gentle kind.'

 . . . .

Now haud your tongue, baith wife and carle,
 And listen, great and sma',
And I will sing of Glenallan's Earl
 That fought on the red Harlaw.

The cronach's cried on Bennachie,
 And doun the Don and a',
And hieland and lawland may mournfu' be
 For the sair field of Harlaw.

They saddled a hundred milk-white steeds,
 They hae bridled a hundred black,
With a chafron of steel on each horse's head,
 And a good knight upon his back.

They hadna ridden a mile, a mile,
 A mile, but barely ten,
When Donald came branking down the brae
 Wi' twenty thousand men.

Their tartans they were waving wide,
 Their glaives were glancing clear,
The pibrochs rung frae side to side,
 Would deafen ye to hear.

The great Earl in his stirrups stood,
 That Highland host to see;
'Now here a knight that's stout and good
 May prove a jeopardie:

'What would'st thou do, my squire so gay,
 That rides beside my reyne,
Were ye Glenallan's Earl the day,
 And I were Roland Cheyne?

'To turn the rein were sin and shame,
 To fight were wond'rous peril;
What would ye do now, Roland Cheyne,
 Were ye Glenallan's Earl?'

'Were I Glenallan's Earl this tide,
 And ye were Roland Cheyne,
The spur should be in my horse's side,
 And the bridle upon his mane.

'If they hae twenty thousand blades,
　　And we twice ten times ten,
Yet they hae but their tartan plaids,
　　And we are mail-clad men.

'My horse shall ride through ranks sae rude,
　　As through the moorland fern,—
Then ne'er let the gentle Norman blude
　　Grow cauld for Highland kerne.'

(The Antiquary, Chapter XL.)

Bannockburn

Unflinching foot 'gainst foot was set,
Unceasing blow by blow was met;
　　The groans of those who fell
Were drown'd amid the shriller clang
That from the blades and harness rang,
　　And in the battle-yell.
Yet fast they fell, unheard, forgot,
Both Southern fierce and hardy Scot;
And O! amid that waste of life,
What various motives fired the strife!
The aspiring Noble bled for fame,
The Patriot for his country's claim;
This Knight his youthful strength to prove,
And that to win his lady's love;
Some fought from ruffian thirst of blood,
From habit some, or hardihood.
But ruffian stern, and soldier good,
　　The noble and the slave,
From various cause the same wild road,
On the same bloody morning, trode,
　　To that dark inn, the Grave!

(The Lord of the Isles, Canto VI, stanza 26.)

Flodden

By this, though deep the evening fell,
Still rose the battle's deadly swell,
For still the Scots, around their King,
Unbroken, fought in desperate ring.
Where's now their victor vaward wing,
    Where Huntly, and where Home?—
O, for a blast of that dread horn,
On Fontarabian echoes borne,
    That to King Charles did come,
When Rowland brave, and Olivier,
And every paladin and peer,
    On Roncesvalles died!
Such blast might warn them, not in vain,
To quit the plunder of the slain,
And turn the doubtful day again,
    While yet on Flodden side,
Afar, the Royal Standard flies,
And round it toils, and bleeds, and dies,
    Our Caledonian pride!
In vain the wish—for far away,
While spoil and havoc mark their way,
Near Sybil's Cross the plunderers stray.
'O, Lady,' cried the Monk, 'away!'
    And plac'd her on her steed,
And led her to the chapel fair,
    Of Tilmouth upon Tweed.
There all the night they spent in prayer,
And at the dawn of morning, there
She met her kinsman, Lord Fitz-Clare.

But as they left the dark'ning heath,
More desperate grew the strife of death.
The English shafts in volleys hail'd,
In headlong charge their horse assail'd;

Front, flank, and rear, the squadrons sweep
To break the Scottish circle deep,
    That fought around their King.
But yet, though thick the shafts as snow,
Though charging knights like whirlwinds go,
Though bill-men ply the ghastly blow,
    Unbroken was the ring;
The stubborn spear-men still made good
Their dark impenetrable wood,
Each stepping where his comrade stood,
    The instant that he fell.
No thought was there of dastard flight;
Link'd in the serried phalanx tight,
Groom fought like noble, squire like knight,
    As fearlessly and well;
Till utter darkness closed her wing
O'er their thin host and wounded King.
Then skilful Surrey's sage commands
Led back from strife his shatter'd bands;
    And from the charge they drew,
As mountain-waves, from wasted lands,
    Sweep back to ocean blue.
Then did their loss his foemen know;
Their King, their Lords, their mightiest low,
They melted from the field as snow,
When streams are swoln and south winds blow
    Dissolves in silent dew.
Tweed's echoes heard the ceaseless plash,
    While many a broken band,
Disorder'd, through her currents dash,
    To gain the Scottish land;
To town and tower, to town and dale,
To tell red Flodden's dismal tale,
And raise the universal wail.
Tradition, legend, tune, and song,

Shall many an age that wail prolong:
Still from the sire the son shall hear
Of the stern strife, and carnage drear,
  Of Flodden's fatal field,
Where shiver'd was fair Scotland's spear,
  And broken was her shield!

Day dawns upon the mountain's side:
There, Scotland! lay thy bravest pride,
Chiefs, knights, and nobles, many a one:
The sad survivors all are gone.
View not that corpse mistrustfully,
Defac'd and mangled though it be;
Nor to yon Border castle high,
Look northward with upbraiding eye;
  Nor cherish hope in vain,
That, journeying far on foreign strand,
The Royal Pilgrim to his land
  May yet return again.
He saw the wreck his rashness wrought;
Reckless of life, he desperate fought,
  And fell on Flodden plain:
And well in death his trusty band,
Firm clench'd within his manly hand,
  Beseem'd the monarch slain.
But, O! how changed since yon blithe night!
Gladly I turn me from the sight,
  Unto my tale again.

(*Marmion*, Canto VI, stanzas 33–35.)

Coronach

He is gone on the mountain,
  He is lost to the forest,
Like a summer-dried fountain,
  When our need was the sorest.

The font, reappearing,
  From the rain-drops shall borrow,
But to us comes no cheering,
  To Duncan no morrow!

The hand of the reaper
  Takes the ears that are hoary,
But the voice of the weeper
  Wails manhood in glory.
The autumn winds rushing
  Waft the leaves that are searest,
But our flower was in flushing,
  When blighting was nearest.

Fleet foot on the correi,
  Sage counsel in cumber,
Red hand in the foray,
  How sound is thy slumber!
Like the dew on the mountain,
  Like the foam on the river,
Like the bubble on the fountain,
  Thou art gone, and for ever!

(*The Lady of the Lake*, Canto III, stanza 16.)

Love

And said I that my limbs were old,
And said I that my blood was cold,
And that my kindly fire was fled,
And my poor wither'd heart was dead,
  And that I might not sing of love?—
How could I to the dearest theme,
That ever warm'd a minstrel's dream,
  So foul, so false a recreant prove!
How could I name love's very name,
Nor wake my heart to notes of flame!

In peace, Love tunes the shepherd's reed;
In war, he mounts the warrior's steed;
In halls, in gay attire is seen;
In hamlets, dances on the green.
Love rules the court, the camp, the grove,
And men below, and saints above;
For love is heaven, and heaven is love.

(*The Lay of the Last Minstrel*, Canto III, stanzas 1 and 2.)

Rosabelle

O listen, listen, ladies gay!
　　No haughty feat of arms I tell;
Soft is the note, and sad the lay,
　　That mourns the lovely Rosabelle.

—'Moor, moor the barge, ye gallant crew!
　　And, gentle ladye, deign to stay!
Rest thee in Castle Ravensheuch,
　　Nor tempt the stormy firth to-day.

'The blackening wave is edg'd with white:
　　To inch and rock the sea-mews fly;
The fishers have heard the Water-Sprite,
　　Whose screams forebode that wreck is nigh.

'Last night the gifted Seer did view
　　A wet shroud swathed round ladye gay;
Then stay thee, Fair, in Ravensheuch:
　　Why cross the gloomy firth to-day?

''Tis not because Lord Lindesay's heir
　　To-night at Roslin leads the ball,
But that my ladye-mother there
　　Sits lonely in her castle-hall.

''Tis not because the ring they ride,
　　And Lindesay at the ring rides well,

But that my sire the wine will chide,
  If 'tis not fill'd by Rosabelle.'

O'er Roslin all that dreary night
  A wondrous blaze was seen to gleam;
'Twas broader than the watch-fire's light,
  And redder than the bright moonbeam.

It glar'd on Roslin's castled rock,
  It ruddied all the copse-wood glen;
'Twas seen from Dryden's groves of oak,
  And seen from cavern'd Hawthornden.

Seem'd all on fire that chapel proud,
  Where Roslin's chiefs uncoffin'd lie,
Each Baron, for a sable shroud,
  Sheath'd in his iron panoply.

Seem'd all on fire within, around,
  Deep sacristy and altar's pale;
Shone every pillar foliage-bound,
  And glimmer'd all the dead men's mail.

Blaz'd battlement and pinnet high,
  Blaz'd every rose-carved buttress fair—
So still they blaze when fate is nigh
  The lordly line of high St. Clair.

There are twenty of Roslin's barons bold
  Lie buried within that proud chapelle;
Each one the holy vault doth hold—
  But the sea holds lovely Rosabelle!

And each St. Clair was buried there,
  With candle, with book, and with knell;
But the sea-caves rung, and the wild winds sung,
  The dirge of lovely Rosabelle.

(*The Lay of the Last Minstrel*, Canto VI, stanza 23.)

A weary lot is thine

'A weary lot is thine, fair maid,
　A weary lot is thine!
To pull the thorn thy brow to braid,
　And press the rue for wine!
A lightsome eye, a soldier's mien,
　A feather of the blue,
A doublet of the Lincoln green,—
　No more of me you knew,
　　　　　　　　　My love!
No more of me you knew.

This morn is merry June, I trow,
　The rose is budding fain;
But she shall bloom in winter snow,
　Ere we two meet again.'
He turn'd his charger as he spake,
　Upon the river shore,
He gave his bridle-reins a shake,
　Said, 'Adieu for evermore,
　　　　　　　　　My love!
And adieu for evermore.'

　　　　　　　　　(*Rokeby*, Canto III, stanza 28.)

Lochinvar

O, young Lochinvar is come out of the west,
Through all the wide Border his steed was the best;
And save his good broadsword he weapons had none,
He rode all unarm'd, and he rode all alone.
So faithful in love, and so dauntless in war,
There never was knight like the young Lochinvar.

He staid not for brake, and he stopp'd not for
    stone,
He swam the Eske river where ford there was
    none;
But ere he alighted at Netherby gate,
The bride had consented, the gallant came late:
For a laggard in love, and a dastard in war,
Was to wed the fair Ellen of brave Lochinvar.

So boldly he enter'd the Netherby Hall,
Among bride's-men, and kinsmen, and brothers, and
    all:
Then spoke the bride's father, his hand on his
    sword,
(For the poor craven bridegroom said never a
    word,)
'O come ye in peace here, or come ye in war,
Or to dance at our bridal, young Lord Lochinvar?'

'I long woo'd your daughter, my suit you denied;—
Love swells like the Solway, but ebbs like its tide—
And now am I come, with this lost love of mine,
To lead but one measure, drink one cup of wine.
There are maidens in Scotland more lovely by far,
That would gladly be bride to the young Lochinvar.'

The bride kiss'd the goblet: the knight took it up,
He quaff'd off the wine, and he threw down the
    cup.
She look'd down to blush, and she look'd up to
    sigh,
With a smile on her lips, and a tear in her eye.
He took her soft hand, ere her mother could bar—
'Now tread we a measure!' said young Lochinvar.

So stately his form, and so lovely her face,
That never a hall such a galliard did grace;
While her mother did fret, and her father did fume,
And the bridegroom stood dangling his bonnet and
    plume;
And the bride-maidens whisper'd, "'Twere better by
    far,
To have match'd our fair cousin with young
    Lochinvar.'

One touch to her hand, and one word in her ear,
When they reach'd the hall-door, and the charger
    stood near;
So light to the croupe the fair lady he swung,
So light to the saddle before her he sprung!
'She is won! we are gone, over bank, bush, and scaur;
They'll have fleet steeds that follow,' quoth young
    Lochinvar.

There was mounting 'mong Græmes of the Netherby
    clan;
Forsters, Fenwicks, and Musgraves, they rode and
    they ran:
There was racing and chasing on Cannobie Lee,
But the lost bride of Netherby ne'er did they see.
So daring in love, and so dauntless in war,
Have ye e'er heard of gallant like young Lochinvar?

             (*Marmion*, Canto v, stanza 12.)

Proud Maisie

Proud Maisie is in the wood,
    Walking so early;
Sweet Robin sits on the bush,
    Singing so rarely.

'Tell me, thou bonny bird,
  When shall I marry me?'
'When six braw gentlemen
  Kirkward shall carry ye.'

'Who makes the bridal bed,
  Birdie, say truly?'
'The grey-headed sexton
  That delves the grave duly.

'The glow-worm o'er grave and stone
  Shall light thee steady.
The owl from the steeple sing,
  "Welcome, proud lady".'

(*The Heart of Midlothian*, Chapter XL.)

Lucy Ashton's Song

Look not thou on beauty's charming,
Sit thou still when kings are arming,
Taste not when the wine-cup glistens,
Speak not when the people listens,
Stop thine ear against the singer,
From the red gold keep thy finger;
Vacant heart and hand and eye,
Easy live and quiet die.

(*The Bride of Lammermoor*, Chapter III.)

Donald Caird[1]

Donald Caird's come again!
Donald Caird's come again!
Tell the news in brugh[2] and glen,
Donald Caird's come again!

[1] caird signifies tinker.   [2] burgh.

Donald Caird can lilt and sing,
Blithely dance the Hieland fling,
Drink till the gudeman be blind,
Fleech till the gudewife be kind;
Hoop a leglin,[1] clout a pan,
Or crack a pow[2] wi' ony man;—
Tell the news in brugh and glen,
Donald Caird's come again.

    Donald Caird's come again!
    Donald Caird's come again!
    Tell the news in brugh and glen,
    Donald Caird's come again.

Donald Caird can wire a maukin,[3]
Kens the wiles o' dun-deer staukin',
Leisters kipper,[4] makes a shift
To shoot a muir-fowl in the drift;
Water-bailiffs, rangers, keepers,—
He can wauk when they are sleepers;
Nor for bountith or rewaird
Dare ye mell wi'[5] Donald Caird.

    Donald Caird's come again!
    Donald Caird's come again!
    Gar the bagpipes hum amain,
    Donald Caird's come again.

Donald Caird can drink a gill
Fast as hostler-wife can fill;
Ilka ane that sells gude liquor
Kens how Donald bends a bicker;
When he's fou he's stout and saucy,
Keeps the cantle o' the causey;[6]
Hieland chief and Lawland laird
Maun gie room to Donald Caird!

[1] milk-pail   [2] head.   [3] hare.   [4] spears fish.
[5] meddle with.   [6] crown of the causeway.

Donald Caird's come again!
Donald Caird's come again!
Tell the news in brugh and glen,
Donald Caird's come again.

Steek the amrie,[1] lock the kist,[2]
Else some gear may weel be mis't;
Donald Caird finds orra[3] things
Where Allan Gregor fand the tings;[4]
Dunts of kebbuck, taits o' woo,[5]
Whiles a hen and whiles a sow,
Webs or duds frae hedge or yaird—
'Ware the wuddie,[6] Donald Caird!

Donald Caird's come again!
Donald Caird's come again!
Dinna let the Shirra ken
Donald Caird's come again.

On Donald Caird the doom was stern,
Craig[7] to tether, legs to airn;
But Donald Caird, wi' mickle study,
Caught the gift to cheat the wuddie;
Rings of airn, and bolts of steel,
Fell like ice frae hand and heel!
Watch the sheep in fauld and glen,
Donald Caird's come again!

Donald Caird's come again!
Donald Caird's come again!
Dinna let the Justice ken,
Donald Caird's come again.

---

[1] cupboard.   [2] chest.   [3] odd.   [4] tongs.
[5] slices of cheese and hanks of wool.   [6] gallows.   [7] neck.

The Sun upon the Weirdlaw Hill

The sun upon the Weirdlaw Hill,
　　In Ettrick's vale, is sinking sweet;
The westland wind is hush and still,
　　The lake lies sleeping at my feet.
Yet not the landscape to mine eye
　　Bears those bright hues that once it bore;
Though evening, with her richest dye,
　　Flames o'er the hills of Ettrick's shore.

With listless look along the plain,
　　I see Tweed's silver current glide,
And coldly mark the holy fane
　　Of Melrose rise in ruin'd pride.
The quiet lake, the balmy air,
　　The hill, the stream, the tower, the tree,—
Are they still such as once they were?
　　Or is the dreary change in me?

Alas, the warp'd and broken board,
　　How can it bear the painter's dye!
The harp of strain'd and tuneless chord,
　　How to the minstrel's skill reply!
To aching eyes each landscape lowers,
　　To feverish pulse each gale blows chill;
And Araby's or Eden's bowers
　　Were barren as this moorland hill.

ANON.

Epitaph on John Murray, 1777

Ah, John, what changes since I saw thee last;
Thy fishing and thy shooting days are past,
Bagpipes and hautboys thou canst sound no more;

Thy nods, grimaces, winks and pranks are o'er.
Thy harmless, queerish, incoherent talk,
Thy wild vivacity, and trudging walk
Will soon be quite forgot. Thy joys on earth—
A snuff, a glass, riddles and noisy mirth—
Are vanished all. Yet blest, I hope, thou art,
For, in thy station, weel thou play'dst thy part.

(From his gravestone in the kirkyard of Kells, Galloway.)

False luve! and hae ye played me this?
(From David Herd's *Scottish Songs*, 1776.)

False luve! and hae ye played me this,
   In the simmer, 'mid the flowers?
I sall repay ye back again,
   In the winter 'mid the showers.

But again, dear luve, and again, dear luve,
   Will ye not turn again?
As ye look to ither women,
   Sall I to ither men.

Kind Robin Lo'es Me
(From David Herd's *Scottish Songs*, 1776.)

Robin is my only joe,[1]
Robin has the art to lo'e,
So to his suit I mean to bow
   Because I ken he lo'es me.
Happy happy was the show'r,
That led me to his birken bow'r,
Whare first of love I fand the pow'r,
   And ken'd that Robin lo'ed me.

[1] sweetheart.

They speak of napkins, speak of rings,
Speak of gloves and kissing strings,
And name a thousand bonny things,
　　And ca' them signs he lo'es me.
But I'd prefer a smack of Rob,
Sporting on the velvet fog,[1]
To gifts as lang's a plaiden wobb,[2]
　　Because I ken he lo'es me.

He's tall and sonsy, frank and free,
Lo'ed by a' and dear to me,
Wi' him I'd live, wi' him I'd die,
　　Because my Robin lo'es me.
My titty Mary said to me,
Our courtship but a joke wad be,
And I, or lang, be made to see
　　That Robin did na lo'e me.

But little kens she what has been,
Me and my honest Rob between,
And in his wooing, O so keen,
　　Kind Robin is that lo'es me.
Then fly ye lazy hours away,
And hasten on the happy day,
When joined our hands Mess John shall say,
　　And mak him mine that lo'es me.

Till then let every chance unite,
To weigh our love and fix delight,
And I'll look down on such wi' spite,
　　Wha doubt that Robin lo'es me.
O hey Robin, quo' she, O hey Robin, quo' she,
　　O hey Robin, quo' she,
　　Kind Robin lo'es me.

　　　[1] moss.　　　[2] web of rough tweed.

THOMAS CAMPBELL
1777–1844

Freedom and Love

How delicious is the winning
Of a kiss at love's beginning,
When two mutual hearts are sighing
For the knot there's no untying!

Ye remember, 'midst your wooing,
Love has bliss, but Love has ruing;
Other smiles may make you fickle,
Tears for other charms may trickle.

Love he comes, and Love he tarries,
Just as fate or fancy carries;
Longest stays, when sorest chidden;
Laughs and flies, when press'd and bidden.

Bind the sea to slumber stilly,
Bind its odour to the lily,
Bind the aspen ne'er to quiver,
Then bind Love to last for ever.

Love's a fire that needs renewal
Of fresh beauty for its fuel:
Love's wing moults when caged and captured,
Only free, he soars enraptured.

Can you keep the bee from ranging
Or the ringdove's neck from changing?
No! nor fetter'd Love from dying
In the knot there's no untying.

Florine

Could I bring back lost youth again
 And be what I have been,
I'd court you in a gallant strain,
 My young and fair Florine.

But mine's the chilling age that chides
 Devoted rapture's glow,
And Love—that conquers all besides—
 Finds Time a conquering foe.

Farewell! we're severed by our fate
 As far as night from noon;
You came into the world too late,
 And I depart so soon.

The River of Life

The more we live, more brief appear
 Our life's succeeding stages:
A day to childhood seems a year,
 And years like passing ages.

The gladsome current of our youth,
 Ere passion yet disorders,
Steals lingering like a river smooth
 Along its grassy borders.

But as the careworn cheek grows wan,
 And sorrow's shafts fly thicker,
Ye stars, that measure life to man,
 Why seem your courses quicker?

When joys have lost their bloom and breath,
    And life itself is vapid,
Why, as we reach the Falls of death,
    Feel we its tide more rapid?

It may be strange—yet who would change
    Time's course to slower speeding,
When one by one our friends have gone
    And left our bosoms bleeding?

Heaven gives our years of fading strength
    Indemnifying fleetness;
And those of youth, a seeming length,
    Proportion'd to their sweetness.

ALLAN CUNNINGHAM

1784–1842

The sun rises bright in France

The sun rises bright in France,
    And fair sets he;
But he has tint[1] the blythe blink he had
    In my ain countree.

O, it's nae my ain ruin
    That saddens aye my e'e,
But the dear Marie I left ahin'
    Wi' sweet bairnies three.

My lanely hearth burn'd bonnie,
    And smiled my ain Marie;
I've left a' my heart behin'
    In my ain countree.

[1] lost.

The bud comes back to summer,
    And the blossom to the bee;
But I'll win back, O never,
    To my ain countree.

O, I am leal to high Heaven,
    Where soon I hope to be,
An' there I'll meet ye a' soon
    Frae my ain countree!

Hame, hame, hame

Hame, hame, hame, O hame fain wad I be—
    O hame, hame, hame, to my ain countree!
When the flower is i' the bud and the leaf is on the
        tree,
The larks shall sing me hame in my ain countree;
Hame, hame, hame, O hame fain wad I be—
O hame, hame, hame, to my ain countree!

The green leaf o' loyaltie's beginning for to fa',
The bonnie White Rose it is withering an' a';
But I'll water 't wi' the blude of usurping tyrannie,
An' green it will graw in my ain countree.

O, there's nocht now frae ruin my country can save,
But the keys o' kind heaven, to open the grave;
That a' the noble martyrs wha died for loyaltie
May rise again an' fight for their ain countree.

The great now are gane, a' wha ventured to save,
The new grass is springing on the tap o' their grave;
But the sun through the mirk blinks blythe in my
        e'e,
'I'll shine on ye yet in your ain countree.'

Hame, hame, hame, O hame fain wad I be—
O hame, hame, hame, to my ain countree!

A wet sheet and a flowing sea

A wet sheet and a flowing sea,
  A wind that follows fast,
And fills the white and rustling sail,
  And bends the gallant mast;
And bends the gallant mast, my boys,
  While, like the eagle free,
Away the good ship flies, and leaves
  Old England on the lee.

O for a soft and gentle wind!
  I heard a fair one cry;
But give to me the snoring breeze,
  And white waves heaving high;
And white waves heaving high, my boys,
  The good ship tight and free—
The world of waters is our home,
  And merry men are we.

There's tempest in yon hornèd moon,
  And lightning in yon cloud;
And hark the music, mariners,
  The wind is piping loud;
The wind is piping loud, my boys,
  The lightning flashing free—
While the hollow oak our palace is,
  Our heritage the sea.

ANON.

Canadian Boat Song

Fair these broad meads—these hoary woods are
    grand;
But we are exiles from our fathers' land.

Listen to me, as when you heard our father
  Sing long ago the song of other shores—
Listen to me, and then in chorus gather
  All your deep voices, as ye pull your oars.

From the lone sheiling of the misty island
  Mountains divide us, and the waste of seas—
Yet still the blood is strong, the heart is Highland,
  And we in dreams behold the Hebrides.

We ne'er shall tread the fancy-haunted valley,
  Where 'tween the dark hills creeps the small clear
    stream,
In arms around the patriarch banner rally,
  Nor see the moon on royal tombstones gleam.

When the bold kindred, in the time long vanish'd,
  Conquered the soil and fortified the keep,—
No seer foretold the children would be banish'd
  That a degenerate lord might boast his sheep.

Come foreign rage—let Discord burst in slaughter!
  O then for clansmen true, and stern claymore—
The hearts that would have given their blood like
    water,
  Beat heavily beyond the Atlantic roar.

LADY JOHN SCOTT

1810–1900

The Comin' o' the Spring

There's no a muir in my ain land but's fu' o' sang
    the day,
Wi' the whaup, and the gowden plover, and the lintie
    upon the brae.

The birk in the glen is springin', the rowan-tree in
    the shaw,
And every burn is rinnin' wild wi' the meltin' o' the
    snaw.

The wee white cluds in the blue lift are hurryin' light
    and free,
Their shadows fleein' on the hills, where I, too, fain
    wad be;
The wind frae the west is blawing, and wi' it seems
    to bear
The scent o' the thyme and gowan thro' a' the caller
    air.

The herd doon the hillside's linkin'. O licht his heart
    may be
Whose step is on the heather, his glance ower muir
    and lea!
On the Moss are the wild ducks gatherin', whar the
    pules like diamonds lie,
And far up soar the wild geese, wi' weird unyirdly
    cry.

In mony a neuk the primrose lies hid frae stranger
    een,
An' the broom on the knowes is wavin' wi' its cludin'[1]
    o' gowd and green;
Ower the first green springs o' heather the muir-fowl
    faulds his wing,
And there's nought but joy in my ain land at the
    comin' o' the Spring!

[1] clothing.

Ettrick

When we first rade down Ettrick,
Our bridles were ringing, our hearts were dancing,
The waters were singing, the sun was glancing,
An' blithely our voices rang out thegither,
As we brushed the dew frae the blooming heather,
  When we first rade down Ettrick.

When we next rade down Ettrick,
The day was dying, the wild birds calling,
The wind was sighing, the leaves were falling,
An' silent an' weary, but closer thegither,
We urged our steeds thro' the faded heather,
  When we next rade down Ettrick.

When I last rade down Ettrick,
The winds were shifting, the storm was waking,
The snow was drifting, my heart was breaking,
For we never again were to ride thegither,
In sun or storm on the mountain heather,
  When I last rade down Ettrick.

ALEXANDER SMITH

1830–1867

Glasgow

City! I am true son of thine;
Ne'er dwelt I where great mornings shine
  Around the bleating pens;
Ne'er by the rivulets I strayed,
And ne'er upon my childhood weighed
  The silence of the glens.
Instead of shores where ocean beats,
I hear the ebb and flow of streets.

Black Labour draws his weary waves.
Into their secret-moaning caves;
   But with the morning light,
The sea again will overflow
With a long weary sound of woe,
   Again to faint in night.
Wave am I in that sea of woes;
Which, night and morning, ebbs and flows.

I dwelt within a gloomy court
Wherein did never sunbeam sport;
   Yet there my heart was stirr'd—
My very blood did dance and thrill,
When on my narrow window-sill,
   Spring lighted like a bird.
Poor flowers—I watched them pine for weeks,
With leaves as pale as human cheeks.

Afar, one summer, I was borne;
Through golden vapours of the morn,
   I heard the hills of sheep:
I trod with a wild ecstasy
The bright fringe of the living sea:
   And on a ruined keep
I sat, and watched an endless plain
Blacken beneath the gloom of rain.

O fair the lightly sprinkled waste,
O'er which a laughing shower has raced!
   O fair the April shoots!
O fair the woods on summer days,
While a blue hyacinthine haze
   Is dreaming round the roots!
In thee, O City! I discern
Another beauty, sad and stern.

Draw thy fierce streams of blinding ore,
Smite on a thousand anvils, roar
   Down to the harbour-bars;
Smoulder in smoky sunsets, flare
On rainy nights, with street and square
   Lie empty to the stars.
From terrace proud to alley base
I know thee as my mother's face.

When sunset bathes thee in his gold,
In wreaths of bronze thy sides are rolled,
   Thy smoke is dusky fire;
And, from the glory round thee poured,
A sunbeam like an angel's sword
   Shivers upon a spire.
Thus have I watched thee, Terror! Dream!
While the blue Night crept up the stream.

The wild Train plunges in the hills,
He shrieks across the midnight rills;
   Streams through the shifting glare,
The roar and flap of foundry fires,
That shake with light the sleeping shires;
   And on the moorlands bare,
He sees afar a crown of light
Hang o'er thee in the hollow night.

At midnight, when thy suburbs lie
As silent as a noonday sky,
   When larks with heat are mute,
I love to linger on thy bridge,
All lonely as a mountain ridge,
   Disturbed but by my foot;
While the black lazy stream beneath,
Steals from its far-off wilds of heath.

And through my heart, as through a dream,
Flows on that black disdainful stream;
   All scornfully it flows,
Between the huddled gloom of masts,
Silent as pines unvexed by blasts—
   'Tween lamps in streaming rows.
O wondrous sight! O stream of dread!
O long dark river of the dead!

Afar, the banner of the year
Unfurls: but dimly prisoned here,
   'Tis only when I greet
A dropt rose lying in my way,
A butterfly that flutters gay
   Athwart the noisy street,
I know the happy Summer smiles
Around thy suburbs, miles on miles.

All raptures of this mortal breath,
Solemnities of life and death,
   Dwell in thy noise alone:
Of me thou hast become a part—
Some kindred with my human heart
   Lives in thy streets of stone;
For we have been familiar more
Than galley-slave and weary oar.

The beech is dipped in wine; the shower
Is burnished; on the swinging flower
   The latest bee doth sit.
The low sun stares through dust of gold,
And o'er the darkening heath and wold
   The large ghost-moth doth flit.
In every orchard Autumn stands,
With apples in his golden hands.

But all these sights and sounds are strange;
Then wherefore from thee should I range?
   Thou hast my kith and kin:
My childhood, youth, and manhood brave;
Thou hast an unforgotten grave
   Within thy central din.
A sacredness of love and death
Dwells in thy noise and smoky breath.

While o'er thy walls the darkness sails,
I lean against the churchyard rails;
   Up in the midnight towers
The belfried spire, the street is dead,
I hear in silence overhead
   The clang of iron hours:
It moves me not, I know her tomb
Is yonder in the shapeless gloom.

Barbara

   On the Sabbath-day,
   Through the churchyard old and gray,
Over the crisp and yellow leaves I held my rustling
   way;
And amid the words of mercy, falling on my soul
   like balms,
'Mid the gorgeous storms of music—in the mellow
   organ-calms,
'Mid the upward-streaming prayers, and the rich and
   solemn psalms,
   I stood careless, Barbara.

   My heart was otherwhere,
   While the organ shook the air,
And the priest, with outspread hands, bless'd the
   people with a prayer;

But when rising to go homeward, with a mild and
 saint-like shine
Gleam'd a face of airy beauty with its heavenly eyes
 on mine—
Gleam'd and vanish'd in a moment—O that face
 was surely thine
  Out of heaven, Barbara!

  O pallid, pallid face!
  O earnest eyes of grace!
When last I saw thee, dearest, it was in another place.
You came running forth to meet me with my love-gift
 on your wrist:
The flutter of a long white dress, then all was lost in
 mist—
A purple stain of agony was on the mouth I kiss'd,
  That wild morning, Barbara.

  I search'd, in my despair,
  Sunny noon and midnight air;
I could not drive away the thought that you were
 lingering there.
O many and many a winter night I sat when you
 were gone,
My worn face buried in my hands, beside the fire
 alone—
Within the dripping churchyard, the rain plashing
 on your stone,
  You were sleeping, Barbara.

  'Mong angels, do you think
  Of the precious golden link
I clasp'd around your happy arm while sitting by
 yon brink?

Or when that night of gliding dance, of laughter and
     guitars,
Was emptied of its music, and we watch'd, through
     lattice-bars,
The silent midnight heaven creeping o'er us with its
     stars,
       Till the day broke, Barbara?

       In the years I've changed;
       Wild and far my heart has ranged,
And many sins and errors now have been on me
     avenged;
But to you I have been faithful whatsoever good I
     lack'd:
I loved you, and above my life still hangs that love
     intact—
Your love the trembling rainbow, I the reckless
     cataract.
       Still I love you, Barbara.

       Yet, Love, I am unblest;
       With many doubts opprest,
I wander like the desert wind without a place of rest.
Could I but win you for an hour from off that starry
     shore.
The hunger of my soul were still'd; for Death hath
     told you more
Than the melancholy world doth know—things
     deeper than all lore
       You could teach me, Barbara.

       In vain, in vain, in vain!
       You will never come again.
There droops upon the dreary hills a mournful fringe
     of rain;

The gloaming closes slowly round, loud winds are in
    the tree,
Round selfish shores for ever moans the hurt and
    wounded sea;
There is no rest upon the earth, peace is with Death
    and thee—
        Barbara!

JAMES THOMSON

1834–1882

The City of Dreadful Night

IV

As I came through the desert thus it was,
As I came through the desert: All was black,
In heaven no single star, on earth no track;
A brooding hush without a stir or note,
The air so thick it clotted in my throat;
And thus for hours; then some enormous things
Swooped past with savage cries and clanking wings:
        But I strode on austere;
        No hope could have no fear.

As I came through the desert thus it was,
As I came through the desert: Eyes of fire
Glared at me throbbing with a starved desire;
The hoarse and heavy and carnivorous breath
Was hot upon me from deep jaws of death;
Sharp claws, swift talons, fleshless fingers cold
Plucked at me from the bushes, tried to hold:
        But I strode on austere;
        No hope could have no fear.

As I came through the desert thus it was,
As I came through the desert: Lo you, there,
That hillock burning with a brazen glare;
Those myriad dusky flames with points a-glow
Which writhed and hissed and darted to and fro;
A Sabbath of the Serpents, heaped pell-mell
For Devil's roll-call and some *fête* of Hell:
   Yet I strode on austere;
   No hope could have no fear.

As I came through the desert thus it was,
As I came through the desert: Meteors ran
And crossed their javelins on the black sky-span;
The zenith opened to a gulf of flame,
The dreadful thunderbolts jarred earth's fixed frame:
The ground all heaved in waves of fire that surged
And weltered round me sole there unsubmerged:
   Yet I strode on austere;
   No hope could have no fear.

As I came through the desert thus it was,
As I came through the desert: Air once more,
And I was close upon a wild sea-shore;
Enormous cliffs arose on either hand,
The deep tide thundered up a league-broad strand;
White foambelts seethed there, wan spray swept and
  flew;
The sky broke, moon and stars and clouds and blue:
   And I strode on austere;
   No hope could have no fear.

As I came through the desert thus it was,
As I came through the desert: On the left
The sun arose and crowned a broad crag-cleft;
There stopped and burned out black, except a rim,

A bleeding eyeless socket, red and dim;
Whereon the moon fell suddenly south-west,
And stood above the right-hand cliffs at rest:
                    Still I strode on austere;
                    No hope could have no fear.

As I came through the desert thus it was,
As I came through the desert: From the right
A shape came slowly with a ruddy light;
A woman with a red lamp in her hand,
Bareheaded and barefooted on that strand;
O desolation moving with such grace!
O anguish with such beauty in thy face!
                    I fell as on my bier,
                    Hope travailed with such fear.

As I came through the desert thus it was,
As I came through the desert: I was twain,
Two selves distinct that cannot join again;
One stood apart and knew but could not stir,
And watched the other stark in swoon and her;
And she came on, and never turned aside,
Between such sun and moon and roaring tide:
                    And as she came more near
                    My soul grew mad with fear.

As I came through the desert thus it was,
As I came through the desert: Hell is mild
And piteous matched with that accursèd wild;
A large black sign was on her breast that bowed,
A broad black band ran down her snow-white shroud;
That lamp she held was her own burning heart,
Whose blood-drops trickled step by step apart;
                    The mystery was clear;
                    Mad rage had swallowed fear.

As I came through the desert thus it was,
As I came through the desert: By the sea
She knelt and bent above that senseless me;
Those lamp-drops fell upon my white brow there,
She tried to cleanse them with her tears and hair;
She murmured words of pity, love, and woe,
She heeded not the level rushing flow:
       And mad with rage and fear,
       I stood stonebound so near.

As I came through the desert thus it was,
As I came through the desert: When the tide
Swept up to her there kneeling by my side,
She clasped that corpse-like me, and they were borne
Away, and this vile me was left forlorn;
I know the whole sea cannot quench that heart,
Or cleanse that brow, or wash those two apart:
       They love; their doom is drear,
       Yet they nor hope nor fear;
       But I, what do I here?

X

The mansion stood apart in its own ground;
   In front thereof a fragrant garden-lawn,
High trees about it, and the whole walled round:
   The massy iron gates were both withdrawn;
And every window of its front shed light,
Portentous in that City of the Night.

But though thus lighted it was deadly still
   As all the countless bulks of solid gloom:
Perchance a congregation to fulfil
   Solemnities of silence in this doom,
Mysterious rites of dolour and despair
Permitting not a breath of chant or prayer?

Broad steps ascended to a terrace broad
   Whereon lay still light fron the open door;
The hall was noble, and its aspect awed,
   Hung round with heavy black from dome to floor;
And ample stairways rose to left and right
Whose balustrades were also draped with night.

I paced from room to room, from hall to hall,
   Nor any life throughout the maze discerned;
But each was hung with its funereal pall,
   And held a shrine, around which tapers burned,
With picture or with statue or with bust,
All copied from the same fair form of dust:

A woman very young and very fair;
   Beloved by bounteous life and joy and youth,
And loving these sweet lovers, so that care
   And age and death seemed not for her in sooth:
Alike as stars, all beautiful and bright,
These shapes lit up that mausoléan night.

At length I heard a murmur as of lips,
   And reached an open oratory hung
With heaviest blackness of the whole eclipse;
   Beneath the dome a fuming censer swung;
And one lay there upon a low white bed,
With tapers burning at the foot and head:

The Lady of the images: supine,
   Deathstill, lifesweet, with folded palms she lay:
And kneeling there as at a sacred shrine
   A young man wan and worn who seemed to pray:
A crucifix of dim and ghostly white
Surmounted the large altar left in night:—

The chambers of the mansion of my heart,
In every one whereof thine image dwells,
Are black with grief eternal for thy sake.

The inmost oratory of my soul,
Wherein thou ever dwellest quick or dead,
Is black with grief eternal for thy sake.

I kneel beside thee and I clasp the cross,
With eyes for ever fixed upon that face,
So beautiful and dreadful in its calm.

I kneel here patient as thou liest there;
As patient as a statue carved in stone,
Of adoration and eternal grief.

While thou dost not awake I cannot move;
And something tells me thou wilt never wake,
And I alive feel turning into stone.

Most beautiful were Death to end my grief,
Most hateful to destroy the sight of thee,
Dear vision better than all death or life.

But I renounce all choice of life or death,
For either shall be ever at thy side,
And thus in bliss or woe be ever well.—

He murmured thus and thus in monotone,
    Intent upon that uncorrupted face,
Entranced except his moving lips alone:
    I glided with hushed footsteps from the place.
This was the festival that filled with light
That palace in the City of the Night.

XX

I sat me weary on a pillar's base,
    And leaned against the shaft; for broad moonlight
O'erflowed the peacefulness of cloistered space,
    A shore of shadow slanting from the right:
The great cathedral's western front stood there,
A wave-worn rock in that calm sea of air.

Before it, opposite my place of rest,
    Two figures faced each other, large, austere;
A couchant sphinx in shadow to the breast,
    An angel standing in the moonlight clear;
So mighty by magnificence of form,
They were not dwarfed beneath that mass enorm.

Upon the cross-hilt of a naked sword
    The angel's hands, as prompt to smite, were held;
His vigilant intense regard was poured
    Upon the creature placidly unquelled,
Whose front was set at level gaze which took
No heed of aught, a solemn trance-like look.

And as I pondered these opposèd shapes
    My eyelids sank in stupor, that dull swoon
Which drugs and with a leaden mantle drapes
    The outworn to worse weariness. But soon
A sharp and clashing noise the stillness broke,
And from the evil lethargy I woke.

The angel's wings had fallen, stone on stone,
    And lay there shattered; hence the sudden sound
A warrior leaning on his sword alone
    Now watched the sphinx with that regard profound
The sphinx unchanged looked forthright, as aware
Of nothing in the vast abyss of air.

Again I sank in that repose unsweet,
  Again a clashing noise my slumber rent;
The warrior's sword lay broken at his feet:
  An unarmed man with raised hands impotent
Now stood before the sphinx, which ever kept
Such mien as if with open eyes it slept.

My eyelids sank in spite of wonder grown;
  A louder crash upstartled me in dread:
The man had fallen forward, stone on stone,
  And lay there shattered, with his trunkless head
Between the monster's large quiescent paws,
Beneath its grand front changeless as life's laws.

The moon had circled westward full and bright,
  And made the temple-front a mystic dream,
And bathed the whole enclosure with its light,
  The sworded angel's wrecks, the sphinx supreme:
I pondered long that cold majestic face
Whose vision seemed of infinite void space.

DAVID GRAY

1838–1861

Sonnet 1

(From *In the Shadows*)

If it must be; if it must be, O God!
  That I die young, and make no further moans;
That, underneath the unrespective sod,
  In unescutcheoned privacy, my bones
Shall crumble soon,—then give me strength to bear
  The last convulsive throe of too sweet breath!
I tremble from the edge of life, to dare
  The dark and fatal leap, having no faith,

No glorious yearning for the Apocalypse;
  But like a child that in the night-time cries
For light, I cry; forgetting the eclipse
  Of knowledge and our human destinies,
O peevish and uncertain soul! obey
  The law of life in patience till the Day.

THOMAS DAVIDSON
1838–1870

And there will I be buried

Tell me not the good and wise
  Care not where their dust reposes—
That to him in death who lies
  Rocky beds are even as roses.

I've been happy above ground;
  I can never be happy under
Out of gentle Teviot's sound—
  Part us not then, far asunder.

Lay me here where I may see
  Teviot round his meadows flowing,
And around and over me
  Winds and clouds for ever going.

Love's Last Suit

Love, forget me when I'm gone!
When the tree is overthrown,
Let its place be digg'd and sown
O'er with grass;—when that is grown,
The very place shall be unknown!
So court I oblivion.
So I charge thee, by our love,
Love, forget me when I'm gone!

Love of him that lies in clay
  Only maketh life forlorn—
Clouding o'er the new-born day
  With regrets of yester morn.
And what is love of him that's low,
  Or sunshine on his grave that floats?
Love nor sunshine reacheth now
  Deeper than the daisy roots!

So, when he that nigh me hovers—
Death—that spares not happy lovers—
Comes to claim his little due,
Love—as thou art good and true—
Proudly give the churl his own,
And forget me when I'm gone!

ANDREW LANG

1844–1912

Almæ Matres

(St. Andrews, 1862.   Oxford, 1865.)

St. Andrews by the Northern Sea,
  A haunted town it is to me!
A little city, worn and grey,
  The grey North Ocean girds it round,
And o'er the rocks, and up the bay,
  The long sea-rollers surge and sound.
And still the thin and biting spray
  Drives down the melancholy street,
And still endure, and still decay,
  Towers that the salt winds vainly beat.
Ghost-like and shadowy they stand
Dim mirrored in the wet sea-sand.

St. Leonard's chapel, long ago
   We loitered idly where the tall
Fresh-budded mountain ashes blow
   Within thy desecrated wall:
The tough roots rent the tomb below,
   The April birds sang clamorous,
We did not dream, we could not know
   How hardly Fate would deal with us!

O, broken minster, looking forth
   Beyond the bay, above the town,
O, winter of the kindly North,
   O, college of the scarlet gown,
And shining sands beside the sea,
   And stretch of links beyond the sand,
Once more I watch you, and to me
   It is as if I touched his hand!

And therefore art thou yet more dear,
   O, little city, grey and sere,
Though shrunken from thine ancient pride
   And lonely by thy lonely sea,
Than these fair halls on Isis' side,
   Where Youth an hour came back to me!

A land of waters green and clear,
   Of willows and of poplars tall,
And, in the spring-time of the year,
   The white may breaking over all,
And Pleasure quick to come at call.
   And summer rides by marsh and wold,
And Autumn with her crimson pall
   About the towers of Magdalen rolled;
And strange enchantments from the past,
   And memories of the friends of old,

And strong Tradition, binding fast
   The 'flying terms' with bands of gold,—
All these hath Oxford: all are dear,
   But dearer far the little town,
The drifting surge, the wintry year,
   The college of the scarlet gown.
      St. Andrews by the Northern Sea,
         That is a haunted town to me!

Clevedon Church

Westward I watch the low green hills of Wales,
   The low sky silver grey,
The turbid Channel with the wandering sails
   Moans through the winter day.
There is no colour but one ashen light
   On tower and lonely tree,
The little church upon the windy height
   Is grey as sky or sea.

But there hath he that woke the sleepless Love
   Slept through these fifty years,
There is the grave that has been wept above
   With more than mortal tears.
And far below I hear the Channel sweep
   And all his waves complain,
As Hallam's dirge through all the years must keep
   Its monotone of pain.

.   .   .   .   .   .

Grey sky, brown waters, as a bird that flies,
   My heart flits forth from these
Back to the winter rose of northern skies,
   Back to the northern seas.

And lo, the long waves of the ocean beat
 Below the minster grey,
Caverns and chapels worn of saintly feet,
 And knees of them that pray.

And I remember me how twain were one
 Beside that ocean dim,
I count the years passed over since the sun
 That lights me looked on him,
And dreaming of the voice that, safe in sleep,
 Shall greet me not again,
Far, far below I hear the Channel sweep
 And all his waves complain.

Lost Love

Who wins his love shall lose her,
 Who loses her shall gain,
For still the spirit woos her,
 A soul without a stain;
And memory still pursues her
 With longings not in vain!

He loses her who gains her,
 Who watches day by day
The dust of time that stains her,
 The griefs that leave her gray—
The flesh that yet enchains her
 Whose grace hath passed away!

Oh, happier he who gains not
 The love some seem to gain:
The joy that custom stains not
 Shall still with him remain;
The loveliness that wanes not,
 The love that ne'er can wane.

In dreams she grows not older
    The lands of dream among;
Though all the world wax colder,
    Though all the songs be sung,
In dreams doth he behold her
    Still fair and kind and young.

Twilight on Tweed

Three crests against the saffron sky,
    Beyond the purple plain,
The dear remembered melody
    Of Tweed once more again.

Wan water from the border hills,
    Dear voice from the old years,
Thy distant music lulls and stills,
    And moves to quiet tears.

Like a loved ghost thy fabled flood
    Fleets through the dusky land;
Where Scott, come home to die, has stood,
    My feet returning stand.

A mist of memory broods and floats,
    The border waters flow;
The air is full of ballad notes,
    Borne out of long ago.

Old songs that sung themselves to me,
    Sweet through a boy's day-dream,
While trout below the blossom'd tree
    Plashed in the golden stream.

.   .   .   .   .   .

Twilight, and Tweed, and Eildon Hill,
   Fair and thrice fair you be;
You tell me that the voice is still
   That should have welcomed me.

ROBERT LOUIS STEVENSON
1850–1894

Blows the wind today

Blows the wind today, and the sun and the rain are
   flying,
   Blows the wind on the moors today and now,
Where about the graves of the martyrs the whaups
   are crying,
   My heart remembers how!

Grey recumbent tombs of the dead in desert places,
   Standing stones on the vacant wine-red moor,
Hills of sheep, and the homes of the silent vanished
   races,
   And winds, austere and pure:

Be it granted me to behold you again in dying,
   Hills of home! and to hear again the call;
Hear about the graves of the martyrs the peewees
   crying,
   And hear no more at all.

In the Highlands

In the highlands, in the country places,
Where the old plain men have rosy faces,
   And the young fair maidens
   Quiet eyes;

Where essential silence cheers and blesses,
And for ever in the hill-recesses
Her more lovely music
Broods and dies.

O to mount again where erst I haunted;
Where the old red hills are bird-enchanted,
And the low green meadows
Bright with sward;
And when even dies, the million-tinted,
And the night has come, and planets glinted,
Lo! the valley hollow
Lamp-bestarred.

O to dream, O to awake and wander
There, and with delight to take and render,
Through the trance of silence,
Quiet breath;
Lo! for there, among the flowers and grasses,
Only the mightier movement sounds and passes;
Only winds and rivers,
Life and death.

Romance

I will make you brooches and toys for your delight
Of bird-song at morning and star-shine at night.
I will make a palace fit for you and me,
Of green days in forests and blue days at sea.

I will make my kitchen, and you shall keep your room,
Where white flows the river and bright blows the
broom,
And you shall wash your linen and keep your body
white
In rainfall at morning and dewfall at night.

And this shall be for music when no one else is near,
The fine song for singing, the rare song to hear!
That only I remember, that only you admire,
Of the broad road that stretches and the roadside
fire.

Requiem

Under the wide and starry sky
Dig the grave and let me lie:
Glad did I live and gladly die,
 And I laid me down with a will.

This be the verse you grave for me:
Here he lies where he long'd to be;
Home is the sailor, home from sea,
 And the hunter home from the hill.

JOHN DAVIDSON

1857–1909

Greenock

        I need
No world more spacious than the region here:
The foam-embroidered firth, a purple path
For argosies that still on pinions speed,
Or fiery-hearted cleave with iron limbs
And bows precipitous the pliant sea;
The sloping shores that fringe the velvet tides
With heavy bullion and with golden lace
Of restless pebble worn and fine spun sand;
The villages that sleep the winter through,
And, wakening with the spring, keep festival
All summer and all autumn: this grey town

That pipes the morning up before the lark
With shrieking steam, and from a hundred stalks
Lacquers the sooty sky; where hammers clang
On iron hulls, and cranes in harbours creak
Rattle and swing, whole cargoes on their necks;
Where men sweat gold that others hoard or spend,
And lurk like vermin in their narrow streets:
This old grey town, this firth, this further strand
Spangled with hamlets, and the wooden steeps,
Whose rocky tops behind each other press,
Fantastically carved like antique helms
High-hung in heaven's cloudy armoury,
Is world enough for me. Here daily dawn
Burns through the smoky east; with fire-shod feet
The sun treads heaven, and steps from hill to hill
Downward before the night that still pursues
His crimson wake; here winter plies his craft,
Soldering the years with ice; here spring appears,
Caught in a leafless brake, her garland torn,
Breathless with wonder, and the tears half-dried
Upon her rosy cheek; here summer comes
And wastes his passion like a prodigal
Right royally; and here her golden gains
Free-handed as a harlot autumn spends;
And here are men to know, women to love.

(From *A Ballad in Blank Verse of the Making of a Poet.*)

In Romney Marsh

As I went down to Dymchurch Wall,
   I heard the South sing o'er the land;
I saw the yellow sunlight fall
   On knolls where Norman churches stand.

And ringing shrilly, taut and lithe,
   Within the wind a core of sound,
The wire from Romney town to Hythe
   Alone its airy journey wound.

A veil of purple vapour flowed
   And trailed its fringe along the Straits;
The upper air like sapphire glowed;
   And roses filled Heaven's central gates.

Masts in the offing wagged their tops;
   The swinging waves pealed on the shore;
The saffron beach, all diamond drops
   And beads of surge, prolonged the roar.

As I came up from Dymchurch Wall,
   I saw above the Downs' low crest
The crimson brands of sunset fall,
   Flicker and fade from out the west.

Night sank: like flakes of silver fire
   The stars in one great shower came down;
Shrill blew the wind; and shrill the wire
   Rang out from Hythe to Romney town.

The darkly shining salt sea drops
   Streamed as the waves clashed on the shore;
The beach, with all its organ stops
   Pealing again, prolonged the roar.

I haunt the hills that overlook the sea

I haunt the hills that overlook the sea.
Here in the Winter like a meshwork shroud
The sifted snow reveals the perished land,

And powders wisps of knotgrass dank and dead
That trail like faded locks on mouldering skulls
Unearthed from shallow burial. With the Spring
The west-wind thunders through the budding hedge
That stems the furrowed steep—a sound of drums,
Of gongs and muted cymbals; yellow breasts
And brown wings whirl in gusts, fly chaffering, drop,
And surge in gusts again; in wooded coombs
The hyacinth with purple diapers
The russet beechmast, and the cowslips hoard
Their virgin gold in lucent chalices;
The sombre furze, all suddenly attired
In rich brocade, the enterprise-in-chief
And pageant of the season, over-rides
The rolling land and girds the bosomed plain
That strips her green robe to a saffron shore
And steps into the surf where threads and scales
And arabesques of blue and emerald wave
Begin to damascene the iron sea;
While faint from upland fold and covert peal
The sheep-bell and the cuckoo's mellow chime.
Then when the sovereign light from which we came,
Of earth enamoured, bends most questioning looks,
I watch the land grow beautiful, a bride
Transfigured with desire of her great lord.
Betrothal-music of the tireless larks,
Heaven-high, heaven-wide possesses all the air,
And wreathes the shining lattice of the light
With chaplets, purple clusters, vintages
Of sound from the first fragrant breath and first
Tear-sprinkled blush of Summer to the deep
Transmuted fire, the smouldering golden moons,
The wine-stained dusk of Autumn harvest-ripe;
And I behold the period of Time,
When Memory shall devolve and Knowledge lapse

Wanting a subject, and the willing earth
Leap to the bosom of the sun to be
Pure flame once more in a new time begun:
Here, as I pace the pallid doleful hills
And serpentine declivities that creep
Unhonoured to the ocean's shifting verge,
Or where the prouder curve and greener sward,
Surmounting peacefully the restless tides,
The cliffed escarpment ends in stormclad strength.

(From *The Testament of a Man Forbid.*)

A Runnable Stag

When the pods went pop on the broom, green broom,
   And apples began to be golden-skinned,
We harboured a stag in the Priory coomb,
   And we feathered his trail up-wind, up-wind,
    We feathered his trail up-wind—
      A stag of warrant, a stag, a stag,
      A runnable stag, a kingly crop,
      Brow, bay and tray and three on top,
      A stag, a runnable stag.

Then the huntsman's horn rang yap, yap, yap,
   And 'Forwards' we heard the harbourer shout;
But 'twas only a brocket that broke a gap
   In the beechen underwood, driven out,
    From the underwood antlered out
      By warrant and might of the stag, the stag,
      The runnable stag, whose lordly mind
      Was bent on sleep, though beamed and tined,
      He stood, a runnable stag.

So we tufted the covert till afternoon
   With Tinkerman's Pup and Bell-of-the-North;

And hunters were sulky and hounds out of tune
　Before we tufted the right stag forth
　Before we tufted him forth,
　　　The stag of warrant, the wily stag,
　　　The runnable stag with his kingly crop,
　　　Brow, bay and tray and three on top,
　　　The royal and runnable stag.

It was Bell-of-the-North and Tinkerman's Pup
　That stuck to the scent till the copse was drawn.
'Tally ho! tally ho!' and the hunt was up,
　The tufters whipped and the pack laid on,
　The resolute pack laid on,
　　　And the stag of warrant away at last,
　　　The runnable stag, the same, the same,
　　　His hoofs on fire, his horns like flame,
　　　A stag, a runnable stag.

Let your gelding be: if you check or chide
　He stumbles at once and you're out of the hunt;
For three hundred gentlemen, able to ride,
　On hunters accustomed to bear the brunt,
　Accustomed to bear the brunt,
　　　Are after the runnable stag, the stag,
　　　The runnable stag with his kingly crop,
　　　Brow, bay and tray and three on top,
　　　The right, the runnable stag.

By perilous paths in coomb and dell,
　The heather, the rocks, and the river-bed,
The pace grew hot, for the scent lay well,
　And a runnable stag goes right ahead,
　The quarry went right ahead—
　　　Ahead, ahead, and fast and far;
　　　His antlered crest, his cloven hoof,
　　　Brow, bay and tray and three aloof,
　　　The stag, the runnable stag.

For a matter of twenty miles and more,
　By the densest hedge and the highest wall,
Through herds of bullocks he baffled the lore
　Of harbourer, huntsman, hounds and all,
　Of harbourer, hounds and all—
　　　The stag of warrant, the wily stag,
　　　For twenty miles, and five and five,
　　　He ran, and he never was caught alive,
　　　This stag, this runnable stag.

When he turned at bay in the leafy gloom,
　In the emerald gloom where the brook ran deep,
He heard in the distance the rollers boom,
　And he saw in a vision of peaceful sleep,
　In a wonderful vision of sleep,
　　　A stag of warrant, a stag, a stag,
　　　A runnable stag in a jewelled bed,
　　　Under the sheltering ocean dead,
　　　A stag, a runnable stag.

So a fateful hope lit up his eye,
　And he opened his nostrils wide again,
And he tossed his branching antlers high
　As he headed the hunt down the Charlock glen,
　As he raced down the echoing glen
　　　For five miles more, the stag, the stag,
　　　For twenty miles, and five and five,
　　　Not to be caught now, dead or alive,
　　　The stag, the runnable stag.

Three hundred gentlemen, able to ride,
　Three hundred horses as gallant and free,
Beheld him escape on the evening tide,
　Far out till he sank in the Severn Sea,
　Till he sank in the depths of the sea—

The stag, the buoyant stag, the stag,
That slept at last in a jewelled bed
Under the sheltering ocean spread,
The stag, the runnable stag.

Thirty Bob a Week

I couldn't touch a stop and turn a screw,
   and set the blooming world a-work for me,
like such as cut their teeth—I hope, like you—
   on the handle of a skeleton gold key;
I cut mine on a leek, which I eat it every week:
   I'm a clerk at thirty bob as you can see.

But I don't allow it's luck and all a toss;
   there's no such thing as being starred and crossed;
it's just the power of some to be a boss,
   and the bally power of others to be bossed:
I face the music, sir; you bet I ain't a cur;
   strike me lucky if I don't believe I'm lost!

For like a mole I journey in the dark,
   a-travelling along the underground
from my Pillared Halls and broad Suburbean Park,
   to come the daily dull official round;
and home again at night, with my pipe all alight,
   a-scheming how to count ten bob a pound.

And it's often very cold and very wet,
   and my misses stitches towels for a hunks;
and the Pillared Halls is half of it to let—
   three rooms about the size of travelling trunks.
And we cough, my wife and I, to dislocate a sigh,
   when the noisy little kids are in their bunks.

But you never hear her do a growl or whine,
    for she's made of flint and roses, very odd;
and I've got to cut my meaning rather fine,
    or I'd blubber, for I'm made of greens and sod:
so perhaps we are in Hell, for all that I can tell,
    and lost and damned and served up hot to God.

I ain't blaspheming, Mr. Silver-Tongue;
    I'm saying things a bit beyond your art:
of all the rummy starts you ever sprung,
    thirty bob a week's the rummiest start!
With your science and your books and your theories
      about spooks,
    did you ever hear of looking in your heart?

I didn't mean your pocket, Mr., no:
    I mean that having children and a wife,
with thirty bob on which to come and go,
    isn't dancing to the tabor and the fife:
when it doesn't make you drink, by Heaven! it makes
      you think,
    and notice curious items about life.

I step into my heart and there I meet
    a god-almighty devil singing small,
who would like to shout and whistle in the street,
    and squelch the passers flat against the wall;
if the whole world was a cake he had the power to
      take,
    he would take it, ask for more, and eat them all.

And I meet a sort of simpleton beside,
    the kind that life is always giving beans;
with thirty bob a week to keep a bride
    he fell in love and married in his teens:
at thirty bob he stuck; but he knows it isn't luck:
    he knows the seas are deeper than tureens.

And the god-almighty devil and the fool
   that meet me in the High Street on the strike,
when I walk about my heart a-gathering wool,
   are my good and evil angels if you like.
And both of them together in every kind of weather
   ride me like a double-seated bike.

That's rough a bit and needs its meaning curled.
   But I've a high old hot un in my mind—
a most engrugious notion of the world,
   that leaves your lightning 'rithmetic behind:
I give it at a glance when I say, 'There ain't no
     chance,
   nor nothing of the lucky-lottery kind.'

And it's this way that I make it out to be:
   no fathers, mothers, countries, climates—none;
not Adam was responsible for me,
   not society, nor systems, nary one:
a little sleeping seed, I woke—I did, indeed—
   a million years before the blooming sun.

I woke because I thought the time had come;
   beyond my will there was no other cause;
and everywhere I found myself at home,
   because I chose to be the thing I was;
and in whatever shape, of mollusc or of ape,
   I always went according to the laws.

I was the love that chose my mother out;
   I joined two lives and from the union burst;
my weakness and my strength without a doubt
   are mine alone for ever from the first:
it's just the very same, with a difference in the name,
   as 'Thy will be done.' You say it if you durst!

They say it daily up and down the land
   as easy as you take a drink, it's true;
but the difficultest go to understand,
   and the difficultest job a man can do,
is to come it brave and meek with thirty bob a week,
   and feel that that's the proper thing for you.

It's naked child against a hungry wolf;
   it's playing bowls upon a splitting wreck;
it's walking on a string across a gulf
   with millstones fore-and-aft about your neck;
but the thing is daily done by many and many a one;
   and we fall, face forward, fighting, on the deck.

The Last Journey

I felt the world a-spinning on its nave,
   I felt it sheering blindly round the sun;
I felt the time had come to find a grave:
   I knew it in my heart my days were done.
I took my staff in hand; I took the road,
And wandered out to seek my last abode.
        Hearts of gold and hearts of lead
          Sing it yet in sun and rain,
           'Heel and toe from dawn to dusk,
           Round the world and home again.'

Oh, long before the bere was steeped for malt,
   And long before the grape was crushed for wine,
The glory of the march without a halt,
   The triumph of a stride like yours and mine
Was known to folk like us, who walked about,
To be the sprightliest cordial out and out!
        Folk like us, with hearts that beat,
          Sang it too in sun and rain—
           'Heel and toe from dawn to dusk,
           Round the world and home again.'

My feet are heavy now, but on I go,
  My head erect beneath the tragic years.
The way is steep, but I would have it so;
  And dusty, but I lay the dust with tears,
Though none can see me weep: alone I climb
The rugged path that leads me out of time—
        Out of time and out of all,
          Singing yet in sun and rain,
          'Heel and toe from dawn to dusk,
          Round the world and home again.'

Farewell the hope that mocked, farewell despair
  That went before me still and made the pace.
The earth is full of graves, and mine was there
  Before my life began, my resting-place;
And I shall find it out and with the dead
Lie down for ever, all my sayings said—
        Deeds all done and songs all sung,
          While others chant in sun and rain,
          'Heel and toe from dawn to dusk,
          Round the world and home again.'

(From *The Testament of John Davidson*.)

VIOLET JACOB

1863–1946

Tam i' the Kirk

O Jean, my Jean, when the bell ca's the congregation
  Owre valley an' hill wi' the ding frae its iron mou',
When a'body's thochts is set on his ain salvation,
        Mine's set on you.

There's a reid rose lies on the Buik o' the Word afore
   ye
   That was growin' braw on its bush at the keek o'
   day,
But the lad that pu'd yon flower i' the mornin's
   glory—
         He canna pray.

He canna pray; but there's nane i' the kirk will heed
   him
   Whar he sits sae still his lane by the side o' the wa',
For nane but the reid rose kens what my lassie gi'ed
   him—
         It an' us twa!

He canna sing for the sang that his ain he'rt raises,
   He canna see for the mist that's afore his e'en,
And a voice drouns the hale o' the psalms an' the
   paraphrases,
         Cryin' 'Jean, Jean, Jean!'

The Wild Geese

'Oh, tell me what was on yer road, ye roarin' norlan'
   wind
As ye cam' blawin' frae the land that's niver frae my
   mind?
My feet they trayvel England, but I'm deein' for the
   north—'
'My man, I heard the siller tides rin up the Firth o'
   Forth.'

'Aye, Wind, I ken them well eneuch, and fine they
   fa' and rise,
And fain I'd feel the creepin' mist on yonder shore
   that lies,

But tell me, ere ye passed them by, what saw ye on
    the way?'
'My man, I rocked the rovin' gulls that sail abune
    the Tay.'

'But saw ye naethin', leein' Wind, afore ye cam' to
    Fife?
There's muckle lyin' yont the Tay that's mair to me
    nor life.'
'My man, I swept the Angus braes ye haena trod for
    years—'
'O Wind, forgie a hameless loon that canna see for
    tears!—'

'And far abune the Angus straths I saw the wild geese
    flee,
A lang, lang skein o' beatin' wings wi' their heids
    towards the sea,
And aye their cryin' voices trailed ahint them on the
    air—'
'O Wind, hae maircy, haud yer whisht, for I daurna
    listen mair!'

MARION ANGUS
1866–1946

Mary's Song

I wad ha'e gi'en him my lips tae kiss,
Had I been his, had I been his;
Barley breid and elder wine,
Had I been his as he is mine.

The wanderin' bee it seeks the rose;
Tae the lochan's bosom the burnie goes;
The grey bird cries at evenin's fa',
'My luve, my fair one, come awa'.'

My beloved sall ha'e this he'rt tae break,
Reid, reid wine and the barley cake,
A he'rt tae break, an' a mou' tae kiss,
Tho' he be nae mine, as I am his.

Alas! Poor Queen

She was skilled in music and the dance
And the old arts of love
At the court of the poisoned rose
And the perfumed glove,
And gave her beautiful hand
To the pale Dauphin
A triple crown to win—
And she loved little dogs
       And parrots
     And red-legged partridges
And the golden fishes of the Duc de Guise
And a pigeon with a blue ruff
She had from Monsieur d'Elboeuf.

Master John Knox was no friend to her;
She spoke him soft and kind,
Her honeyed words were Satan's lure
The unwary soul to bind.
'Good sir, doth a lissome shape
And a comely face
Offend your God His Grace
Whose Wisdom maketh these
Golden fishes of the Duc de Guise?'
She rode through Liddesdale with a song;
'Ye streams sae wondrous strang,
Oh, mak' me a wrack as I come back
But spare me as I gang.'

While a hill-bird cried and cried
Like a spirit lost
By the grey storm-wind tost.

Consider the way she had to go,
Think of the hungry snare,
The net she herself had woven,
Aware or unaware,
Of the dancing feet grown still,
The blinded eyes—
Queens should be cold and wise,
And she loved little things,
      Parrots
    And red-legged partridges
And the golden fishes of the Duc de Guise
And the pigeon with the blue ruff
She had from Monsieur d'Elboeuf.

DAVID RORIE

1867–1946

The Pawky Duke

There aince was a very pawky duke,
   Far kent for his joukery-pawkery,
Wha owned a hoose wi' a gran' outlook,
   A gairden an' a rockery.
Hech mon! The pawky duke!
   Hoot ay! An' a rockery!
For a bonnet laird wi' a sma' kailyaird
   Is naethin' but a mockery!

He dwalt far up a Heelant glen
   Where the foamin' flood an' the crag is,
He dined each day on the usquebae
   An' he washed it doon wi' haggis.

Hech mon! The pawky duke!
   Hoot ay! An' a haggis!
For that's the way that the Heelanters dae
   Whaur the foamin' flood an' the crag is!

He wore a sporran an' a dirk,
   An' a beard like besom bristles,
He was an elder o' the kirk
   And he hated kists o' whistles![1]
Hech mon! The pawky duke!
   An' doon on kists o' whistles!
They're a' reid-heidit fowk up North
   Wi' beards like besom bristles!

His hair was reid as ony rose,
   His legs was lang an' bony,
He keepit a hoast an' a rubbin'-post
   An' a buskit cockernony!
Hech mon! The pawky duke!
   An' a buskit cockernony!
Ye ne'er will ken true Heelantmen
   Wha'll own they hadna ony!

An' if he met a Sassenach,
   Attour in Caledonia,
He gart him lilt in a cotton kilt
   Till he took an acute pneumonia!
Hech mon! The pawky duke!
   An' a Sassenach wi' pneumonia!
He lat him feel that the Land o' the Leal
   'S nae far frae Caledonia!

Then aye afore he socht his bed
   He danced the Gillie Callum,
An' wi's Kilmarnock[2] owre his neb
   What evil could befall him!

       [1] church organ.   [2] bonnet.

Hech mon! The pawky duke!
  What evil could befall him?
When he cast his buits an' soopled his cuits[1]
  Wi' a gude-gaun Gillie Callum!

But they brocht a joke, they did indeed,
  Ae day for his eedification,
An' they needed to trephine his heid
  Sae he deed o' the operation!
Hech mon! The pawky duke!
  Wae's me for the operation!
For weel I wot this typical Scot
  Was a michty loss to the nation!

RACHEL ANNAND TAYLOR

1876–1960

The Princess of Scotland

'Who are you that so strangely woke,
  And raised a fine hand?'
Poverty wears a scarlet cloke
  In my land.

'Duchies of dreamland, emerald, rose
  Lie at your command?'
Poverty like a princess goes
  In my land.

'Wherefore the mask of silken lace
  Tied with a golden band?'
Poverty walks with wanton grace
  In my land.

---

[1] ankles.

'Why do you softly, richly speak
  Rhythm so sweetly scanned?'
Poverty hath the Gaelic and Greek
      In my land.

'There's far-off scent about you seems
  Born in Samarkand.'
Poverty hath luxurious dreams
      In my land.

'You have wounds that like passion-flowers you hide:
  I cannot understand.'
Poverty hath one name with Pride
      In my land.

'Oh! Will you draw your last sad breath
  'Mid bitter bent and sand?'
Poverty begs from none but Death
      In my land.

HAROLD MONRO

1879–1932

Week-End Sonnet No. 1

The train! The twelve o'clock for Paradise.
  Hurry, or it will try to creep away.
Out in the country everyone is wise:
  We can be wise only on Saturday.
There you are waiting, little friendly house:
  Those are your chimney stacks, with you between.
Surrounded by old trees and strolling cows,
  Staring through all your windows at the green.

Your homely floor is creaking for our tread:
 The smiling teapot with contented spout
Thinks of the boiling water, and the bread
 Longs for the butter. All their hands are out
To greet us, and the gentle blankets seem
Purring and crooning:—'Lie in us, and dream.'

Solitude

When you have tidied all things for the night,
And while your thoughts are fading to their sleep,
You'll pause a moment in the late firelight,
Too sorrowful to weep

The large and gentle furniture has stood
In sympathetic silence all the day
With that old kindness of domestic wood;
Nevertheless the haunted room will say;
'Some one must be away.'

The little dog rolls over half awake,
Stretches his paws, yawns, looking up at you,
Wags his tail very slightly for your sake,
That you may feel he is unhappy too.

A distant engine whistles, or the floor
Creaks, or the wandering night-wind bangs a door.

Silence is scattered like a broken glass.
The minutes prick their ears and run about,
Then one by one subside again and pass
Sedately in, monotonously out.

You bend your head and wipe away a tear.
Solitude walks one heavy step more near.

SIR ALEXANDER GRAY
1882–

Scotland

Here in the Uplands
The soil is ungrateful;
The fields, red with sorrel,
Are stony and bare.
A few trees, wind-twisted—
Or are they but bushes?—
Stand stubbornly guarding
A home here and there.

Scooped out like a saucer,
The land lies before me,
The waters, once scattered,
Flow orderedly now
Through fields where the ghosts
Of the marsh and the moorland
Still ride the old marches,
Despising the plough.

The marsh and the moorland
Are not to be banished;
The bracken and heather,
The glory of broom,
Usurp all the balks
And the fields' broken fringes,
And claim from the sower
Their portion of room.

This is my country,
The land that begat me.
These windy spaces
Are surely my own.

And those who here toil
In the sweat of their faces
Are flesh of my flesh
And bone of my bone.

Hard is the day's task—
Scotland, stern Mother!—
Wherewith at all times
Thy sons have been faced:
Labour by day,
And scant rest in the gloaming,
With Want an attendant,
Not lightly outpaced.

Yet do thy children
Honour and love thee.
Harsh is thy schooling
Yet great is thy gain:
True hearts and strong limbs,
The beauty of faces,
Kissed by the wind
And caressed by the rain.

On a Cat, Ageing

He blinks upon the hearth-rug,
 And yawns in deep content,
Accepting all the comforts
 That Providence has sent.

Louder he purrs and louder,
 In one glad hymn of praise
For all the night's adventures,
 For quiet restful days.

Life will go on for ever,
    With all that cat can wish;
Warmth and the glad procession
    Of fish and milk and fish.

Only—the thought disturbs him—
    He's noticed once or twice,
The times are somehow breeding
    A nimbler race of mice.

The Deil o' Bogie

When I was young, and ower young,
I wad a deid-auld wife;
But ere three days had gane by,
    Gi-Ga-Gane-by,
I rued the sturt[1] and strife.

Sae to the Kirk-yaird furth I fared,
And to the Deil I prayed:
'O, muckle Deil o' Bogie,
    Bi-Ba-Bogie,
Come, tak the runkled[2] jade.'

When I got hame, the soor auld bitch
Was deid, ay, deid eneugh.
I yokkit the mare to the dung-cairt,
    Ding-Dang-Dung-cairt,
And drove her furth—and leuch!

And when I cam to the place o' peace,
The grave was howked, and snod:
'Gae canny wi' the corp, lads,
    Ci-Ca-Corp, lads,
You'll wauk her up, by God!

      [1] commotion.   [2] wrinkled.

Ram in, ram in the bonnie yird[1]
Upon the ill-daein wife.
When she was hale and herty,
   Hi-Ha-Herty,
She plagued me o' my life.'

But when I gat me hame again,
The hoose seemed toom[2] and wide.
For juist three days I waited,
   Wit-Wat-Waited,
Syne took a braw young bride.

In three short days my braw young wife
Had ta'en to lounderin[3] me.
'Gie's back, dear Deil o' Bogie,
   Bi-Ba-Bogie,
My auld calamitie!'

ANDREW YOUNG

1885–1971

The Scarecrow

He strides across the grassy corn
That has not grown since it was born,
A piece of sacking on a pole,
A ghost, but nothing like a soul.

Why must this dead man haunt the spring
With arms anxiously beckoning?
Is spring not hard enough to bear
For one at autumn of his year?

---

    [1] earth.   [2] empty.   [3] beating.

The Dead Crab

A rosy shield upon its back,
That not the hardest storm could crack,
From whose sharp edge projected out
Black pin-point eyes staring about;
Beneath, the well-knit cote-armure
That gave to its weak belly power;
The clustered legs with plated joints
That ended in stiletto points;
The claws like mouths it held outside:—
I cannot think this creature died
By storm or fish or sea-fowl harmed
Walking the sea so heavily armed;
Or does it make for death to be
Oneself a living armoury?

HELEN B. CRUICKSHANK

1886–1975

Shy Geordie

Up the Noran Water,
In by Inglismaddy,
Annie's got a bairnie
That hasna got a daddy.
Some say it's Tammas's
And some say it's Chay's;
An' naebody expec'it it,
Wi' Annie's quiet ways.

Up the Noran Water,
The bonnie little mannie
Is dandlit an' cuddlit close
By Inglismaddy's Annie.

Wha the bairnie's faither is
The lassie never says;
But some think it's Tammas's,
And some think it's Chay's.

Up the Noran Water,
The country folk are kind;
An' wha the bairnie's daddy is
They dinna muckle mind.
But oh! the bairn at Annie's breist,
The love in Annie's e'e!
They mak' me wish wi' a' my micht
The lucky lad was me!

The Wishin' Well

A lass cam' sabbin'
    Tae my brink,
Tae dip her hand
    An' wishin', drink.
'O, water, water,
    Gi'e tae me
This wish I wish,
    Or else I dee!'

Back cam' the lass
    Years efter-hend,
An' peered again
    At my dancin' sand.
'I mind,' she said,
    'O' drinkin' here,
But—Losh keep me,
    What *did* I speir?'[1]

[1] ask.

EDWIN MUIR

1887–1959

Scotland, 1941

We were a tribe, a family, a people,
Wallace and Bruce guard now a painted field,
And all may read the folio of our fable,
Peruse the sword, the sceptre and the shield.
A simple sky roofed in that rustic day,
The busy corn-fields and the haunted holms,
The green road winding up the ferny brae.
But Knox and Melville clapped their preaching palms
And bundled all the harvesters away,
Hoodicrow Peden in the blighted corn
Hacked with his rusty beak the starving haulms.
Out of that desolation we were born.

Courage beyond the point and obdurate pride
Made us a nation, robbed us of a nation.
Defiance absolute and myriad-eyed
That could not pluck the palm plucked our damna-
       tion.
We with such courage and the bitter wit
To fell the ancient oak of loyalty,
And strip the peopled hill and the altar bare,
And crush the poet with an iron text,
How could we read our souls and learn to be?
Here a dull drove of faces harsh and vexed,
We watch out cities burning in their pit,
To salve our souls grinding dull lucre out,
We, fanatics of the frustrate and the half,
Who once set Purgatory Hill in doubt.
Now smoke and death and money everywhere,
Mean heirlooms of each fainter generation,

And mummied housegods in their musty niches,
Burns and Scott, sham bards of a sham nation,
And spiritual defeat wrapped warm in riches,
No pride but pride of pelf. Long since the young
Fought in great bloody battles to carve out
This towering pulpit of the Golden Calf.
Montrose, Mackail, Argyle, perverse and brave,
Twisted the stream, unhooped the ancestral hill.
Never had Dee or Don or Yarrow or Till
Huddled such thriftless honour in a grave.

Such wasted bravery idle as a song,
Such hard-won ill might prove Time's verdict wrong,
And melt to pity the annalist's iron tongue.

The Little General

Early in spring the little General came
  Across the sound, bringing the island death,
And suddenly a place without a name,
  And like the pious ritual of a faith,

Hunter and quarry in the boundless trap,
  The white smoke curling from the silver gun,
The feather curling in the hunter's cap,
  And clouds of feathers floating in the sun,

While down the birds came in a deafening shower,
  Wing-hurricane, and the cattle fled in fear.
Up on the hill a remnant of a tower
  Had watched that single scene for many a year,

Weaving a wordless tale where all were gathered
  (Hunter and quarry and watcher and fabulous
    field),
A sylvan war half human and half feathered,
  Perennial emblem painted on the shield

Held up to cow a never-conquered land
Fast in the little General's fragile hand.

The Road

There is a road that turning always
  Cuts off the country of Again.
Archers stand there on every side
  And as it runs time's deer is slain,
  And lies where it has lain.

That busy clock shows never an hour.
  All flies and all in flight must tarry.
The hunter shoots the empty air
  Far on before the quarry,
  Which falls though nothing's there to parry.

The lion couching in the centre
  With mountain head and sunset brow
Rolls down the everlasting slope
  Bones picked an age ago,
  And the bones rise up and go.

There the beginning finds the end
  Before the beginning ever can be,
And the great runner never leaves
  The starting and the finishing tree,
  The budding and the fading tree.

There the ship sailing safe in harbour
  Long since in many a sea was drowned.

The treasure burning in her hold
  So near will never be found,
  Sunk past all sound.

There a man on a summer evening
  Reclines at ease upon his tomb
And is his mortal effigy.
  And there within the womb,
  The cell of doom,

The ancestral deed is thought and done,
  And in a million Edens fall
A million Adams drowned in darkness,
  For small is great and great is small,
  And a blind seed all.

The Old Gods

Old gods and goddesses who have lived so long
Through time and never found eternity,
Fettered by wasting wood and hollowing hill,

You should have fled our ever-dying song,
The mound, the well, and the green trysting tree
They are forgotten, yet you linger still.

Goddess of caverned breast and channelled brow
And cheeks slow hollowed by millenial tears,
Forests of autumn fading in your eyes,

Eternity marvels at your counted years
And kingdoms lost in time, and wonders how
There could be thoughts so bountiful and wise

As yours beneath the ever-breaking bough,
And vast compassion curving like the skies.

One foot in Eden

One foot in Eden still, I stand
And look across the other land.
The world's great day is growing late,
Yet strange these fields that we have planted
So long with crops of love and hate.
Time's handiworks by time are haunted,
And nothing now can separate
The corn and tares compactly grown.
The armorial weed in stillness bound
About the stalk; these are our own.
Evil and good stand thick around
In the fields of charity and sin
Where we shall lead our harvest in.

Yet still from Eden springs the root
As clean as on the starting day.
Time takes the foliage and the fruit
And burns the archetypal leaf
To shapes of terror and of grief
Scattered along the winter way.
But famished field and blackened tree
Bear flowers in Eden never known.
Blossoms of grief and charity
Bloom in these darkened fields alone.
What had Eden ever to say
Of hope and faith and pity and love
Until was buried all its day
And memory found its treasure trove?
Strange blessings never in Paradise
Fall from these beclouded skies.

In love for long

I've been in love for long
With what I cannot tell

And will contrive a song
For the intangible
That has no mould or shape,
From which there's no escape.

It is not even a name,
Yet is all constancy;
Tried or untried, the same,
It cannot part from me;
A breath, yet as still
As the established hill.

It is not any thing,
And yet all being is;
Being, being, being,
Its burden and its bliss.
How can I ever prove
What it is I love?

This happy happy love
Is sieged with crying sorrows,
Crushed beneath and above
Between todays and morrows;
A little paradise
Held in the world's vice.

And there it is content
And careless as a child,
And in imprisonment
Flourishes sweet and wild;
In wrong, beyond wrong,
All the world's day long.

This love a moment known
For what I do not know
And in a moment gone
Is like the happy doe

That keeps its perfect laws
Between the tiger's paws
And vindicates its cause.

A Birthday

I never felt so much
Since I have felt at all
The tingling smell and touch
Of dog-rose and sweet briar,
Nettles against the wall,
All sours and sweets that grow
Together or apart
In hedge or marsh or ditch.
I gather to my heart
Beast, insect, flower, earth, water, fire,
In absolute desire,
As fifty years ago.

Acceptance, gratitude:
The first look and the last
When all between has passed
Restore in ingenuous good
That seeks no personal end,
Nor strives to mar or mend.
Before I touched the food
Sweetness ensnared my tongue;
Before I saw the wood
I loved each nook and bend,
The track going right and wrong;
Before I took the road
Direction ravished my soul.
Now that I can discern
It whole or almost whole,

Acceptance and gratitude
Like travellers return
And stand where they first stood.

C. M. GRIEVE ('Hugh MacDiarmid')

1892–1978

The Eemis-Stane

I' the how-dumb-deid[1] o the cauld hairst[2] nicht
The warl' like an eemis-stane[3]
Wags i the lift;[4]
An my eerie memories fa'
Like a yowdendrift.[5]

Like a yowdendrift so's I couldna read
The words cut oot i the stane
Had the fug[6] o fame
An history's hazelraw[7]
No' yirdit thaim.[8]

In the Hedge-Back

It was a wild black nicht,
But i' the hert o't we
Drave back the darkness wi' a bleeze o' licht,
Ferrer than een could see.

It was a wild black nicht,
But o' the snell[9] air we
Kept juist eneuch to hinder the heat
Meltin' us utterly.

---

[1] depths. [2] harvest. [3] insecure stone. [4] sky.
[5] gale driving down. [6] moss. [7] lichen.
[8] not covered them over. [9] keen.

It was a wild black nicht,
But o' the win's roar we
Kept juist eneuch to hear oor her's beat
Owre it triumphantly.

It was a wild black nicht,
But o' the Earth we
Kept juist eneuch underneath us to ken
That a warl' used to be.

The Watergaw

Ae weet forenicht i' the yow-trummle[1]
I saw yon antrin[2] thing,
A watergaw[3] wi its chitterin' licht
Ayont the on-ding;[4]
An' I thocht o' the last wild look ye gied
Afore ye dee'd!

There was nae reek i' the laverock's hoose[5]
That nicht—an' nane i' mine;
But I hae thocht o' that foolish licht
Ever sin syne;
An' I think that mebbe at last I ken
What your look meant then.

O Jesu Parvule

*'Followis ane sang of the birth of Christ, with the
tune of Baw lu la law.'*

THE GUDE AND GODLIE BALLATIS

His mither sings to the bairnie Christ
Wi' the tune o' *Baw lu la law.*

---

[1] ewe-tremble, i.e. the cold weather that comes in July when
the sheep are sheared.
[2] odd.   [3] an indistinct rainbow.   [4] down-pour.
[5] it was a dark and stormy night (reek-smoke; laverock-lark).

The bonnie wee craturie lauchs in His crib
An' a' the starnies an' he are sib.
  Baw, baw, my loonikie, baw, balloo.

'Fa' owre, ma hinny, fa' owre, fa' owre,
A' body's sleepin' binna oorsels.'
She's drawn Him in tae the bool o' her briest
But the byspale's nae thocht o' sleep i' the least.
  Balloo, wee mannie, balloo, balloo.

Wheesht, Wheesht

    Wheesht,[1] wheesht, my foolish hert,
    For weel ye ken
    I widna ha'e ye stert
    Auld ploys again.

    It's guid to see her lie
    Sae snod an' cool,
    A' lust o' lovin' by—
    Wheesht, wheesht, ye fule!

The Love-sick Lass

As white's the blossom on the rise
The wee lass was.
That 'bune the green risp i' the fu' mune
Cannily blaws.

Sweet as the cushie's croud[2] she sang
Wi' 'r wee reid mou'—
Wha sauch-like i' the lowe[3] o' luve
Lies sabbin' noo!

---

[1] hush.   [2] cushat-dove's song.   [3] flame.

Scunner[1]

Your body derns[2]
In its graces again
As the dreich[3] grun' does
In the gowden grain,
And oot o' the daith
O' pride you rise
Wi' beauty yet
For a hauf-disguise.

The skinklan'[4] stars
Are but distant dirt.
Tho' fer owre near
You are still—whiles—girt
Wi' the bonnie licht
You bood ha'e tint
—And I lo'e Love
Wi' a scunner in't.

Empty Vessel

I met ayont the cairney
A lass wi' tousie hair
Singin' till a bairnie
That was nae langer there.

Wunds wi warlds to swing
Dinna sing sae sweet,
The licht that bends owre a' thing
Is less ta'en up wi't.

[1] disgust.   [2] hides.   [3] dull.   [4] glittering.

O wha's the bride?

O wha's the bride that cairries the bunch
O' thistles blinterin'[1] white?
Her cuckold bridegroom little dreids
What he sall ken this nicht.

For closer than gudeman can come
And closer to'r than hersel',
Wha dicna need her maidenheid
Has wrocht his purpose fell.

O wha's been here afore me, lass,
And hoo did he get in?
—*A man that deed or was I born*
This evil thing has din.

And left, as it were on a corpse,
Your maidenheid to me?
—*Nae lass, gudeman, sin' Time began*
'S hed ony mair to gi'e.

But I can gi'e ye kindness, lad,
And a pair o' willin' hands,
And you sall ha'e my breists like stars,
My limbs like willow wands.

And on my lips ye'll heed nae mair,
And in my hair forget,
The seed o' a' the men that in
My virgin womb ha'e met. . . .

Milk-wort and bog-cotton

Cwa'een like milk-wort and bog-cotton hair!
I love you, earth, in this mood best o' a'
When the shy spirit like a laich[2] wind moves

[1] **gleaming.** [2] low.

And frae the lift nae shadow can fa'
Since there's nocht left to thraw a shadow there
Owre een like milk-wort and milk-white cotton hair.

Wad that nae leaf upon anither wheeld
A shadow either and nae root need dem[1]
In sacrifice to let sic beauty be!
But deep surroondin' darkness I discern
Is aye the price o' licht. Wad licht revealed
Naething but you, and nicht nocht else concealed.

O ease my spirit

*'And as for their appearances they had one likeness as if a
wheel had been in the midst of a wheel'*

EZEKIEL

O ease my spirit increasingly of the load
Of my personal limitations and the riddling differ-
    ences
Between man and man, with a more constant insight
Into the fundamental similarity of all activities.
And quicken me to the gloriously and terribly
    illuminating
Integration of the physical and the spiritual, till I
    feel how easily
I could put my hand gently on the whole round
    world,
As on my sweetheart's head, and draw it to me.

With the Herring Fishers

'I see herrin','—I hear the glad cry
And 'gainst the moon see ilka blue jowl
In turn as the fishermen haul on the nets
And sing: 'Come, shove in your heids and growl.'

[1] hide.

'Soom on, bonnie herrin', soom on,' they shout,
Or 'Come in, O come in, and see me'
'Come gie the auld man something to dae.
It'll be a braw change frae the sea.'

O it's ane o' the bonniest sichts in the warld
To watch the herrin' come walkin' on board
In the wee sma' 'oors o' a simmer's mornin'
As if o' their ain accord.

For this is the way that God sees life,
The haill jing-bang o's appearin'
Up owre frae the edge o' naethingness
—It's his happy cries I'm hearin'.

'Left, right—O come in and see me,'
Reid and yellow and black and white
Toddlin' up into Heaven thegither
At peep o' day frae the endless night.

'I see herrin',' I hear his glad cry,
And 'gainst the moon see his muckle blue jowl,
As he handles buoy-tow and bush-raip
Singin': 'Come, shove in your heids and growl!'

Cattle Show

I shall go among red faces and virile voices,
See stylish sheep, with fine heads and well-woolled,
And great bulls mellow to the touch,
Brood mares of marvellous approach, and geldings
With sharp and flinty bones and silken hair.

And through the enclosure draped in red and gold
I shall pass on to spheres more vivid yet
Where countesses' coque feathers gleam and glow
And, swathed in silks, the painted ladies are
Whose laughter plays like summer lightning there.

C. M. GRIEVE

From *The Glass of Pure Water*

> '*In the de-oxidisation and re-oxidisation of hydrogen
> in a single drop of water we have before us,
> truly, so far as force is concerned, an epitome of
> the whole life. . . . The burning of coal to
> move an iron wheel differs only in detail and
> not in essence, from the decomposition of a
> muscle to effect its own concentration.*'
> James Hinton

> '*We must remember that his analysis was done
> not intellectually but by an immediate process of
> intuition; that he was able, as it were, to taste
> the hydrogen and oxygen in his glass of water.*'
> Aldous Huxley (of D. H. Lawrence)

> '*Praise of pure water is common in Gaelic poetry.*'
> W. J. Watson, *Bardachd Ghaidhlig*

Hold a glass of pure water to the eye of the sun!
It is difficult to tell the one from the other
Save by the tiny hardly visible trembling of the water.
This is the nearest analogy to the essence of human
    life
Which is even more difficult to see.
Dismiss anything you can see more easily;
It is not alive—it is not worth seeing.
There is a minute indescribable difference
Between one glass of pure water and another
With slightly different chemical constituents.

The difference between one human life and another
Is no greater; colour does not colour the water:
You cannot tell a white man's life from a black man's.
But the lives of these particular slum people
I am chiefly concerned with, like the lives of all
The world's poorest, remind me less
Of a glass of water held between my eyes and the sun
—They remind me of the feeling they had

Who saw Sacco and Vanzetti in the death cell
On the eve of their execution.
—One is talking to God.

I dreamt last night that I saw one of His angels
Making his centennial report to the Recording Angel
On the condition of human life.
Look at the ridge of skin between your thumb and
      forefinger.
Look at the delicate lines on it and how they change
—How many different things they can express—
As you move out or close in your forefinger and
      thumb.
And look at the changing shapes—the countless
Little gestures, little miracles of line—
Of your forefinger and thumb as you move them.
And remember how much a hand can express,
How a single slight movement of it can say more
Than millions of words—dropped hand, clenched fist,
Snapping fingers, thumb up, thumb down,
Raised in blessing, clutched in passion, begging,
Welcome, dismissal, prayer, applause,
And a million other signs, too slight, too subtle,
Too packed with meaning for words to describe,
A universal language understood by all.
And the Angel's report on human life
Was the subtlest movement—just like that—and no
      more;
A hundred years of life on the Earth
Summed up, not a detail missed or wrongly assessed,
In that little inconceivably intricate movement.

The only communication between man and man
That says anything worth hearing
—The hidden well-water; the finger of destiny;—
Moves as that water, that angel, moved.

Truth is the rarest thing and life
The gentlest, most unobtrusive movement in the
    world.
I cannot speak to you of the poor people of all the
    world
But among the people in these nearest slums I know
This infinitesimal twinkling, this delicate play
Of tiny signs that not only say more
Than all speech, but all there is to say,
All there is to say and to know and to be.
There alone I seldom find anything else,
Each in himself or herself a dramatic whole,
An 'agon' whose validity is timeless.
Our duty is to free that water, to make these gestures,
To help humanity to shed all else,
All that stands between any life and the sun,
The quintessence of any life and the sun;
To still all sound save that talking to God;
To end all movements save movements like these.

EWART ALAN MACKINTOSH
1893–1916

In Memoriam, Private D. Sutherland
*killed in action in the German trench 16 May 1916,
and the others who died*

So you were David's father,
And he was your only son,
And the new-cut peats are rotting
And the work is left undone,
Because of an old man weeping,
Just an old man in pain,
For David, his son David,
That will not come again.

Oh, the letters he wrote you
And I can see them still,
Not a word of the fighting
But just the sheep on the hill
And how you should get the crops in
Ere the year got stormier,
And the Bosches have got his body,
And I was his officer.

You were only David's father,
But I had fifty sons
When we went up in the evening
Under the arch of the guns,
And we came back at twilight—
O God! I heard them call
To me for help and pity
That could not help at all.

Oh, never will I forget you,
My men that trusted me,
More my sons than your fathers',
For they could only see
The little helpless babies
And the young men in their pride.
They could not see you dying,
And hold you when you died.

Happy and young and gallant,
They saw their first-born go,
But not the strong limbs broken
And the beautiful men brought low,
The piteous writhing bodies,
They screamed 'Don't leave me, sir,'
For they were only your fathers
But I was your officer.

WILLIAM SOUTAR

1898–1943

The Gowk

Half doun the hill, whaur fa's the linn
Far frae the flaught o' fowk,
I saw upon a lanely whin
A lanely singin' gowk:
Cuckoo, cuckoo;
And at my back
The howie hill stüde up and spak:
Cuckoo, cuckoo.

There was nae soun': the loupin' linn
Hung frostit in its fa':
Nae bird was on the lanely whin
Sae white wi' fleurs o' snaw:
Cuckoo, cuckoo;
I stüde stane still;
And saftly spak the howie hill:
Cuckoo, cuckoo.

The Tryst

O luely, luely, cam she in
And luely she lay doun:
I kent her be her caller lips
And her breists sae sma' and roun'.

A' thru the nicht we spak nae word
Nor sinder'd bane frae bane:
A' thru the nicht I heard her hert
Gang soundin' wi' my ain.

It was about the waukrife hour
Whan cocks begin to craw
That she smool'd saftly thru the mirk
Afore the day wud daw.

Sae luely, luely, cam she in
Sae luely was she gaen;
And wi' her a' my simmer days
Like they had never been.

The Children

Upon the street they lie
Beside the broken stone:
The blood of children stares from the broken stone.

Death came out of the sky
In the bright afternoon:
Darkness slanted over the bright afternoon.

Again the sky is clear
But upon earth a stain:
The earth is darkened with a darkening stain:

A wound which everywhere
Corrupts the hearts of men:
The blood of children corrupts the hearts of men.

Silence is in the air:
The stars move to their places:
Silent and serene the stars move to their places:

But from earth the children stare
With blind and fearful faces:
And our charity is in the children's faces.

ROBERT GARIOCH

1909–1981

Sisyphus

Bumpity doun in the corrie gaed whuddran[1] the
    pitiless whun stane.
Sisyphus, pechan and sweitan, disjaskit, forfeuchan[2]
    and broun'd-aff,
sat on the heather a hanlawhile, houpan the Boss
    didna spy him,
seein the terms of his contract includit nae mention of
    tea-breaks,
syne at the muckle big scunnersom[3] boulder he
    trauchlit[4] aince mair.
Ach! hou kenspeckle[5] it was, that he ken'd ilka
    spreckle and blotch on't.
Heavin awa at its wecht, he manhaunnlit the bruitt[6]
    up the braeface,
takkan the easiest gait[7] he had fand in a fudder of
    dour years,
haudan awa frae the craigs[8] had affrichtit him maist
    in his youth-heid,
feelin his years aa the same, he gaed cannily,[9] tenty[10]
    of slipped discs.
Eftir an hour and a quarter he warslit[11] his wey to the
    brae's heid,
hystit his boulder richt up on the tap of the
    cairn—and it stude there!
streikit[12] his length on the chuckie-stanes, houpan the
    Boss wadna spy him,

---

[1]bumping   [2]panting and sweating, worn out,
exhausted   [3]disgusting   [4]labourer   [5]well known
[6]burden   [7]way   [8]rocks   [9]carefully
[10]wary   [11]wrestled   [12]stretched

had a wee look at the scenery, feenisht [1] a pie and a
    cheese-piece.
Whit was he thinking about, that he jist gied the
    boulder a wee shove?
Bumpity doun in the corrie gaed whuddran the
    pitiless whun stane,
Sisyphus dodderan eftir [2] it, shair of his cheque at the
    month's end.

And they were richt

    I went to see 'Ane Tryall of Hereticks'
by Fionn MacColla, treatit as a play;
a wyce-like wark, [3] but what I want to say
is mair taen-up wi halie politics

    nor wi the piece itsel; the kinna tricks
the unco-guid [4] get up til whan they hae
their wey. Yon late-nicht ploy on Setturday
was thrang [5] wi Protestants and Catholics,

    an eydent [6] audience, wi fowth [7] of bricht
arguments wad hae kept them gaun till Monday.
It seemed discussion wad last out the nicht,

    hadna the poliss, [8] sent by Mrs Grundy,
pitten us out at twelve. And they were richt!
Wha daur [9] debait religion on a Sunday?

[1] finished   [2] staggering
[3] clever work   [4] self-consciously, over-righteous
[5] crowded   [6] eager   [7] plenty   [8] police   [9] dare

Nemo canem impune lacessit

I kicked an Edinbro dug-luver's dug,
leastweys I tried; my timing wes owre late.
It stopped whit it wes daein til my gate
and skelpit aff to find anither mug.

Whit a sensation! If a clockwark thug
suid croun ye wi a brolly[1] owre yir pate,[2]
the Embro folk wad leave ye til yir fate:
it's you, maist like, wad get a flee in yir lug.[3]

But kick the Friend of Man! Or hae a try!
The Friend of Wummin, even, that's faur waur
a felony, mair dangerous forbye.

Meddle wi puir dumb craiturs gin ye daur;
that maks ye a richt cruel bruitt, my! my!
And whit d'ye think yir braw front yett is for?

GEORGE BRUCE

1909–

The Fisherman

As he comes from one of those small houses
Set within the curve of the low cliff
For a moment he pauses
Foot on step at the low lintel
Before fronting wind and sun.
He carries out from within something of the dark
Concealed by heavy curtain,
Or held within the ship under hatches.

[1]umbrella   [2]head   [3]ear   [4]gate

Yet with what assurance
The compact body moves,
Head pressed to wind,
His being at an angle
As to anticipate the lurch of earth.

Who is he to contain night
And still walk stubborn
Holding the ground with light feet
And with a careless gait?

Perhaps a cataract of light floods,
Perhaps the apostolic flame.
Whatever it may be
The road takes him from us.
Now the pier is his, now the tide.

Tom on the Beach

With bent back, world's curve on it
I brood over my pretty pool
And hunt the pale, flat, sand-coloured
Fish, with cupped hands, in the cold.

Ah, but my warm heart, with hope
Wrapped in it in the bright afternoon,
Feet glittering in the sand,
Eyes on my pale prey, was sure.

Suns have passed, suns have passed,
Skies purple above the thin sand.
With bent back brooding on the round
World, over my shoulder

I feel the touch of a future
In the cold. The little fish
Come not near me, cleaving
To their element and flattening on the sand.

How many years since with sure heart
And prophecy of success
Warmed in it
Did I look with delight on the little fish,

Start with happiness, the warm sun on me?
Now the waters spread horizonwards.
Great skies meet them.
I brood upon uncompleted tasks.

Kinnaird Head

I go North to cold, to home, to Kinnaird,
Fit monument for our time.
This is the outermost edge of Buchan.
Inland the sea birds range,
The tree's leaf has salt upon it,
The tree turns to the low stone wall.
And here a promontory rises towards Norway,
Irregular to the top of thin grey grass
Where the spindrift in storm lays its beads.
The water plugs in the cliff sides,
The gull cries from the clouds
This is the consummation of the plain.

O impregnable and very ancient rock,
Rejecting the violence of water,
Ignoring its accumulations and strategy,
You yield to history nothing.

A Gateway to the Sea—St. Andrews

Pause stranger at the porch: nothing beyond
This framing arch of stone, but scattered rocks
And sea and these on the low beach
Original to the cataclysm and the dark.

Once one man bent to the stone, another
Dropped the measuring line, a third and fourth
Together lifted and positioned the dressed stone
Making wall and arch; yet others
Settled the iron doors on squawking hinge
To shut without the querulous seas and men.
Order and virtue and love (they say)
Dwelt in the town—but that was long ago.
Then the stranger at the gates, the merchants,
Missioners, the blind beggar with the dog,
The miscellaneous vendors (duly inspected)
Were welcome within the wall that held from sight
The water's brawl. All that was long ago.
Now the iron doors are down to dust,
But the stumps of hinge remain. The arch
Opens to the element—the stones dented
And stained to green and purple and rust.
Pigeons settle on the top. Stranger,
On this winter afternoon pause at the porch,
For the dark land beyond stretches
To the unapproachable element; bright
As night falls and with the allurement of peace,
Concealing under the bland feature, possession.
Not all the agitations of the world
Articulate the ultimate question as do those waters
Confining the memorable and the forgotten;
Relics, records, furtive occasions—Caesar's politics
And he who was drunk last night:

Rings, diamants, snuff boxes, warships.
Also the less worthy garments of worthy men.

Prefer then this handled stone, now ruined
While the sea mists wind about the arch.
The afternoon dwindles, night concludes,
The stone is damp, unyielding to the touch
But crumbling in the strain and stress
Of the years: the years winding about the arch,
Settling in the holes and crevices, moulding
The dressed stone. Once, one man bent to it,
Another dropped the measuring line, a third
And fourth positioned to make wall and arch
Theirs. Pause, stranger, at this small town's edge—
The European sun knew those streets
'O Jesu parvule; Christus Victus, Christus Victor,'
The bells singing from their towers, the waters
Whispering to the waters, the air tolling
To the air—the faith, the faith, the faith.

All this was long ago. The lights
Are out, the town is sunk in sleep,
The boats are rocking at the pier,
The vague winds beat about the streets—
Choir and altar and chancel are gone.
Under the touch the guardian stone remains.
Holding memory, reproving desire, securing hope
In the stop of water, in the lull of night
Before dawn kindles a new day.

NORMAN MacCAIG

1910–

Summer Farm

Straws like tame lightnings lie about the grass
And hang zigzag on hedges. Green as glass

The water in the horse-trough shines.
Nine ducks go wobbling by in two straight lines.

A hen stares at nothing with one eye,
Then picks it up. Out of an empty sky
A swallow falls and, flickering through
The barn, dives up again into the dizzy blue.

I lie, not thinking, in the cool, soft grass,
Afraid of where a thought might take me—as
This grasshopper with plated face
Unfolds his legs and finds himself in space.

Self under self, a pile of selves I stand
Threaded on time, and with metaphysic hand
Lift the farm like a lid and see
Farm within farm, and in the centre, me.

Water Tap

There was this hayfield,
You remember, pale gold
If it weren't hazed
With a million clover heads.

A rope of water
Frayed down—the bucket
Hoisted up a plate
Of flashing light.

The thin road screwed
Into hills; all ended
Journeys were somewhere,
But far, far.

You laughed, by the fence;
And everything that was
Hoisting water
Suddenly spilled over.

Byre

The thatched roof rings like heaven where mice
Squeak small hosannahs all night long,
Scratching its golden pavements, skirting
The gutter's crystal river-song.

Wild kittens in the world below
Glare with one flaming eye through cracks,
Spurt in the straw, are tawny brooches
Splayed on the chests of drunken sacks.

The dimness becomes darkness as
Vast presences come mincing in,
Swagbellied Aphrodites, swinging
A silver slaver from each chin.

And all is milky, secret, female.
Angels are hushed and plain straws shine.
And kittens miaow in circles, stalking
With tail and hindleg one straight line.

Aspects

Clean in the light, with nothing to remember,
The fox fur shrivels, the bone beak drops apart;
Sludge on the ground, the dead deer drips his heart.

Clean in the weather, trees crack and lean over;
Mountain bows down and combs its scurfy head
To make a meadow and its own deathbed.

Clean in the moon, tides scrub away their islands,
Unpicking gulls. Whales that have learned to drown,
Ballooning up, meet navies circling down.

Clean in the mind, a new mind creeps to being,
Eating the old. . . . Ancestors have no place
In such clean qualities as time and space.

November Night, Edinburgh

The night tinkles like ice in glasses.
Leaves are glued to the pavement with frost.
The brown air fumes at the shop windows,
Tries the doors, and sidles past.

I gulp down winter raw. The heady
Darkness swirls with tenements.
In a brown fuzz of cottonwool
Lamps fade up crags, die into pits.

Frost in my lungs is harsh as leaves
Scraped up on paths.—I look up, there,
A high roofs sails, at the mast-head
Fluttering a grey and ragged star.

The world's a bear shrugged in his den.
It's snug and close in the snoring night.
And outside like chrysanthemums
The fog unfolds its bitter scent.

Street Preacher

Every Sunday evening at seven o'clock
He howls outside my window. He howls about God.
No tattered prophet: a rosy bourgeois, he lifts
His head and howls. He addresses me as a friend.

One day I'll open the window and howl at him
And so betray his Enemy. I'll call him Brother.
Who'd laugh the louder, the Devil or God, to see
Two rosy bourgeois howling at each other?

When he goes coughing home, does he speak to his
    wife
Of the good fight well fought, the shaft well sped,
Before he puts God's teeth in a glass and, taking
His sensible underclothes off, rolls into bed?

SYDNEY TREMAYNE

1912–

North of Berwick

Slowly the sea is parted from the sky:
The light surprises, crinkling on the water.
The white sun hardens; cliffs solidify.
A long coast of red rock where three swans fly
Engraves itself in calm, deceptive weather.

Three swans fly north, a diesel thumping south
Draws out of sight along the rusting railway,
All windows clouded with a communal breath.
Fields flash in the sunlight, far beneath
The sea turns in its scales, well in a seal's way.

No boat invades that shining emptiness.
Because the waves are distant, the sky windless,
That pale line round the shore looks motionless.
Hearing such border warfare lost in space
You say the breathing of the sea is endless.

What is the one thing constant? Can you say?
The loneliness that we are born to merges
Perhaps with such a place on such a day.
No stones cry out because we cannot stay.
Through all our absences the long tide surges.

The Galloway Shore

Sand white as frost: the moon stayed hard and high.
Far off, the lights around the Irish coast
Leapt up like salmon. An Iscariot sea
Chinked on the rocks. Within a shadow cast
By broken cliffs, a place of slippery stones,
I faced the speaking lights, small human signs
Of hidden rocks and granite patiences.
Among the sounds of night a slithering wind,
Darkness on dark, in fitful cadences
Phrased the fresh world. There is no older sound.

Never was stillness here, where I began
To watch alone, to be an emptiness,
To let the strongly running world come in
As seldom can be done: this was to pass
Into no trance but a most brilliant waking,
Active as light upon the deep tide snaking
Before my sight, so lately lost in crowds.
The force that moves all things and lives me out
Made me its filament; all that divides
Time into stints could be no longer thought.

To be had no past tense: all sense was new.
There was destruction of irrelevance.
A listener to the world, I heard it flow
So huge, so slow, it seemed like permanence
Experienced for an eye-blink. Darting knives
Made slits of light. My years, those forty thieves
Crowded together in one brimming jar,
Left me no wish to grieve for. All this hoard
Was poured out in an instant to the air,
While I was bankrupt even of a word.

Was it some trick to steal the peace of the dead?
It was not peace but power, surely the source
Of every light lit in a transient head
From Genesis to Einstein. In this place
(Austere, coherent, callous) all deeds done,
Bastilles of knowledge, crumpled. The moon's lane,
Quickened with silver, ran; all near was dark,
The land behind most dark. Spread round the sea,
Pinpricks of light timed out a few men's work,
Wakeful in cells impenetrable by me.

Our time seeks for an idol. There is none.
The image that you want is not a city,
Nothing so pitiable; the sea pours in
And shears your dwellings down, ignores your duty
To house a purpose, bears you to extreme.
The lights were warning lights by which I came
As polar travellers come to what is real
In all their banished days. The sight was calm.
There is not any will, or wall, or cell
Would keep this calmness out. Give it no name.

Growing, the poem's dumb, planted in change
Immeasurable and ineluctible.
It flowers in light. We reach outside our range
Into the sureness, indestructible,
That sings us out of time. Whose is our voice?
It is the voice of stones that waste, of seas
That cannot rest, of air transfixed by light:
That is to say a human voice, that tries,
Always in solitude, aided by night,
To be identified with all of these.

The sun's white shadow darkened all the sea
With cool and bearable light. I knew this dark;
It was the earth between me and the day

And this my turning place, a boundary mark.
The brittle sea fractured along the coast.
The Irish lights jigged on, fixed points that placed
My world on stone foundations. They put space
A little farther off where men marooned
In granite kept their watch. The moon was glass.
I leaned against a rock, out of the wind.

DOUGLAS YOUNG

1913–1973

The Ballant o' the Laird's Bath

In Switzerland lang syne befell
    a deed o great renoun,
i the Whyte Buik o Sarnen
    was trulie scryveit[1] doun.

Alzellen's Laird rade out his lane
    ae simmer mornin early;
midmaist the wuids of Uri
    he sune gat wandert fairlie.

He's socht the wey baith aist and wast,
    but canna win back hame;
the shelt[2] grows mair disjeskit[3] aye,
    the Laird mair wud wi grame.[4]

Near lowsin-time[5] he cam at last,
    aa clortit[6] owre wi stour,[7]
til a bonnie bit hous in a gair[8] o park,
    and breenged[9] intil the bouer.[10]

---

[1] written.   [2] pony.   [3] fatigued.   [4] mad with rage.
[5] end of the working day.   [6] filthied.   [7] dust.   [8] patch.
[9] burst.   [10] women's apartments.

'Guidwife,' quo he, 'gae fetch to me
   a tassie o caller wine,
and thraw a fat hen's craig[1] about.
   Alzellen's Laird maun dine.

But saft . . . I pray thee pardon, dame,
   I suldna been sae reoch,
nou that I see your bonnie blee,
   your weel-faur'd[2] briest and hough.

Anither thochtie I hae thocht.
   Fair dame, I'ld speir at thee,
mak het a chaudron a clear watter
   and syne come bath wi me.'

The douce guidwife was michtilie fleggit[3]
   at sic an orra demand,
the mair that she kent Alzellen's Laird
   was a sair man to withstand.

Nocht answeran him she brocht the wine,
   pit on the pat to boil,
syne threw a pullet's craig about,
   and prayed a prayer the while:

'O Mary, mither o charitie,
   ressave me frae this shame;
haud back the Laird frae his intent
   whill[4] my guidman wins hame.'

She's plied the Laird wi monie a tass
   o the sweet Riesling wine,
and staad[5] his wame[6] wi dentie meats
   fit for King Charlemagne.

Syne she's duin aff his braw sword-belt,
   wi gentie mien and douce,
his cordinant[7] shuin and the lave o his claes,
   and taen them ben the hous.

---

[1] throat.   [2] well-favoured.   [3] startled.   [4] until.   [5] stuffed.
[6] stomach.   [7] of Cordova leather.

He's lowpit intil the warm watter,
   crouse[1] as the Deil was he;
then bydan on that dame's return
   he sings fou lustilie.

Thon randy ballant echoes loud
   amang the wuids o Uri,
the guidman's heard it frae the byre,
   and hame cam he in a furie.

He's breenged inby wi birsslan baird,[2]
   swingan his cleaver-axe;
he's chappit the naukit Laird in twa,
   and syne in eichty-sax.

The wan watter i the bress chaudron[3]
   rins reid wi bree[4] o bluid.
Let that be a lesson to Lairds and the lave
   nae to get tint[5] in a wuid.

Last Lauch

   The Minister said it wald dee,
     the cypress buss I plantit.
   But the buss grew til a tree,
     naething dauntit.

   It's growan, stark and heich,
     derk and straucht and sinister,
   kirkyairdie-like and dreich.
     But whaur's the Minister?

RUTHVEN TODD

1914–1978

To A Very Beautiful Lady

And when you walk the world lifts up its head,
Planets are haloed by the unembarrassed stars,

[1] merry. [2] bristling beard. [3] brass cauldron. [4] mixture. [5] lost.

The town lies fallow at your feet, the ancient dead
Recall their loves, their queens and emperors,
Their shepherds and the quiet pastoral scene.
For less than you Troy burned and Egypt fell,
The corn was blasted while it still stood green,
And Faustus went protesting into Hell.

Be careful, sweet, adored by half the world,
Time to its darlings is not always kind,
There lie the lovelies whom the years have scored
Deeper than all the hearts which once repined.
The knife you hold could cut an empire low
Or in your own breast place the suicidal blow.

G. S. FRASER

1915–1980

Flemish Primitive

Soft petals fell out of a brooding air
Like blossoms of the apple or the pear,

Soft magic, like the feathers of a dove,
Fell on this lady and her little love.

Up in the inn, the travellers sat to dine,
Pouring hot spices in their steaming wine.

Out on the street, the sentry stamped and swore,
Knowing his guard must last for one hour more.

The Three Wise Kings were on their homeward road,
Their hearts unburdened of the ruler's load,

While Herod slept; but, dreaming of disaster,
He felt his heart, that nightmare, beat the faster.

Back on the hill, a Shepherd scratched his head
To find the sense of what the Angels said.

But in her dark Byzantine green and gold,
This sleeping miracle repelled the cold.

The green was fodder, and the gold was straw;
And Mary sang a lullaby and saw

Azure and gilt around her; the intense
And choking fragrance of the frankincense

Swirled in her dream. A thought of stillness was
Sick longing in her soul. She wished to pause

From thought, from movement, and from grief; to
    rest
For ever with the baby at her breast.

To a Scottish Poet

Goddess or ghost, you say, by shuddering,
    And ominous of evil to our land,
Twisting to ugliness the mouths that sing,
    Parching the lover's moist and balmy hand.

Goddess or ghost, you say, by silence known,
    The silence ticking in the rotten wood
Like our numb pain, that can no longer groan:
    A grief so old, it gives the mind no food.

I also on bleak nights in Causewayend
    Where the slate sky distorts the slaty stone
And the shawled women to their burrows wend,
    Have felt my country suffering alone.

The slate sea splashes on the slaty pier
  In lost St. Andrews, where no poets now
Defy the crocodile to shed its tear
  Or take what time the bitter years allow.

And the same sea is loud in Aberdeen:
  Passing the gas-works and the fish-and-chips
One comes in summer on the radiant scene,
  The golden beach, the girls with golden hips,

The sun that cooks and savours all their sex:
  Then I have thought my country might arise
Like these half-sleeping girls with tawny necks
  And summer's sensual softness in their eyes.

These skies bled warmth: and while my blood stays
    young,
  That starving peace, or this protracted war,
Vows broken, or friends lost, or songs unsung
  Shall leave no permanent and vexing scar.

Goddess or ghost, you say, by shuddering,
  And ominous of evil to our land . . .
I say, defy her, while our blood can sing;
  While we stand insolent, as poets stand.

The traveller has regrets

The traveller has regrets,
For the receding shore
That with its many nets
Has caught, not to restore,
The white lights in the bay,
The blue lights on the hill,
Though night with many stars
May travel with him still,

But night has nought to say,
Only a colour and shape
Changing like cloth shaking,
A dancer with a cape
Whose dance is heart-breaking,
Night with its many stars
Can warn travellers
There's only time to kill
And nothing much to say:
But the blue lights on the hill,
The white lights in the bay
Told us the meal was laid
And that the bed was made
And that we could not stay.

On the Persistence of Humanity

I often wonder if the race should die:
My restless body and my fuddled mind,
Machine-like work and torpid lethargy;
The self-importance of my fumbling kind;
The filthy cruelty; the waste of words;
The social goodness with its bony thumbs;
The packet recipe for cream and curds,
Pussy watch sparrow, sparrow watch the crumbs!
I think of happy men who work, eat, sleep,
Watch Television, in the quiet night perish;
I think of managers whc never weep;
Yet there is something still that I can cherish.
I knew love best in hells of fear and grief;
And love outlasts belief, and disbelief.

I want the bloody human race to run
Over the hurdles of its tinny cars
Until that black star pops, that dying sun
We imitate in our preposterous wars:

Murders, lies, wars! And yet I like my sort,
Because I am the sort of clot they are:
Come Judgement Day, and what is my retort?—
'I loved that session in a public bar;
I loved a pussy, loved a little bird;
One ate the other, in a natural way;
I served up misery in a tasty word;
I never wasn't glad to greet the day.
For all the noisy interfering pain,
Given a chance, I'd run the tape again!'

Fearful of dark, for silliest light I cry:
The bawling sergeant on the barrack square,
The bishop's guff, the advertiser's lie,
The chemist's gloss upon my loved one's hair,
The rigged hoarse cheers at the inane mass meeting.
The tartiest weeklies, their most snide reviews.
Long journeys ending in a brush-off greeting,
The sweet fresh morning and its stale sour news!
Friend beneath enemy, O human face,
And loving enemy behind old friend,
Dear deadpan propping failure and disgrace
And in all endings live, unending end,
Unpardonable, we shall carry on:
And other clots like us, when we are gone.

GEORGE CAMPBELL HAY

1915–

The Old Fisherman

Greet the bights that gave me shelter,
they will hide me no more with the horns of their
    forelands.
I peer in a haze, my back is stooping;
my dancing days for fishing are over.

The shoot that was straight in the wood withers,
the bracken shrinks red in the rain and shrivels,
the eyes that would gaze in the sun waver;
my dancing days for fishing are over.

The old boat must seek the shingle,
her wasting side hollow the gravel,
the hand that shakes must leave the tiller;
my dancing days for fishing are over.

The sea was good night and morning,
the winds were friends, the calm was kindly—
the snow seeks the burn, the brown fronds scatter;
my dancing days for fishing are over.

Still gyte, man?

'Still gyte, man? Stude I in yere claes
I'd thole nae beggar's nichts an' days,
chap-chappan, whidderan lik a moose,
at ae same cauld an' steekit hoose!

'What stane has she tae draw yere een?
What gars ye, syne she aye has been
as toom an' hertless as a hoor,
gang sornan kindness at her dure?'

'*Though ye should talk a hunner year,*
the windblown wave will seek the shore,
the muirlan watter seek the sea.
Then, wheesht man. Sae it is wi me.'

SYDNEY GOODSIR SMITH

1915–1975

Loch Leven

Tell me was a glorie ever seen
As the morn I left ma lass
'Fore licht in the toun o' snaw

And saw the dawn
O' burnan crammassie [1]
Turn the grey ice
O' Mary's Loch Leven
Tae sheenan bress—
And kent the glorie and the gleen [2]
Was but the waukenin o' her een?

Elegy XIII

(i)

I got her in the Black Bull
(The Black Bull o Norroway),
Gin I mynd richt, in Leith Street,
Doun the stair at the corner forenent [3]
The Fun Fair and Museum o Monstrosities,
   The Tyke-faced Loun, the Cunyiars Den
     And siclike.
I tine [4] her name the nou, and cognomen for that—
Aiblins it was Deirdre, Ariadne, Calliope,
Gaby, Jacquette, Katerina, Sandra,
   Or sunkots; exotic, I expeck.
A wee bit piece
   O' what our faithers maist unaptlie
   But romanticallie designatit 'Fluff'.
My certie! Nae muckle o Fluff
   About the hures o Reekie!
Dour as stane, the like stane
As biggit [5] the unconquerable citie
Whar they pullulate,
              Infestan
The wynds and closes, squares
And public promenads
    —The bonnie craturies!
        —But til our winter's tale.

[1] crimson. [2] gleam, glance. [3] over against. [4] forget. [5] built.

(ii)

Fou as a puggie, I, the bardic ee
In a fine frenzie rollan,
Drunk as a fish wi sevin tails,
Purpie as Tiberio wi bad rum and beerio,
      (Io! Io! Iacche! Iacche, Io!)

—Sevin nichts and sevin days
      (A modest bout whan aa's dune,
      Maist scriptural, in fack)
Was the Makar on his junketins
      (On this perticular occasioun
      O' the whilk we tell the nou
      Here in the records, for the benefit
      O' future putative historians)
Wi sindrie cronies throu the wastage-land
O' howffs[1] and dancins, stews
And houses o assignatioun
I' the auntient[2] capital.

—Ah, she was a bonnie cou!
Ilka pennie I had she teuk,
Scoffed the halicarnassus lot,
As is the custom, due
And meet and mensefu,
Proper and proprietous,
   Drinkan hersel to catch up wi me
   That had a sevin-day stert on her
     —O' the whilk conditioun
Nae smaa braggandie was made at the time
Here and yont about the metropolis—
   And mysel drinkan me sober again
For reasouns ower obvious

        [1] dens.   [2] ancient.

To needcessitate descriptioun,
                  Explanatioun,
                      Or ither.

Nou, ye canna ging lang at yon game
And the hour cam on at length
That the Cup-bearer did refuse
The provision of further refreshment

—Rochlie, I mynd, and in a menner
Wi the whilk I amna uised,
   Uncomformable wi my lordlie spreit,
   A menner unseemlie, unbefittan
   The speakin-til[1] or interlocutioun
   O' a Bard and Shennachie,
        Far less a Maister o Arts,
        —The whilk rank and statioun I haud
        In consequence and by vertue
        O' unremittan and pertinacious
        Applicatioun til the bottle
        Ower a period no exceedan
        Fowr year and sax munce or moneths
(The latter bean a *hiatus* or *cæsura*
For the purposes o rusticatioun
Or *villeggiatura* 'at my place in the country'):
   Aa the whilk was made sufficient plain
Til the Cup-bearer at the time—
   Losh me, what a collieshangie![2]
Ye'd hae thocht the man affrontit
   Deeplie, maist mortallie
     And til the hert.
Ay, and I cried him Ganymede,
   Wi the whilk address or pronomen
     He grew incensed.

               [1] addressing.   [2] row.

'Run, Ganymede!' quo I,
  'Stay me wi flagons!'
                 (Or maybe tappit-hens)
   —But I digress.
It was rum, I mynd the nou, rum was the bree,[1]
Rum and draucht Bass.
               —Sheer *hara-kiri!*

           (iii)

—Ah, she was a bonnie cou!
Saxteen, maybe sevinteen, nae mair,
Her mither in attendance, *comme il faut*
Pour les jeunes filles bien élevées,
  Drinkan like a bluidie whaul tae!
Wee breists, round and ticht and fou
Like sweet Pomona in the oranger grove;
Her shanks were lang, but no ower lang, and plump,
  A lassie's shanks,
Wi the meisurance o Venus—
  Achteen inch the hoch[2] frae heuchle-bane[3] til
    knap,[4]
  Achteen inch the cauf frae knap til cuit[5]
As is the true perfectioun calculate
By the Auntients efter due regaird
For this and that,
               The true meisurance
  O' the Venus dei Medici,
  The Aphrodite Anadyomene
And aa the goddesses o hie antiquitie—
  Siclike were the shanks and hochs
O' Sandra the cou o the auld Black Bull.
  Her een were, naiturallie, expressionless,
Blank as chuckie-stanes, like the bits

---

[1] brew.   [2] thigh.   [3] hip-bone.   [4] knee.   [5] ankle.

O' blae-green gless ye find by the sea.
     —Nostalgia! Ah, sweet regrets!—
 Her blee[1] was yon o sweet sexteen,
Her lyre as white as Dian's chastitie
 In yon fyle, fousome, clartie slum.
Sound the tocsin, sound the drum!
The Haas o Balclutha ring wi revelrie!
The Prince sall dine at Hailie Rude the nicht!

(iv)

The lums o the reikan toun
Spreid aa ablow, and round
As far as ye coud leuk
The yalla squares o winnocks
Lit ilkane by a nakit yalla sterne
Blenkan, aff, syne on again,
Out and in and out again
As the thrang mercat throve,
 The haill toun at it
Aa the lichts pip-poppan
 In and out and in again
  I' the buts and bens
   And single ends,
    The banks and braes
 O' the toueran cliffs o lands,
Haill tenements, wards and burghs, counties,
 Regalities and jurisdictiouns,
  Continents and empires
  Gien ower entire
Til the joukerie-poukerie!
Hech, sirs, whatna feck of fockerie!
Shades o Knox, the hochmagandie!
 My bonie Edinburrie,

[1]complexion.

Auld Skulduggerie!
Flat on her back sevin nichts o the week,
Earnan her breid wi her hurdies' sweit.

—And Dian's siller chastitie
Muved owre the reikan lums,
Biggan a ferlie toun o jet and ivorie
That was but blackened stane
Whar Bothwell rade and Huntly
And fair Montrose and aa the lave
Wi silken leddies doun til the grave.
    —The hoofs strak siller on the causie!
        And I mysel in cramasie!

(v)

There Sandra sleepan, like a doe shot
I' the midnicht wuid, wee paps
Like munes, mune-aipples gaithert
    I' the Isles o Youth,
Her flung straucht limbs
A paradisal archipelagie
Inhaudan divers bays, lagoons,
Great carses, strands and sounds,
Islands and straits, peninsulies,
    Whar traders, navigators,
    Odyssean gangrels, gubernators,
    Mutineers and maister-marineers,
And aa sic outland chiels[1] micht utilise wi ease
Cheap flouered claiths and beads,
Gawds, wire and sheenan nails
    And siclike flichtmafletherie
In fair and just excambion

[1] fellows.

For aa the ferlies[1] o the southren seas
That chirm[2] in thy deep-dernit creeks,
— My Helen douce as aipple-jack
  That cack't the bed in exstasie!
Ah, belle nostalgie de la boue!

— Sandra, princess-leman o a nicht o lust,
  That girdelt the fishie seas
  Frae Leith til Honolulu,
Maistress o the white mune Cytherean,
  Tak this bardic tribute nou!
Immortalitie sall croun thy heid wi bays,
  Laurel and rosemarie and rue!
You that spierit me nae questions,
  Spierit at me nocht,
    Acceptit me and teuk me in
    A guest o the house, nae less;
Teuk aa there was to gie
  (And yon was peerie[3] worth),
Gied what ye didna loss—
    A bien and dernit fleeman's-firth
    And bodie's easement
    And saft encomfortin!
O Manon! Marguerite! Camille!
    And maybe tae the pox—
                    Ach, weill!

(From *Under the Eildon Tree*.)

---

[1] wonders.   [2] noise of waters rippling.   [3] small.

Ye spier me

Ye spier[1] me, luve, a question,
As we spin through the abyss
Whar is nae sterne[2] or compass,
Ye spier me what it is
That in the nicht o' passion
And the langorie[3] o' dawin
Rairs[4] in the tideless ocean
Whar we byde[5] as in a dwaum[6] ...?
It is the lava thunderan out
Frae the burst craters o' the hairt.

Hamewith

'*En ma fin est mon commencement.*'

MARIE STUART

Man at the end
Til the womb wends,
Fisher til sea,
Hunter to hill,
Miner the pit seeks,
Sodjer the bield.[7]

As bairn on breist
Seeks his first need
Makar[8] his thocht prees,
Doer his deed,
Sanct his peace
And sinner remeid.

Man in dust is lain
And exile wins hame.

---

[1] ask. [2] star. [3] langour. [4] roars.
[5] wait. [6] dream. [7] shelter. [8] poet.

W. S. GRAHAM

1917–

From *The Nightfishing*

We are at the hauling then hoping for it
The hard slow haul of a net white with herring
Meshed hard. I haul, using the boat's cross-heave
We've started, holding fast as we rock back,
Taking slack as we go to. The day rises brighter
Over us and the gulls rise in a wailing scare
From the nearest net-floats. And the unfolding water
Mingles its dead.

Now better white I can say what's better sighted,
The white net flashing under the watched water,
The near net dragging back with the full belly
Of a good take certain, so drifted easy
Slow down on us or us hauled up upon it
Curved in a garment down to thicker fathoms.
The hauling nets come in sawing the gunwale
With herring scales.

The air bunches to a wind and roused sea-cries.
The weather moves and stoops high over us and
There the forked tern, where my look's whetted on
    distance,
Quarters its hunting sea. I haul slowly
Inboard the drowning flood as into memory,
Braced at the breathside in my net of nerves.
We haul and drift them home. The winds slowly
Turn round on us and

Gather towards us with dragging weights of water
Sleekly swelling across the humming sea

And gather heavier. We haul and hold and haul
Well the bright chirpers home, so drifted whitely
All a blinding garment out of the grey water.
And, hauling hard in the drag, the nets come in,
The headrope a sore pull and feeding its brine
Into our hacked hands.

Over the gunwhale over into our deep lap
The herring come in, staring from their scales,
Fruitful as our deserts would have it out of
The deep and shifting seams of water. We haul
Against time fallen ill over the gathering
Rush of the sea together. The calms dive down.
The strident kingforked airs roar in their shell.
We haul the last

Net home and the last tether off the gathering
Run of the started sea. And then was the first
Hand at last lifted getting us swung against
Into the homing quarter, running that white grace
That sails me surely ever away from home.
And we hold into it as it moves down on
Us running white on the hull heeled to light.
Our bow heads home

Into the running blackbacks soaring us loud
High up in open arms of the towering sea.
The steep bow heaves, hung on these words, towards
What words your lonely breath blows out to meet it.
It is the skilled keel itself knowing its own
Fathoms it further moves through, with us there
Kept in its common timbers, yet each of us
Unwound upon

By a lonely behaviour of the all common ocean.
I cried headlong from my dead. The long rollers,

Quick on the crests and shirred with fine foam,
Surge down then sledge their green tons weighing
    dead
Down on the shuddered deck-boards. And shook off
All that white arrival upon us back to falter
Into the waking spoil and to be lost in
The mingling world.

So we started back over that sea we
Had worked widely all fish-seasons and over
Its shifting grounds, yet now risen up into
Such humours, I felt like a farmer tricked to sea.
For it sailed sore against us. It grew up
To black banks that crossed us. It stooped, beaked.
Its brine burnt us. I was chosen and given.
It rose as risen.

Treachery becomes myself, to clip me amorously
Off from all common breath. Those fires burned
Sprigs of the foam and branching tines of water.
It rose so white, soaring slowly, up
On us, then broke, down on us. It became a mull
Against our going and unfastened under us and
Curdled from the stern. It shipped us at each blow.
The brute weight

Of the living sea wrought us, yet the boat sleeked lean
Into it, upheld by the whole sea-brunt heaved,
And hung on the swivelling tops. The tiller raised
The sliding tide to wrench us and took a good
Ready hand to hold it. Yet we made a seaway
And minded all the gear was fast, and took
Our spell at steering. And we went keeled over
The streaming sea.

                          (Part III, stanzas 19–29.)

TOM SCOTT

1918–

Auld Sanct-Aundrians—Brand the Builder

On winter days, about the gloamin[1] hour,
Whan the knock on the college touer
Is chappan[2] lowsin[3]-time,
And ilka mason packs his mell and tools awa
Ablow his banker,[4] and bien forenenst the waa
The labourer haps the lave o the lime
Wi soppan secks, to keep it frae a frost, or faa
O suddent snaw
Duran the nicht,
And scrawnie craws flap in the shell-green licht
Towards yon bane-bare rickle[5] o trees
That heeze
Up on the knowe[6] abuin the toun,
And the red goun
Is happan[7] mony a student frae the snell[8] nor-easter,
Malcolm Brand, the maister,
Seean the last hand thru the yett[9]
Afore he bars and padlocks it,
Taks ae look round his stourie[10] yaird
Whaur chunks o stane are liggan
Like the ruins o some auld-farrant biggin:
Picks a skelf out o his beard,
Scliffs his tackety buits and syne
Clunters hamelins doun the wyn'.[11]

Alang the shore,
The grienan[12] white sea-owsen[13] ramp and roar.

---

[1]between daylight and dark.   [2]knocking.   [3]release.   [4]bench.
[5]collection.   [6]hill.   [7]wrapping.   [8]biting.   [9]gate.   [10]dusty.
[11]lane.   [12]complaining.   [13]oxen.

The main street echoes back his clinkan fuit-faas
Frae its waas,
Whaur owre the kerb and causeys[1] yellow licht
Presses back the mirk nicht
As shop fronts flude the pavin-stanes in places,
Like the peintit faces
Whures pit on, or actresses, —ay, or meenisters—
To please their several customers.
But aye the nordren nicht, cauld as rumour,
Taks command,
Chills the toun wi his militarie humour,
And plots his map o starns wi deadly hand.

Doun by the sea,
Murns the white swaw[2] owre the wrack ayebydanlie.[3]
Stoupan throu the anvil pend
Gaes Brand,
And owre the coort wi the twa-three partan[4] creels,
The birss air fu
O the smell o the sea, and fish, and meltit glue,
Draws up at his door, and syne,
Hawkan his craig[5] afore he gangs in ben,
Gies a bit scrape at the grater wi his heels.

The kail-pat on the hob is hotteran fu
O the usual hash o Irish stew,
And by the grate, a red-haired bewtie frettit thin,
His wife is kaain a spurtle[6] round.
He swaps his buits for his baffies[7] but a sound.
The twa-three bairnies ken to mak nae din
Whan faither's in,
And sit on creepies[8] round about.
Brand gies a muckle yawn, and howks his paper out.

[1] middle of the road.   [2] wave.   [3] constantly.
[4] baskets of crabs.   [5] clearing his throat.
[6] a wooden stick for stirring.   [7] slippers.   [8] low stools.

Tither side the fire,
The kettle sings like a telephone wire.

    'Lord, for what we are about to receive
    Help us to be truly thankful—Amen—
    Wumman, ye've pit ingans in't again.'

    'Gae wa ye coorse auld hypocrite!
    Thank the Lord for your maet, syne grue at it!'

Wi chowks[1] drawn ticht in a speakless sconner
He glowers on her:
Syne on the quate and straucht-faced bairns:
Faulds his paper doun by his eatin-airns,
And, til the loud tick-tockan o the knock,
Sups, and reads, wi nae ither word nor look.
The warld outside
Like a lug-held[2] sea-shell, roars wi the rinnan tide.

The supper owre, Brand redds up[3] for the nicht.
Aiblins[4] there's a schedule for to price,
Or somethin nice
On at the picters—sacont hoose—
Or some poleetical meetin wants his licht,
Or aiblins, wi him t-total aa his life,
No able to seek the pub to flee the wife,
Daunders[5] out the West Sands 'on the loose'.
Whatever tis,
The waater slorps frae his elbucks as he synds his
    phiz.

And this is aa the life he kens there is.

---

[1] jowls.   [2] ear-held.   [3] tidies up.   [4] mebbe.   [5] strolls.

MAURICE LINDSAY

1918–

Hurlygush

The hurlygush[1] and hallyoch[2] o the watter
a-skinklan[3] i the moveless simmer sun
harles[4] aff the scaurie mountain wi a yatter[5]
that thru ten-thoosan centuries has run.

Wi cheek against the ash o wither't bracken
I ligg[6] at peace and hear nae soun at aa
but yonder hurlygush that canna slacken
thru time and space mak never-endan faa:

as if a volley o the soun had brocht me
doun tae the pool whaur timeless things begin,
and e'en this endless faa'an that had claucht[7] me
wi ilka ither force was gether't in.

At Hans Christian Andersen's Birthplace, Odense, Denmark

Sunlight folds back pages of quiet shadows
against the whitewashed walls of his birthplace.
                              Tourists move
through crowded antiseptic rooms and ponder
what row after row of glass-cased paper ought to prove.

Somehow the long-nosed gangling boy who was only
at home in fairy-land, has left no clues.
The tinder-box of Time we rub
answers us each the way we choose.

For kings have now no daughters left for prizes.

---

[1] noise made by running water.   [2] noise made by water over stones.
[3] glittering.   [4] peels.   [5] noise of talking.   [6] lie.   [7] caught

Swineherds must remain swineherds; not a spell
can make the good man prince; psychiatrists
have dredged up wonder from the wishing well.

The whole of his terrible, tiny world might be
dismissed as a beautiful madman's dream, but that
                each of us knows
whenever we move out from the warmth of our lone-
    liness
we may be wearing the Emperor's new clothes.

Shetland Pony

A loose fold of steam idling,
slumped in a roll of wet grass:
bridle in hand, me, soothing, sidling
up to its rest. One move to pass

the loop round its passivity,
and eyes clench, nostrils itch,
its breath flaring activity
as hocks and neck bend in a twitch

that plucks it up to throw a plunging
proud parabola. It shakes
the field's roots, and leaves me lunging
blundered angles out. It makes

knots in the wide circumference
of centuries it darkly flings
around that less old arrogance
by which my domination clings:

then suddenly trundle-bellies in
from what it's proved to where I stand
haltered in sweat; and, duty done,
nuzzles confinement from my hand.

Picking Apples

Apple time, and the trees brittle with fruit.
My children climb the bent, half-sapping branches
to where the apples, cheeked with the hectic flush
of Autumn, hang. The children bark their haunches

and lean on the edge of their balance. The apples
    are out
of reach; so they shake the tree. Through a tussle of
    leaves and laughter
the apples thud down; thud on the orchard grasses
in rounded, grave finality, each one after

the other dropping; the muffled sound of them
    dropping
like suddenly hearing the beats of one's own heart
falling away, as if shaken by some storm
as localised as this. Loading them into the cart,

the sweet smell of their bruises moist in the sun,
their skins' bloom tacky against the touch,
I experience fulfilment, suddenly aware
of some ripe, wordless answer, knowing no such

answers exist; only questions, questions, the beating
    years,
the dropped apples . . . the kind of touch and go
that poetry makes satisfactions of;
reality, with nothing more to show

than a brush of branches, time and the apples falling,
and shrill among the leaves, children impatiently
    calling.

ALEXANDER SCOTT

1920–

Scrievin

I walkit air, I walkit late
By craigs[1] o gloamin-coloured stane,
I heard the sea-maws skirl and keen
Like sclate-pens[2] scraichan ower a sclate.

I walkit late, I walkit air
By parks that winter smairged[3] wi snaw,
I saw the spoor o pad and claw
Like ink on paper mirkened[4] there.

I lippened[5] syne, I lookit syne,
But cudna richt jalouse[6] ava
A word o what I heard or saw
Scrievit[7] by hands sae unlike mine.

Haar in Princes Street

The heicht o the biggins[8] is happit in rauchens o
    haar,[9]
        The statues alane
    Stand clearlie, heid til fit in stane,
And lour frae *then* and *thonder* at *hencefurth* and *here*.

The past on pedestals, girnan[11] frae ilka feature,
        Wi granite frouns
    They glower at the present's feckless loons,
Its gangrels tint[11] i the haar that fankles the future.

[1]rocks   [2]slate-pencils   [3]smeared   [4]darkened
[5]paid attention   [6]recognize   [7]written
[8]buildings.   [9]fog.   [10]complaining.   [11]lost.

The fowk o flesh, stravaigan wha kens whither,
  And come frae whar,
 Hudder lik ghaists i the gastrous haar,
Forfochten[1] and wae i the smochteran smore o the
  weather.

They swaiver[2] and flirn i the freeth like straes i the sea,
  An airtless swither,
 Steeran awa the t'ane frae t'ither,
Alane, and lawlie aye to be lanesome sae.

But heich i the lift[3] (whar the haar is skailan[4] fairlie
  In blufferts o wind)
 And blacker nor nicht whan starns are blind,
The Castle looms, a fell, a fabulous ferlie.[5]

Dragonish, darksome, dourlie grapplan the Rock
  Wi claws o stane
 That scart[6] our historie bare til the bane,
It braks like Fate throu Time's wanchancy reek.

Recipe: To mak a ballant

To mak a ballant:
tak onie image sclents frae the dark o your mind,
sieve it through twal years' skill
i the fewest words can haud it
(meantime steeran in your hert's bluid),
spice wi wit, saut wi passion,
bile i the hettest fire your love can kindle,
and serve at the scaud in your strangmaist stanza
(the haill process aa to be dune at aince)

Syne rin like hell afore the result explodes!

---

[1] exhausted.   [2] move aimlessly.   [3] sky.
   [4] dissolving.   [5] marvel   [6] scratch.

Ballade of Beauties

Miss Israel Nineteen-Sixty-Eight is new,
A fresh-poured form her swimsuit moulds to
    sleekness,
Legs long, breasts high, the shoulders firm and true,
The waist a lily-wand without a weakness,
The hair, *en brosse* and black, is shorn to bleakness,
Yet shines as stars can make the midnight do—
But still my mind recalls more maiden meekness,
Miss Warsaw Ghetto Nineteen-Forty-Two.

Her masters filmed her kneeling stripped to sue
The mercy barred as mere unmanning weakness,
Or raking rubbish-dumps for crusts to chew,
Or licking boots to prove her slavish meekness,
Or baring loins to lie beneath the bleakness
Of conquerors' lust (and forced to smile it through),
Her starving flesh a spoil preferred to sleekness,
Miss Warsaw Ghetto Nineteen-Forty-Two.

The prize she won was given not to few
But countless thousands, paid the price of meekness,
And paid in full, with far too high a due,
By sadist dreams transformed to functioned sleekness,
A pervert prophet's weakling hate of weakness
Constructing a mad machine that seized and slew,
The grave her last reward, the final bleakness,
Miss Warsaw Ghetto Nineteen-Forty-Two.

Princesses, pale in death or sunned in sleekness,
I dedicate these loving lines to you,
Miss Israel Sixty-Eight and (murdered meekness)
Miss Warsaw Ghetto Nineteen-Forty-Two.

EDWIN MORGAN

1920–

Aberdeen Train

Rubbing a glistening circle
on the steamed-up window I framed
a pheasant in a field of mist.
The sun was a great red thing somewhere low,
struggling with the milky scene. In the furrows
a piece of glass winked into life,
hypnotized the silly dandy; we
hooted past him with his head cocked,
contemplating a bottle-end.
And this was the last of October,
a Chinese moment in the Mearns.

King Billy

Grey over Riddrie the clouds piled up,
dragged their rain through the cemetery trees.
The gates shone cold. Wind rose
flaring the hissing leaves, the branches
swung, heavy, across the lamps.
Gravestones huddled in drizzling shadow,
flickering streetlight scanned the requiescats,
a name and an urn, a date, a dove
picked out, lost, half regained.
What is this dripping wreath, blown from its grave
red, white, blue, and gold
'To Our Leader of Thirty Years Ago'—

Bareheaded, in dark suits, with flutes
and drums, they brought him here, in procession
seriously, King Billy of Brigton, dead,
from Bridgeton Cross: a memory of violence,

brooding days of empty bellies,
billiard smoke and a sour pint,
boots or fists, famous sherrickings,
the word, the scuffle, the flash, the shout,
bloody crumpling in the close,
bricks for papish windows, get
the Conks next time, the Conks ambush
the Billy Boys, the Billy Boys the Conks till
Sillitoe scuffs the razors down the stank—
No, but it isn't the violence they remember
but the legend of a violent man
born poor, gang-leader in the bad times
of idleness and boredom, lost in better days,
a bouncer in a betting club,
a quiet man at last, dying
alone in Bridgeton in a box bed.
So a thousand people stopped the traffic
for the hearse of a folk hero and the flutes
threw 'Onward Christian Soldiers' to the winds
from unironic lips, the mourners kept
in step, and there were some who wept.
Go from the grave. The shrill flutes
are silent, the march dispersed.
Deplore what is to be deplored,
and then find out the rest.

Absence

My shadow—
I woke to a wind swirling the curtains light and dark
and the birds twittering on the roofs, I lay cold
in the early light in my room high over London.
What fear was it that made the wind sound like a
    fire
so that I got up and looked out half-asleep
at the calm rows of street-lights fading far below?

Without fire
only the wind blew.
But in the dream I woke from, you
came running through the traffic, tugging me, cling-
     ing
to my elbow, your eyes spoke
what I could not grasp—
Nothing, if you were here!

The wind of the early quiet
merges slowly now with a thousand rolling wheels.
The lights are out, the air is loud.
It is an ordinary January day.
My shadow, do you hear the streets?
Are you at my heels? Are you here?
And I throw back the sheets.

From the Domain of Arnheim

And so that all these ages, these years
we cast behind us, like the smoke-clouds
dragged back into vacancy when the rocket springs—
The domain of Arnheim was all snow, but we were
     there.
We saw a yellow light thrown on the icefield
from the huts by the pines, and laughter came up
floating from a white corrie
miles away, clearly.
We moved on down, arm in arm.
I know you would have thought it was a dream
but we were there. And those were trumpets—
tremendous round the rocks—
while they were burning fires of trash and mammoths'
     bones.
They sang naked, and kissed in the smoke.
A child, or one of their animals, was crying.

Young men blew the ice crystals off their drums.
We came down among them, but of course
they could see nothing, on their time-scale.
Yet they sensed us, stopped, looked up—even into
    our eyes.
To them we were a displacement of the air,
a sudden chill, yet we had no power
over their fear. If one of them had been dying
he would have died. The crying
came from one just born: that was the cause
of the song. We saw it now. What had we stopped
but joy?
I know you felt
the same dismay, you gripped my arm, they were
    waiting
for what they knew of us to pass.
A sweating trumpeter took
a brand from the fire with a shout and threw it
where our bodies would have been—
we felt nothing but his courage.
And so they would deal with every imagined power
seen or unseen.
There are no gods in the domain of Arnheim.

We signalled to the ship; got back;
our lives and days returned to us, but
haunted by deeper souvenirs than any rocks or seeds.
From time the souvenirs are deeds.

GEORGE MACKAY BROWN

1921–

The Lodging

The stones of the desert town
Flush; and, a star-filled wave,
Night steeples down.

From a pub door here and there
A random ribald song
Leaks on the air.

The Roman in a strange land
Broods, wearily leaning
His lance in the sand.

The innkeeper over the fire
Counting his haul, hears not
The cry from the byre;

But rummaging in the till
Grumbles at the drunken shepherds
Dancing on the hill;

And wonders, pale and grudging,
If the queer pair below
Will pay their lodging.

Wedding

With a great working of elbows
The fiddlers ranted

   —Joy to Ingrid and Magnus!

With much boasting and burning
The whisky circled

   —Wealth to Ingrid and Magnus!

With deep clearings of the throat
The minister intoned
　　　　—Thirdly, Ingrid and Magnus. . . .

Ingrid and Magnus stared together
When midnight struck
At a white unbroken bed.

Old Fisherman with Guitar

A formal exercise for withered fingers.
　　The head is bent,
　　　　the eyes half closed, the tune
Lingers
　　And beats, a gentle wing the west had thrown
　　Against his breakwater wall with salt
　　　　　　　　　　savage lament.

So fierce and sweet the song on the plucked string,
　　Know now for truth
　　These hands have cut from the net
The strong
　　Crab-eaten corpse of Jock washed from a boat
　　One old winter, and gathered the mouth of Thora
　　　　　　　　to his mouth.

IAN HAMILTON FINLAY

1925–

Bedtime

　　So put your nightdress on
　　It is so white and long
　　And your sweet night-face
　　Put it on also please

It is the candle-flame
It is the flame above
Whose sweet shy shame
My love, I love, I love.

Twice

(i)

It is a little pond
And it is frail and round

And it is in the wood,
A doleful mood

Of birches (white) and stale
Very old thin rain grown pale.

(ii)

It is a little pond
And it is brown; around

It (like the eye
Of a cow) soft emerald

Grasses and things
Grow up. The tall white harlequins

Sway again
And again, in the bright new clean rain.

ALASTAIR MACKIE

1925–

Mongol Quine

Elbucks[1] on the herbour waa
the mongol quine[2]
collogues[3]
wi hersel.

Her blonde baa-heid[4] wags
frae side to side.
Noo she's a clock-hand
noo a croon.[5]

Wha said grace and grouwin
tae this mistak?
A ban was on her
frae furder[6] back.

Nievie nievie nack nack
whit hand'll ye tak tak?
She got the wrang hand
and didna pan oot.[7]

She's got pig's een,
a bannock face,
and hurdies[8] that rowed
like twa muckle bools.[9]

She wints[10] for naething. Yet
she's singin till the distance.
Ayont[11] the hert-brak her een
are set for ever on an unkent airt.[12]

[1]elbows   [2]girl   [3]talks to   [4]ball head
[5]crown   [6]further   [7]work out   [8]hips
[9]bowls   [10]wants   [11]beyond   [12]unknown direction

In Absentia

'We've no heard frae God this while,'
said ane o the angels.
It was at a synod
o the metaphors.

Cam a wind;
it was aabody speirin[1]
'Wha?'
intill themsels.

It was heard by the sauls
o Baudelaire and Pascal.
They fell thro the muckle[2] hole
opened by the question.

I the boddom[3] Jesus sweatit
'Consummatum est.'
And Nietzsche
hou he laucht[4] and laucht.

The maist o fowk bein neither
philosophers or theologians
kept gaun tae the kirk.
Whiles, like.

Syne God said: 'Noo I'm awa,
mak a kirk or a mill o't.'[5]

And God gaed tae the back o beyond
i the midst o aathing.[6].

[1]asking   [2]great   [3]bottom   [4]laughed
[5]make what you like of it   [6]everything

IAIN CRICHTON SMITH

1928–

Old Woman

And she, being old, fed from a mashed plate
as an old mare might droop across a fence
to the dull pastures of its ignorance.
Her husband held her upright while he prayed

to God who is all-forgiving to send down
some angel somewhere who might land perhaps
in his foreign wings among the gradual crops.
She munched, half dead, blindly searching the spoon.

Outside, the grass was raging. There I sat
imprisoned in my pity and my shame
that men and women having suffered time
should sit in such a place, in such a state

and wished to be away, yes, to be far away
with athletes, heroes, Greeks or Roman men
who pushed their bitter spears into a vein
and would not spend an hour with such decay.

'Pray God', he said, 'we ask you, God,' he said.
The bowed back was quiet. I saw the teeth
tighten their grip around a delicate death.
And nothing moved within the knotted head

but only a few poor veins as one might see
vague wishless seaweed floating on a tide
of all the salty waters where had died
too many waves to mark two more or three.

Luss Village

Such walls, like honey, and the old are happy
in morphean air like gold-fish in a bowl.
Ripe roses trail their margins down a sleepy
mediaeval treatise on the slumbering soul.

And even the water, fabulously silent,
has no salt tales to tell us, nor make jokes
about the yokel mountains, huge and patient,
that will not court her but read shadowy books.

A world so long departed! In the churchyard
the tilted tombs still gossip, and the leaves
of stony testaments are read by Richard,
Jean and Carol, pert among the sheaves

of unscythed shadows, while the noon day hums
with bees and water and the ghosts of psalms.

At the Firth of Lorne

In the cold orange light we stared across
to Mull and Kerrera and far Tiree.
A setting sun emblazoned your bright knee
to a brilliant gold to match your hair's gold poise.

Nothing had changed: the world was as it was
a million years ago. The slaty stone
slept in its tinged and aboriginal iron.
The sky might flower a little, and the grass

perpetuate its sheep. But from the sea
the bare bleak islands rose, beyond the few
uneasy witticisms we let pursue
their desolate silences. There was no tree

nor other witness to the looks we gave
each other there, inhuman as if tolled
by some huge bell of iron and of gold,
I no great Adam and you no bright Eve.

Two Girls Singing

It neither was the words nor yet the tune.
Any tune would have done and any words.
Any listener or no listener at all.

As nightingales in rocks or a child crooning
in its own world of strange awakening
or larks for no reason but themselves.

So on the bus through late November running
by yellow lights tormented, darkness falling,
the two girls sang for miles and miles together

and it wasn't the words or tune. It was the singing
It was the human sweetness in that yellow,
the unpredicted voices of our kind.

ALASTAIR REID

1926–

Isle of Arran

Where no one was was where my world was stilled
into hills that hung behind the lasting water,
a quiet quilt of heather where bees slept,
and a single slow bird in circles winding
round the axis of my head.

Any wind being only my breath, the weather
stopped, and a woollen cloud smothered the sun.

Rust and a mist hung over the clock of the day.
A mountain dreamed in the light of the dark
and marsh mallows were yellow for ever.

Still as a fish in the secret loch alone
I was held in the water where my feet found ground
and the air where my head ended,
all thought a prisoner of the still sense—
till a butterfly drunkenly began the world.

The Fall

He teeters along the crumbling top
of the garden wall and calls, 'Look up,
Papa, look up! I'm flying . . .' till,
in a sudden foreseen spasm, I see him fall.

Terrible
when fear cries to the senses, when the whirl
of the possible drowns the real. Falling
is a fright in me. I call
and move in time to catch
his small, sweat-beaded body,
still thrilled with the air.
'I flew, Papa, I flew!'
'I know, child, I know.'

TOM BUCHAN

1931–

The Week-end Naturalist

My humanoid friend, myself, a limited animal
in love with the planet
escaping across the dumb topographies of Assynt
with maps and a compass

taking incorrect fixes on anonymous Bens
staring into bog-pools

entertaining myself with half-formulated notions
of a non-utilitarian character
and applying my ragbag of ecological data
to flowers which I recognize
absentmindedly as if they were old friends
whose names I've forgotten

timidly leaping backwards at the green skeleton
of a ewe
scared out of my wits by an equally terrified stag
and always very much conscious
of my wet socks, my deaf ear, balding pate
and over-filled gut

but retaining even here persistent after-images
of my bank-balance
the impersonal malevolence of ill-paid officials
the pretensions
of well-paid academics, the dishonesties of
        shopkeepers
car-salesmen and politicians

until my vague fountain of speculative ideas
coalesces into irritability
and these innocent towers of darkening gneiss
stand over me
like tax inspectors as I trip on a delinquent peat
and fall on my face.

The Everlasting Astronauts

These dead astronauts cannot decay—
they bounce on the quilted walls of their tin grave
and very gently collide with polythene balloons
full of used mouthwash, excrements and foodscraps.

They were chosen not for their imagination
but for their compatibility with machines—
glancing out at the vast America of the universe
they cried, 'Gee boys, it's great up here!'

Now, tumbling and yawing, their playpen hurries
into the continuum and at last they are real explorers
voyaging endlessly among unrecorded splendours
with Columbus, Peary, Magellan and Drake.

STEWART CONN

1936–

Visiting Hour

In the pond of our new garden
were five orange stains, under
inches of ice. Weeks since anyone
had been there. Already by far
the most severe winter for years.
You broke the ice with a hammer.
I watched the goldfish appear,
blunt-nosed and delicately clear.

Since then so much has taken place
to distance us from what we were.
That it should come to this.
Unable to hide the horror
in my eyes, I stand helpless
by your bedside and can do no more
than wish it were simply a matter
of smashing the ice and giving you air.

Todd

My father's white uncle became
Arthritic and testamental in
Lyrical stages. He held cardinal sin
Was misuse of horses, then any game

Won on the sabbath. A Clydesdale
To him was not bells and sugar or declension
From paddock, but primal extension
Of rock and soil. Thundered nail

Turned to sacred bolt. And each night
In the stable he would slaver and slave
At cracked hooves, or else save
Bowls of porridge for just the right

Beast. I remember I lied
To him once, about oats: then I felt
The brand of his loving tongue, the belt
Of his own horsey breath. But he died,

When the mechanised tractor came to pass.
Now I think of him neighing to some saint
In a simple heaven or, beyond complaint,
Leaning across a fence and munching grass.

JAMES AITCHISON

1939 –

Landscape with Lapwings

It's another April, and a day
with all the seasons in it, with lapwings
falling out of sunlight into rain,
stalling on a squall and then tumbling
over the collapsing wall of air
to float in zones of weightlessness again.

And on a day like this in such a place—
a few square miles of moorland in a round
of rounded hills, rain clouds and scattered trees,
with water flowing clearly over stone—
in such a place I feel the weights slip off
the way a lapwing would if it were me.

The place might form a frame of reference
for calculating weightlessness, and all
the weathers that are in one April day,
for drawing what conclusions can be drawn
from lapwings tumbling in and out of light
with such a total lack of gravity.

DOUGLAS DUNN

1942–

The Drying-Green

A housewife on her drying-green,
Beneath her high-poled ropes, holds back
White sheets, rectangular whitenesses
That flag the cleanliness of Monday.

One white billow, then another, held
By a hemmed edge, between finger
And thumb, a tented labyrinth,
Prepare a sooty coalman's entrance.

Four times this happens, four sacks of coal . . .
He walks burdened. His coal rushes
in a black spill of mineral noise.
She parts the white sheets; he passes through

Her glades of laundry. Back again
To the bunker . . . He is leathery,
A man from a dirty, servile past.
She smiles, as if there is a moral in it.

There is none, only black and white
Both clean on Monday afternoon
In a wind that is good for drying,
The faultless clouds, the April sky.

Listening

From the unoiled wheels of a bicycle
I heard a squeak become a human cry.
In those silent lamentations
When rose-petals fall, I heard
My sorrows murdered by aesthetics.
When laughter from a fire-lit barbecue
Travelled with woodsmoke across the gardens,
I saw an apple hold its skin against an apple—
Two blushing faces kissing in the dark.
In the orchard of listening fruit
Woodsmoke and voices crowded the foliage,
Rummaging for the sweet bite together.
I felt I almost heard the secrets of a tree—
The fruits falling, the birds fluttering,
The music danced to under coloured lights.

The Harp of Renfrewshire

Contemplating a map

Annals of the trilled R, gently stroked L,
Lamenting O of local literature,
Open, on this, their one-page book, a still
Land-language chattered in a river's burr.

Small-talk of herdsmen, rural argument—
These soft disputes drift over river-meadows,
A darg of conversations, a verbal scent—
Tut-tutted discourse, time of day, word-brose.

Named places have been dictionaried in
Ground's secret lexicon, its racial moan
Of etymology and cries of pain
That slit a summer wind and then were gone.

A mother calls her daughter from her door.
Her house, my stone illusion, hugs its hill.
From Eaglesham west to the rocky shore
Her cry is stretched across bog-asphodel.

The patronymic miles of grass and weddings,
Their festivals of gender, covenants,
Poor pre-industrially scattered steadings,
Ploughed-up davochs—old names, inhabitants.

And on my map is neither wall or fence,
But men and women and their revenue,
As, watching them, I utter into silence
A granary of whispers rinsed in dew.

War Blinded

For more than sixty years he has been blind
Behind that wall, these trees, with terrible
Longevity wheeled in the sun and wind
On pathways of the soldiers' hospital.

For half that time his story's troubled me—
That showroom by the ferry, where I saw
His basketwork, a touch-turned filigree
His fingers coaxed from charitable straw;

Or how he felt when young, enlisting at
Recruiting tables on the football pitch,
To end up slumped across a parapet,
His eye-blood running in a molten ditch;

Or how the light looked when I saw two men,
One blind, one in a wheelchair, in that park,
Their dignity, which I have not forgotten,
Which helps me struggle with this lesser dark.

That war's too old for me to understand
How he might think, nursed now in wards of want,
Remembering that day when his right hand
Gripped on the shoulder of the man in front.

ALAN BOLD

1943–

Space for Colour

The space between the hysterical squeals
Of gulls and the hangdog heads of seals

Is full of colour. The colour of fishing boats,
Of fur and feathers, of scarlet lobster floats.

And as these colours furiously try to merge
Between the wind's insistence and the sea's surge

They end by changing spaces so that seablue
Mirrors skygreen and the seals chamelon too.

Meanwhile in a sudden fluttering downward flash
Seagulls squabble over a single fish

Whose gleaming waterproof gull-vulnerable green
      scales
Are colourfully torn apart between hysterical squeals.

The Realm of Touching

Between my lips the taste of night-time blends
And then dissolves. It is blank as my eyelids close.
For a flickering of time I concentrate on how time
      ends.

It should be present, the scent of the rose
We bought, though one petal has begun to fall.
Somehow that simplifies the girl I chose.

Night music must be the sweetest sound of all.
It is made to overwhelm with virtuosity.
But every night it is the same pounding on the same
    wall.

Nocturnal images are said to be the ones that stay
Longest, with exploitation of the dark half-tone.
This I disregard and watch for the day.

A touch in the realm of touching alone
Adds presence to the absence of light.
A clasp of hands, then bodies, my own
And hers is when I welcome the blindness of night.

STANLEY ROGER GREEN

1944–

Death's-Head Moth

I saw it settle like a stain
On the dusk, each tired wing
Spread flat upon the window pane

Yet the angles were less than bad,
The design of its parts persuasive,
So I picked up a sketching pad,

Traced out the furtive symmetry,
Coaxed light round furred edges,
And wondered why it disgusted me,

It lacked the frenetic sly
Grace and rainbow hues
Of the madcap butterfly,

An outcast cousin on a probe,
I guessed, a skeleton in the closet
Come to plunder in my wardrobe,

A pirate on a textile raid
Who never filibusters flowers
Or seeks gold booty in a bosky glade,

Who reminds me less of summer
Than of dust and mortality,
A flame-drawn deathwish mummer.

Moth, I need no reminders; look
Where I will, a shadow falls,
Even on the pages of a book.

I've opened up the window pane—
Out you go to the heedless world,
There! the dusk is clear again.

The Old Bing

A century ago deep dripping galleries were gutted
To build this monument above the wooded carse;
Now the bing is overwhelmed by dog-rose and
        bramble,
Veins of wild strawberry throb under bracken.

In winter keen hill winds and valley rains
Strip it bare revealing a gaunt memorial;
Stark in its grandeur the bing rears from the carse
Like the tumulus of a long-dead jarl or thane.

At its base a slow river ambles reflecting tall
Hills and still herons heraldic in twilight;

Not even the sighs of evening winds can recall
The anguished grunts of those nameless toilers

Who hacked a sparse living from grudging seams,
Cursed at roof-falls, mourned lost comrades,
Indifferent as moles to the cenotaph above them
Each day darkly rising, shouldering the sun.

LIZ LOCHHEAD
1948–

Tam Lin's Lady

'O I forbid you maidens a'
who wear gowd in your hair—
to come or go to Carterhaugh
for young Tam Lin is there.'

So you met him in a magic place?
O.K.
But that's a bit airy fairy for me.
I go for the specific—you could, for instance,
say that when he took you for a coffee
before he stuck you on the last bus
there was one of those horrible congealed-on
plastic tomatoes on the table . . . oh don't
ask me
I don't know why everything has to be so sordid these
        days . . .
I can take *some* sentiment
tell me how charmed you were
when he wrote both your names and a heart in spilt
        coffee—

anything except that he carved them on the eldern
    tree.
But have it your own way.
Picking apart your personal
dream landscape of court and castle and greenwood
isn't really up to me.
So call it magical. A fair country.
Anyway you were warned.

And if, as the story goes
nine times out of ten—
he took you by the milkwhite hand & by the
    grassgreen sleeve
& laid you on the bonnie bank & asked of you no
    leave,
well, so what?
You're not the first to fall for it,
good green girdle and all—
with your schooltie rolled up in your pocket
trying to look eighteen. I know.
All perfectly forgiveable.
Relax.

What I do think was a little dumb
if only you'd trust him just this once
was to swallow that old one about you being
the only one who could save him.

Oh I see—there was this lady
he couldn't get free of.
Seven years and more he said he'd sacrificed himself
and if you didn't help him he'd end up
a fairy for ever! Enslaved.

Or worse still in hell without you.

Well, well.
So he stopped you from wandering in the forest
and picking pennyroyal and foxgloves
and making appointments and borrowing money for
    the abortion.
He said all would be well
if only you'd trust him just this once
and go through
what he was honest enough to admit in advance
would be hell and highwater for you.
So he told you which relatives to pander to
and which to ignore.
How to snatch him from the Old One
and hold on through thick and thin
through every change that happened.
Oh but it was terrible!
It seemed earlier, you see,
he'd been talking in symbols (like
adder-snake, wild savage bear
brand of bright iron red-hot from the fire)
and as usual the plain unmythical truth was worse.
At any rate you were good and brave, you did
hang on, hang on tight.
And in the end of course
everything turned out conventionally right
with the old witch banished to her corner lamenting,
cursing his soft heart and the fact she couldn't keep
    him,
and everyone sending out for booze for the wedding.

So we're all supposed to be happy?
But how about you, my fallen fair maiden
now the drama's over, tell me
how goes the glamourie?
After the twelve casks of good claret wine

and the twelve and twelve of muskadine,
tell me
what about you?
How do you think Tam Lin will take
all the changes you go through?

ANDREW GREIG

1951–

Sapper

Yard by yard I let you
sap my resistance
and undermine
my easy independence.

Your smiles and warm ways
burrowed burning
into my cool brain; your firmness
honeycombed my heart.

Then you laid in
barrel-loads of love
and laid a powder trail
to the ammunition dump

of my desire. And now
I've caught you, hand
on my fuse. And I say
'Yes, love'.

The Glove

This room need not speak of her.
It is enough
the air is hard to breathe.

On the table, a flattened glove.
Nothing has moved
since she slipped out.

There is no calling from kitchen or shore.

For a ghost as subtle as a lack
there are rituals of banishment
in time:

vacuums are filled, rooms aired,
furniture shifted, walls painted,
a new lodger—

and one day the glove is gone
edged out of this world
as things are when we have no room

even for their absence.

In Galloway

In Galloway the drystane dykes that curl
like smoke over the shoulder of the hill
are built with holes
through which sky shows and spindrift birls,
so the wind is baffled but not barred
lest drifting snow smoors a sheltering herd.

There is an art in framing holes
and in the space between the stones.
Structures pared to the bone—
the line that pleases by what's not there
or drydykes laced across the whirling air.

INDEX OF FIRST LINES